FIFTY YEARS AND COUNTING

# YATRIK

## A JOURNEY INTO THEATRICAL ART

Dedicated to the memory of
JOY MICHAEL
1926-2018

FIFTY YEARS AND COUNTING

# YATRIK

# A JOURNEY INTO THEATRICAL ART


**DIWAN SINGH BAJELI**

**Editors**
**Indu Ramchandani, Bhaskar Ghose, Sunit Tandon, and Ranjit Mathur**



PAPER MISSILE

NIYOGI BOOKS

Published by
**NIYOGI BOOKS**
Block D, Building No. 77,
Okhla Industrial Area, Phase-I,
New Delhi-110 020, INDIA
Tel: 91-11-26816301, 26818960
Email: niyogibooks@gmail.com
Website: www.niyogibooksindia.com



Editor: Saachi Khurana
Design: Shashi Bhushan Prasad

ISBN: 978-93-86906-31-1
Publication: 2019



Printed at: Niyogi Offset Pvt. Ltd., New Delhi, India

# CONTENTS

# DIRECTOR'S NOTE

**This book is the result of a collaborative project between Yatrik and the Raza Foundation. Yatrik gratefully acknowledges the invaluable collaboration of the Raza Foundation in bringing out this important publication on Delhi theatre.**

Yatrik was founded as a bilingual repertory theatre company in 1964 with the objective of projecting theatre as a dynamic, living force by providing regular performances of rich and meaningful theatre. Its founder members were Joy Michael, Rati Bartholomew, Sushma Seth, Roshan Seth, Kusum Haidar, Nigam Prakash, Marcus Murch, and Sneih Das.

Yatrik has many 'firsts' to its credit. It was the first to establish and maintain weekend repertory theatre and the first to produce plays for children. With the aim of promoting theatre in education, Yatrik began holding workshops in schools and colleges and staging its plays in educational institutions. Yatrik was also among the very first to enter the formidable world of musicals, the staging of which has always been a deterrent to most amateur groups.

Yatrik has from the outset sponsored original Indian plays both in Hindi and English, and has also encouraged translations of regional Indian plays and adaptations of foreign plays, bringing to the Delhi stage several classics of Western and regional drama and, most recently, some of modern India's finest plays. Yatrik has produced over 300 plays in English, Hindi, Urdu, and Punjabi since 1964, surely living up to its objective of providing regular and sustained theatre!

Yatrik has also travelled extensively with its plays in India and abroad to Dubai, South Africa, Pakistan, and Russia. Several plays of Yatrik have won awards and recognition at national and international theatre festivals, and at least four of them have been selected by the Sahitya Kala Parishad in its annual selection for 'The Best Plays of the Year' and two for the National School of Drama's annual Bharat Rang Mahotsav.

The list of those who have worked with Yatrik over the last four decades is indeed impressive—Zohra Sehgal, Pearl Padamsee, Roshan Seth, Sai Paranjpye, Alyque Padamsee, Sushma Seth, Rati Bartholomew, Kusum Haider, Ebrahim Alkazi, Rajinder Nath, Ram Gopal Bajaj, Salima Raza, Marcus Murch, Chaman Bagga, Mohan Maharishi, B.V. Karanth, Barry John, Kulbhushan Kharbanda, Gerson da Cunha, Bhaskar Ghose, Sabina Mehta Jaitly, M.K. Raina, Madhuri Bhatia, Vinay Capila, Ajay Balram, Sant Juneja, Prabha Tonk, Deepak Kejriwal, Bhaskar Bhattacharji, Tejeshwar Singh, Ranjit Mathur, Jasbir Malik, Surinder Dugal, Ramesh Thakur, Prakash Bhatia, Avijit Dutt, Pradeep Kapoor, Tannishtha Chatterjee…the list goes on. It is creditable that several of these thespians continue to work with Yatrik even today.

Joy Michael, Yatrik's former director and one of its founder members, steered the group for forty years, taking it forward through times good and bad, with great courage, imagination and commitment. She has received several awards in recognition of her contribution to Indian theatre, including the Padma Shri and and Sangeet Natak Akademi Award. Other directors of the group have included Sabina Mehta Jaitly, Prakash Bhatia, and Avijit Dutt.

As Yatrik completed five decades of its continuous existence, I found myself being elected the director of the group. This is a position that I did not want and certainly never imagined I would hold when I first joined the group in 1979–80. I have some small cause for satisfaction in the fact that, despite facing the most challenging financial position, we managed to revive two of our more significant productions of recent years to celebrate our Golden Jubilee in 2014: *The Virtuous Burglar* and *Metamorphoses*.

This book is another contribution to the commemoration of 50 years of Yatrik, and it has been a dream project for Joy Michael for several years now. It is perhaps the first ever book on an entire Indian theatre group, which has made its writing and compilation a far more complex and time-consuming task than a book on a single director, actor, or playwright.

It was only when the noted theatre critic and scholar Mr Diwan Singh Bajeli very kindly agreed to undertake this project at the initiative of Avijit Dutt, a prime mover of the book project, that it finally got off the ground. Mr Bajeli produced the solid core of the book, which was then fleshed out with contributions from as many regular Yatrik members as could be reached, under the supervision of that marvellous professional book editor we are lucky enough to have amongst the ranks of senior members of Yatrik—Indu Ramchandani. With guidance from Bhaskar Ghose and Ranjit Mathur and with the blessings and concurrence of Mr Bajeli, Indu worked indefatigably to give this book its final shape. Without the contribution of these key persons, this book may not have seen the light of day. I owe a debt of eternal gratitude to Mr Bajeli and also to Indu, Bhaskar, and Ranjit for all that they have done.

In 2017, I completed 40 years in theatre. I can only hope that while I would like to continue my involvement with the group as long as is possible, younger and more capable hands will come forward to take this unique, collegial, all-embracing group forward with renewed energy, commitment, and determination in its sixth and subsequent decades.

**Sunit Tandon**<br>
*Director, Yatrik*<br>
2018

# GENESIS OF YATRIK...
## As the Story Begins

*...Art is necessary in order that man should be able to recognize and change the world. But art is also necessary by virtue of the magic inherent in it.*

*The Necessity of Art*
**Ernst Fisher**

## A Seed is Sown

This is the story of some unique people who were drawn together by one common attraction for the stage. Few thrills can compare with a stage actor's euphoria when he or she senses or knows that he or she has captured the hearts and appreciation of an audience...and it was with such a thrill that this group was aglow. It was a comparatively young group—the eldest in her early thirties, the youngest still in college. Their tiredness, as they finally returned home to Delhi in a train, could not dampen their enthusiasm, as they thought of and talked about the shared experiences of the previous year and a half.

During that time, they had travelled together to many parts of India, staging two plays in cities, schools, and colleges. Everywhere they had been received with enthusiasm. Their shows were a tremendous success. They realised they had a common passion for theatre and they had banded themselves into a harmonious and responsible team. "Now we should not disband," they said. "We must work together." Just as the stations, big and small, passed swiftly by, and as thoughts and ideas were delightfully in sync, it emerged: the decision to form a repertory company with the ambitious goal of full-time stagecraft.

And so, before that train journey ended, another journey was set to begin, but could this group nurture the seed they had pledged to sow? This is the story of that journey and of that group.

## The Fertile Background

After Independence, the cultural world of Delhi had begun to vibrate with new hope, vitality, and spirit of experiment to evolve new forms of art and to infuse them with modern sensitivity and indigenous idiom. The formation of the Sangeet Natak Akademi in 1952 and the Sahitya Akademi in 1954 gave a boost to creativity, attracting new talents. In 1959, the National School of Drama, the premier national dramatic institution, was opened and its performing wing—the Repertory Company—was set up in 1964, which opened a whole new world of modern dramatic art to the audience. The opening of these national cultural bodies made Delhi a unique hub of pulsating drama. Ebrahim Alkazi, the doyen of contemporary Indian theatre, with his students at the National School of Drama, produced works of art, especially dramatic works of the West. His production of Dharamvir Bharati's verse play *Andha Yug* in Hindi presented in the open air against the backdrop of the historic Feroz Shah Kotla heralded a new epoch in the history of contemporary theatre in India.

The period of the 1950s and 1960s also saw significant plays from various Indian regions finding a platform on the Delhi stage. Several plays were translated into Hindi. Bohurupee, formed in 1948 under the leadership of Sombhu Mitra, frequently brought its production to Delhi, displaying its highly innovative approach, especially with its productions of Rabindranath Tagore's evergreen dramatic works. Delhi also witnessed productions under the direction of Utpal Dutt, revealing his Marxist vision, analysing the antagonistic forces in a class society. Hindi versions of plays by Vijay Tendulkar (Marathi), P.L. Deshpande (Marathi), Badal Sircar (Bengali), Sriranga (Kannada), and Girish Karnad (Kannada) were staged, and catapulted these significant playwrights to national fame.

These plays further ignited the theatrical scene in the capital. Qudsia Zaidi had already unfurled the flag of professional theatre on the landscape of Delhi theatre with the formation of Hindustani Theatre in 1954. Her associate Habib Tanvir produced his celebrated productions of *Agra Bazar* and *Mitti ki Gaadi*. Later, he formed Garage Theatre on Kasturba Gandhi Marg with Monica Mishra Tanvir and subsequently renamed it Naya Theatre Company. Award-winning Urdu playwright Revati Sharan Sharma set up Kala

Sadhana Mandir. Hindi writer and playwright Dr Laxmi Narain Lal formed Samvad in 1961. The pioneer of the Punjabi musical theatre movement Sheila Bhatia formed Delhi Arts Theatre along with Hali in Delhi with the staging of *Call of the Valley* in 1951, after she migrated from Lahore in the wake of the Partition. Graduates of the National School of Drama formed another significant group Dishantar in 1967. The founder members of the group were highly talented artists such as Om Shivpuri, Sudha Sharma Shivpuri, Ram Gopal Bajaj, Mohan Maharishi, Wamdev Sinha, and Anjala Maharishi. The group set new standards of theatrical art. One of the leading dramatic groups of the decade was Yavanika, formed in 1967 with the blessings of the then Information and Broadcasting Minister K.K. Shah. Abhiyan was another outstanding group formed by gifted theatre practitioners in 1967. Prof. Frank Thakurdas and veteran theatre director Rajinder Nath were among its founders.

The opening of the Delhi branch of the Indian People's Theatre Association (IPTA) by the then vice president of India Dr S. Radhakrishnan in 1958 enabled a politically conscious audience to watch sharp-edged satires that sought to expose unjust economic and political systems. In the early stages of their careers, Pankaj Kapoor, Neelima Azim, Pawan Malhotra, Om Puri, and Naseeruddin Shah were associated with IPTA. Leading theatre practitioner and former NSD director B.M. Shah was associated with Little Theatre Group's repertory during his initial days. In 1972, as director, he produced five plays on an average annually, which bore the stamp of his superb craftsmanship. Earlier, in collaboration with B.V. Karanth and J.N. Kaushal, he put up Rangmanch in 1964, which produced *Trishanku* in 1969, considered to be a major breakthrough in contemporary Indian theatre. One of the groups that regaled Delhi audiences with a touch of moral messages was the Three Arts Club, founded in 1943 by Om Sharma, Devi Chand Kayasth, and R.M. Kaul. Later, Ramesh

Mehta, a popular playwright, and M.N. Kapoor, the late principal of Modern School, joined the club. In 1968, expatriate folk artists from the region of present-day Uttarakhand started the Parvatiya Kala Kendra with Mohan Upreti as its artistic director under the creative collaboration of two geniuses of the region—B.M. Shah and B.L. Shah. The Kendra recreated immortal ballads of the hills as operas of great beauty.

## The Emergence of Theatre Groups

Against this backdrop, several amateur theatre groups emerged. Most of these groups that displayed great promise and presented memorable productions faded out with time, as their gifted performers left Delhi for greener pastures. Their place was taken by other hurriedly formed groups, but most of them disappeared after one or two productions. Among those which continued to function were Yatrik, Yavanika, Parvatiya Kala Kendra, Abhiyan, Three Arts Club, and IPTA.

Forming an amateur group was relatively easy, and the enthusiasm of the beginning was the boost, but it needed a lot of resources in terms of organisational skill, commitment, and perseverance to continue the creative journey in the face of formidable problems and to compete with other groups founded by great names in the Delhi theatre world. The United States Information Service and the British Council, which patronised English dramatic activities in Delhi, drew some talent from these amateur groups. Among those that came from Unity Theatre was one particular amateur group.

The founder members of this group were Joy Michael, Sushma Mathur (now Seth), Rati Bartholomew, Kusum Bahl (now Haidar), Sneh Das, and college students Roshan Seth, Nigam Prakash, and Marcus Murch. The founders were soon to be joined by Salima Raza.

In August 1964, Yatrik registered itself as a bilingual repertory company with the objective of projecting the Arts as a dynamic living force by providing regular sustained performances of theatre and other arts and building up an audience for them. In 1964–65, its first year, Yatrik produced seven plays: *All the King's Men*, *Azar Ka Khwab* (an Urdu translation by Begum Qudsia Zaidi of George Bernard Shaw's *Pygmalion*), *The Government Inspector*, *Hotel Paradiso*, *Who's Afraid of Virginia Woolf?*, *Five Finger Exercise*, and *The Matchmaker*.

## Debut as Weekend Repertory Theatre

With *All the King's Men*, Yatrik was the first to establish and maintain a weekend repertory theatre. From 1964–72, for six to seven months in the year, they staged regular performances every Saturday and Sunday, first at the mini theatre on Mahadev Road and then in the bat-and-pigeon-ridden Defence Pavilion auditorium in the exhibition grounds, which are now part of Pragati Maidan. Brochures listing the season's programmes were issued in September, and theatre lovers were invited to become members and buy season tickets at a reduced rate. The emphasis was on variety, quality, and experimentation. Wherever possible, plays mounted in the winter were taken on tour in the summer to schools and colleges or to cities such as Lucknow and Chandigarh.

*All the King's Men* was staged at the Mahadev Road Auditorium (now the Films Division Auditorium), near Gole Dak Khana (Gole Post Office). Nigam Prakash had the honour to direct the play with Roshan Seth and Rati Bartholomew performing. A stage version of the American novel by Robert Penn Warren, it revolves round Willie who rises from abysmal poverty to the post of governor. It is set in the Deep South of the United States of America during the 1930s.

The rise and fall of its main character, who resorts to blackmail and bullying tactics to silence his enemies and his radical populist policies, were presented with dramatic intensity. Says Nigam, "In the lead role, Roshan Seth gave a superb performance."

Robert Penn Warren's play was a difficult and daring choice. But, as Yatrik's founder member Rati Bartholomew asserts, "The idea was to start with something unusual that would hold the imagination and break away from the drawing-room routine. The first problem that the group had to face was the small pocket-size stage at the Assembly Hall—20-ft x 16-ft proscenium with a back wall of 10 feet. Erecting a 24-ft x 8-ft wooden forestage, projecting into the auditorium, one foot lower in height than the main stage, surmounted this problem. Not only did this enlarge the acting area, but made for considerable variation in acting levels and established greater intimacy with the audience. This became a permanent feature of subsequent plays produced by the group during this session. Secondly, for practical reasons and as an experiment, the front curtain was dispensed with, necessitating a simplification of sets and scene changes depending upon the efficiency of stage management and split-second timing of light changes."

The play was a challenge in that it was episodic in character, consisting of straight dramatic incidents and flashbacks, the whole knitted together by the figure of the professor, who narrated and commented as the chorus. The playwright himself had envisaged an open stage with no set changes, but moving the story "by a fluid shifting of light from one acting area to another". The director based his production on the same lines, but had to cope with a small stage. Wooden platforms of different levels and sizes, with the action switching from one to the other with the help of well-timed light changes, the stage clad in sombre black, and abstract music by Bartok and Miles Davis created the fluidity and continuity required of the play.

*All the King's Men*

Yatrik made a graceful debut…If the performance is any indication, Yatrik has a promising future. —*The Times of India*

Yatrik opens the season with a gripping play…directed with a splendid tempo and with verve. As a maiden offering, this is fine stuff and highly competent. —*The Statesman*

...this play is a triumph of devotion. The stage is kept near-bare, set in multiple tiers. Change of scenes is effected through changing spots…It also launches Yatrik as a repertory theatre.—*Thought*

The Director dressed the play on a bare stage—moods and emphasis being established by a clever play of lights and shifting of the action from one level of the stage to another.—*Link*

Nigam recalls, "It was a small and intimate theatre. There was not enough space to use huge sets; so our sets were minimal. Since we were doing mainly English theatre, we had audiences from Delhi University, the embassies, and senior government officers and bureaucrats. We staged a new play every month with weekend shows. The tickets were sold at a low cost. Our aim was to develop professional theatre in the capital. The cast and crew of the play were doing theatre as a hobby. Subsequently, the government acquired the Mahadev Road auditorium and we shifted to a bigger venue at Pragati Maidan, which was allotted to us by the Ministry of Defence. My other memorable play at Pragati Maidan was *The Italian Straw Hat* by Eugene Labiche and Marc-Michel, adapted by Thomas Walton."

*All the King's Men*—Sushma Seth (left)

*All the King's Men*—Roshan Seth and Rati Bartholomew

*All the King's Men*—Kusum Bahl (Haidar) (left)

## The Group with Many Firsts

Yatrik was the first to start producing plays for children and teenagers. *Abe Lincoln* appealed to school children and *Sabrina Fair* to a slightly older group. This play was most attractively produced in the garden of the Michaels' house in Kaka Nagar when a young Kusum Bahl played the star role. Subsequent productions had Sushma Seth in this role, supported by stalwarts Marcus Murch, Roshan Seth, and Salima Raza.

But, in addition to plays like these, the really little ones were initiated into the fun of teamwork with the founding of Yatrik's Young Stagers' Club, which met up regularly. The club enjoyed playing in *The Land of Cards*, produced by Sai Paranjpye (1967–68), David Horsburgh's *The Ungrateful Man, Dancing Donkey* (1970–71), and *The Sleeping Beauty,* which was a pantomime for Christmas (1971–72). Barry John produced some delightful plays for children—*The Snow Queen* (1970–71) and *Trudi and the Minstrel* (1971–72). Others working with children were Meena Swaminathan and Feisal Alkazi.

In 1971, Yatrik ran into difficulties in finding space for its work. Max Mueller Bhavan (MMB), with accommodation in Connaught Circus, lent its premises, and the first summer workshop was conducted there. The group called itself "The Rooftop Theatre". Graduates from the National School of Drama helped with course productions. *The Shoemaker's Prodigious Wife* by Lorca was produced by Joy Michael in English, and Gorky's *Lower Depths* by M.K. Raina in Hindustani. With this venture, several budding talents were launched on their dramatic careers. Max Mueller Bhavan has given tremendous support and encouragement over the years. It has been a venue for rehearsals, visual enactments, and the production of plays. Irpinder Puri wrote a play based upon the life of Max Mueller, which was presented in 1982 as *Ek Roshan Awaaz* in Hindi.

*Abe Lincoln in Illinois*—Roshan Seth and Joy Michael

## Yatrik and the Renaissance of Theatre

The contour of the landscape of the theatrical movement in Delhi during the early three decades after Independence reveals a great creative upsurge. In such a landscape, Yatrik was not only part of this renaissance, but also contributed immensely to enrich it, playing the role of a catalyst. Commenting on this vibrant scene, Prof. Devendra Raj Ankur, eminent theatre artist and former director of the National School of Drama, said, "Because of its high artistic standard and sustained activities, Yatrik established its distinct identity in the theatre world of Delhi. Initially it was a group producing only English plays, but it expanded its field and soon enough it earned the reputation of a multilingual theatre group. Its productions, such as *Azar Ka Khwab*, symbolised the pinnacle of its creativity. This was the period of cooperation between various groups. The competition was healthy. Sushma Seth, Sudha Chopra, Sudha Shivpuri, and Om Shivpuri not only worked for Yatrik, but also acted in plays produced by Abhiyan. One of the distinct features of Yatrik was that it introduced a large number of talented directors, such as Marcus Murch, Barry John, and M.K. Raina. Raina directed for Yatrik Gorky's *Lower Depths*, which is considered a landmark production. It also organised drama competitions. In the first competition, 1967–68, Kulbhushan Kharbanda's *Koi Hai*, an adaptation in Hindi of William Saroyan's *Hello Out There!*, won the best play award. It was a significant event in the history of Delhi theatre. The play had several shows."

An early play *Abe Lincoln in Illinois,* produced by Unity Theatre, was the progenitor of Yatrik, and the group travelled to Calcutta (present-day Kolkata), Jaipur, and Jodhpur and then to Dehra Dun, Nainital, Mussoorie, and Shimla.

Decades have elapsed, but the participants in these touring shows continue to remember their exciting experiences when they were young and dreamt of beautiful things in life.

# NURTURED BY JOY...
## FRIEND, PHILOSOPHER, AND GUIDE

*The eternal simplicities generate the enrichment of art from their own bosoms not only because they are eternal, but also because change is the condition of their existence. Thus art is one of the conditions of man's realization of himself, and in its turn is one of the realities of man.*

**Christopher Caudwell**

When we talk of Yatrik, a face that radiates charm, intelligence, great warmth, and affection comes to mind instantly...that of Joy Michael, because Yatrik is to Joy as Joy is to Yatrik. This is the face that sheds its brilliance on all aspects of Yatrik's creativity and organisational structure. It is the face of a friend, philosopher, and guide, and has continued to be an integral part of Yatrik for over five decades.

Joy Michael has vibrantly kept alive on the stage an array of characters from the classics and contemporary dramatic masterpieces that have left indelible impressions on audiences. She is one of India's greatest scholars of Western theatre and drama, a practitioner and a cultural ambassador of her country to acquaint the West with India's great dramatic heritage. She has carried her team, Yatrik, through 50 glorious years, in spite of many vicissitudes, with courage, determination, and commitment. She has, in the real sense, nurtured the group. Her life in the theatre presents an inspired saga of an artist's struggle to achieve excellence. She is a woman who dared to enter a field dominated by men through single-minded dedication, fecundity of imagination, scholarly grasp of theatrical arts, and organisational skills. She emerged as one of our finest theatre artists, leaving an indelible mark on the Delhi stage. As a leader, she has always inspired her dedicated band of theatre persons to create works of theatrical art to be admired by a discerning audience.

Over the years, Joy has produced more than 250 plays for Yatrik and portrayed wide-ranging characters, which bear the stamp of her brilliant artistry. As an artist and human being, Joy has always sought happiness for her artistic collaborators and for herself through creativity. As a creative person with poetic vision, she has enlarged the dimension of education, and as an educationist, she has deepened the human essence in her art. She stressed the role of theatre in the cultural and aesthetic development of youth and promoted theatre in schools as a part of basic education. As she matured into a fine artist,

Joy Michael in *Tartuffe*

*The Importance of Being Earnest*—Joy Michael

so did Yatrik and with her, all those who joined the journey in pursuit of excellence of the theatrical art.

**Early days:** Joy was born in 1924 in Asansol, West Bengal, where her father worked for the Maharaja of Darbanga. In Calcutta, she was initiated into theatre right from childhood. She followed her hobby to act in all school productions. When she joined St. Stephen's College, Delhi, her hobby matured into a passion for theatre and she became the first female secretary of the Shakespeare Society of the college. Full of youthful energy, she used to cycle to college while she was staying in Civil Lines with her parents.

Along with founding Yatrik, Joy had started the Young Stagers' Club in the 1960s, which would regularly put on a play or a musical in the 60s with child actors. This group was popular.

**Reminiscences:** My father was a chief engineer in Bihar. I had to go to Patna to attend school. I came to Delhi when I was 10 years old and joined Presentation Convent Higher Secondary School. As a child, I was very naughty, mischievous, and always ready for pranks.

We were in Delhi during the pre-Independence riots and in Calcutta during the communal riots; I was deeply affected by them. Such memories leave indelible scars. It was in Calcutta where I met Hugh Michael. He was a young army officer and he helped rescue my family from a riot-affected area.

I used to go to my college on bicycle. It was an exciting experience. I did my MA in English Literature in 1950. St. Stephen's College made me what I am today. While I was in college, I used to work with theatre groups such as Unity Theatre and the UK High Commission, which had a strong drama group. I also did a play for the Army Headquarters' dramatic society. During those days Hindi theatre was uncommon, until Ebrahim Alkazi came here and started the National School of Drama.

In the late 1950s, Roshan Seth and Nigam Prakash, also students of St. Stephen's College, joined me. The United States Information Service (USIS) was the hub of American plays. We, a group of six now, Sushma, Rati, Kusum, Roshan, and Nigam, with Salima joining us soon thereafter, produced plays for them, toured with productions throughout the country, and gave 73 performances. We travelled in air-conditioned compartments. We had such a wonderful experience and with it came the conviction that theatre activities must be continued. This convinced us to form a group of our own.

In the summer of 1964, we finally formed our group. It was named Yatrik, as suggested by Nigam Prakash. Planned by young people with a lot of energy, imagination, and experience, Yatrik grew into an institution with more and more talented people joining it at different points of time. We attracted young people through conducting

A scene from *Goa*

*Goa*—a simple and effective set

theatre workshops. I wanted them to develop their potential and to find fulfilment in doing something to enjoy.

In 1970, Yatrik merged with the Indian National Theatre and with Sheila Bharat Ram; I laid the foundation of the Shri Ram Centre. I was the first director, and opened the season with Asif Currimbhoy's *Goa*. At that time, we had perhaps the first full-time professional theatre team in the history of theatre in India—full-time stage manager, the irrepressible Marcus Murch, assistant stage manager Barry John, who had just returned from England, full-time actor Kulbhushan Kharbanda, manager Ranbir Singh, costume-in-charge Prema Karanth, and our dedicated carpenter Charan Singh.

I left for America in 1971 to accept an appointment to direct and lecture on Indian drama. I returned in 1972 to find that the merger had failed. Yatrik had lost everything and faced dissolution. The future was bleak, but the courage, determination, commitment, and support of my family—my husband, my mother, my daughters

Meriel and Kristine—and of some stalwarts pulled us through. 1973 onwards were difficult years of struggle for survival. Marcus started Stagedoor, Barry established Theatre Action Group (TAG), and some founder members had left the country. We had to regroup and re-establish. It was heartbreaking and frustrating, and I felt disillusionment but not despair. Max Mueller Bhavan came to our rescue and allowed us to use its Connaught Place premises, where we established a rooftop theatre.

Soon thereafter, I became the principal of St. Thomas School, where I was able to promote and encourage creative drama. From 1975, it was a steady, slow, hard revival and rejuvenation to reassure our audiences that we were still active. During that interim period of many years, Yatrik sponsored original plays, was keen on good translations, appreciated and promoted Indo-Anglian drama, enjoyed producing the classics and, importantly, presented brilliant, outstanding Hindi plays, both original and adapted.

In 2003–04, Yatrik celebrated 40 glorious years of theatre activity with 250 plays to its credit. We performed for two weeks at the British Council and two weeks at the India Habitat Centre—six full-length plays were played to full houses, allowing free entry. My daughter Kristine designed a brilliant and outstanding record of plays, pictures, exhibition of costumes, display of programmes, newspaper articles, and theatre memorabilia. Our chronicler Lola Chatterji wrote a delightful, interesting history of Yatrik, which is now part of this book.

So that is what theatre is about—success and disappointment, frustration and renewed hope. What seems impossible slowly but surely shows rays of light, human strengths and frailties, and enduring warm friendships. Yatrik has been always in my mind and I am fully conscious of the duty of the artist towards society, which is mirrored and communicated on this unique stage of life. Theatre is a way of life. An artist has to assert his or her freedom and build a bridge to connect with people. This is also the artistic credo of Yatrik.

Meet **Joy Michael**, the guiding light for the Yatrik Theatre Group.

In the late 1950s, Joy trained at the London Academy of Music and Dramatic Arts (LAMDA), the Royal Academy of Music and the British Drama League, London, on a British Council Scholarship. She has lectured and directed Indian plays at the University of Virginia, Russell Sage College, New York, Sweet Briar College and Punjab University, Chandigarh. Visiting lecturer in Indian drama, Mary Washington College, University of Virginia, Fredericksburg, Virginia, Joy taught a general course in Sanskrit drama and Indian folk theatre, and directed Mohan Rakesh's *One Day in Ashadh* in an English translation and David Horsburgh's *The Ungrateful Man*—a story from the *Panchatantra*. As an executive at the United States Educational Foundation in India (USEFI), she travelled widely, witnessing theatre productions abroad.

As principal of St. Thomas School, New Delhi, Joy Michael's production of the play *Stree,* based on interviews with Aruna Asaf Ali and Kamaladevi Chattopadhyay, was a theatrical masterpiece in that it was both educative and entertaining. Presented by the school, Joy conceived and directed it with choreography by Madhuri Bhatia and music composition by Robida. This dance-drama opened with an ode to Mother India, a poem dedicated to the glorification of the achievements of great Indian women, such as Rukmini Devi Arundale, an exponent of classical dance in the quest of a modern idiom; Kamaladevi Chattopadhyay, leader of the Indian cultural renaissance; and Rajkumari Amrit Kaur, a disciple of Mahatma Gandhi and the first woman to hold a cabinet rank in Independent India, as Union Health Minister. Highlighting various facets of the life of Indian women, their struggle for a free, meaningful, and dignified life, the dance-drama culminated with women as a vehicle for socio-economic change.

As a pioneer of Indian theatre, Joy has been honoured by a number of leading cultural bodies and awards, such as the Rockefeller Award for work in professional theatre in New York, the Delhi Natya Sangh Theatre Award, the Sahitya Kala Parishad Award, the Raja Ram Mohan Roy National Education Award, the Poorva South Asian Women's Director Award, the Emeritus Director Theatre Award, Government of India, and the Chaman Lal Memorial Award. She was acclaimed, recognised, and felicitated for her lifelong contribution and service to theatre at the Asian Women's Directors' Conference in Delhi in January 2003; she received the Sangeet Natak Akademi Award in 2009 for theatre direction. Joy was honoured with the fourth-highest civilian award, the Padma Shri, in 2012. In February 2016, as she received the National School of Drama's Bharat Rang Mahotsav Award, her response to the question of how she managed to keep Yatrik going for over 50 years was, "Love."

## The Michael Family

Before we can reflect on or talk about the extended Yatrik family, we must look at the incredible support that Joy and Yatrik got from her immediate family. Her family was, and continues to be, completely involved in what could be described as creative fanaticism.

**Lt Col. Hugh E. Michael,** Joy's husband ("Hubie" as he was affectionately called), was her staunch supporter. He was himself a rich baritone singer and took part in any play that needed singing. He played important singing roles in *The Fantasticks* and *Oliver*. He was the organiser of all "front of house" activities for many years. He

*Oliver*—Jamila Verghese and Hugh Michael

actually did everything on the outside that was integral to staging a play—printing and selling tickets, delivery of tickets to various outlets, publicity, printing of brochures, getting police permissions, and the difficult and delicate task of procuring entertainment tax exemptions.

One of his quiet but invaluable roles was that of being the public face of the group. He supervised the seating of audiences in the auditorium, interacting with all of them. He knew most of them by name and would be happy to joke around and provide a personal touch. He would encourage them to not only enjoy the play but also to come again and spread the word. Hugh Michael trained all the children in how to usher, sell brochures, and keep accounts. He was a great favourite with all the children whose working parents sometimes had to bring them to shows and rehearsals. He was always ready with fascinating stories to keep bored kids amused. His constant support and encouragement were incredibly important for Joy and the rest of the Yatrik family in those early years.

**Ruby Christian,** Joy's mother, was a skilled seamstress and would undertake all the alterations of the costumes for the plays. She was especially good with hats and they were indispensable in *The Matchmaker*, the play that later became popular as *Hello, Dolly!* The action took place in a hat shop. Most of the "period" plays involved actors wearing her costume jewellery.

Ruby Christian's greatest contribution, however, was keeping starving actors fed. In those days, there were few small restaurants, especially since most actors were students who couldn't afford anything but hostel and canteen food. She was famous for the broth and bread she would serve as supper. In fact, whenever the group worked late, especially on dress rehearsal nights, she would provide food for the entire cast and crew. The supper theatre, which Yatrik ran for a few years at the Films Division Auditorium at Mahadev Road, was also catered for with her vegetable broth and served with

*The Road to Mecca*—Ramesh Thakur and Kristine Michael

bread. We kids would always wait eagerly for the enormous *degchi* filled with steaming hot broth and had to be restrained from eating up everyone's share.

Joy Michael's two daughters—Meriel and Kristine—started acting on the stage from their childhood, graduating to play major roles. First it was with the Young Stagers' Club, and then with Yatrik. While Meriel's stage appearances were more frequent in the earlier years, Kristine was seen on stage in several plays through the years.

**Meriel Michael** recalls: My active association with Yatrik was in my younger days, because later, once I was in government service, most of my adult years were spent outside of Delhi. But in those early years with Yatrik, most of the time I was backstage helping out with whatever needed to be done. I acted in Luigi Pirandello's

*Six Characters in Search of an Author*, *South Pacific*, and *Our Town*, to mention a few that I can remember.

Our several homes over the years—in Kaka Nagar, in St. Thomas School, in the Asian Games Village—have always been Yatrik's homes, the nerve centres. Yatrik is an extension of the Michael family. Working in Yatrik is a family affair for all of its members and the togetherness engendered by Joy creates an atmosphere of camaraderie.

Up to the age of 10, we used to travel with the group which was to become Yatrik. I remember our travelling with Tom Noonan of the USIS, who was a puppeteer by profession, with the play *Abe Lincoln in Illinois*. We travelled with Rati Bartholomew and her children Sushma Seth, Nigam Prakash, and others. There was not much money, so we, the group, used to hire a complete railway compartment (possibly second class) and we kids had a whale of a time. When we got to the college where the adults would perform, it was our duty to clean the stage, help set up the set and props, and help with costume changes. I remember that there were only a few places with dressing rooms; otherwise, most of the costume changes were done behind bed sheets.

One of the great things about Yatrik in those years was the feeling of togetherness and lack of class distinctions. Actors of all ages and positions would willingly help with all kinds of menial tasks. For us, as children, it was wonderful as no one talked down to us and we were accepted and encouraged to do our little bit to help. Apart from cleaning the stage, helping with the props and carpentry, setting up the costumes, ushering, and working as stagehands, we were allowed to do anything including direct and act in our own productions for the public. The shy and socially inept were soon jollied out of their shells. When a production was over, everyone helped bring down the sets and clean up. No aftershow parties were permitted until everything was cleared and the stage was left bare and clean for the next user. No snobs or "prima donnas" were accepted. There was basic

*The Land of Cards*—Meriel Michael (left)

*The Land of Cards*—Meriel Michael (right)

discipline and cooperation; everyone was bound by a strong esprit de corps. There was a great opportunity available for anyone to develop his or her talents, and this attracted the young and the old alike to the group.

Some of my poignant memories are with the Young Stagers' Club. We were popular with other children who came to watch our shows. Among the many plays we did were *The Land of Cards* and *Alice in Wonderland*. In one play, the boy playing the king forgot his lines and the entire cast prompted him, loud and clear, right there on stage. In David Horsburgh's *The Ungrateful Man*, there was a scene where some members of the audience were invited to the stage. One of the boys picked up one of the "monkeys" and tried to carry her off to his house as a pet, not realising it was a girl in costume. The shocked "monkey" was Chandrika Grover, if I remember correctly. In another scene during the same play, the king was to be informed that his daughter had been bitten by a snake and would die soon. The 12-year-old playing the princess' attendant forgot to take off her spectacles when she came on stage to break this news. She got so flustered that she blurted out, "The princess has bitten the snake," much to the merriment of the young cast members and the audience.

A scene from *Alice in Wonderland*

Kristine Michael (left) in *A Doctor in Spite of Himself*

Kristine Michael in the makeup room

*Uncle Vanya*—Kristine Michael and Kusum Haidar

Kusum Haidar was acting in *The Seagull*, which was staged at Pragati Maidan's Defence Pavilion. She had to play her part poised over a small tank outside in the rundown garden, since the director decided to have the play there. There were a lot of big frogs and we kids spent a lot of time trying to catch them to frighten her during the performance. Unfortunately, we were unsuccessful.

## Ode to Joy

Some enchanted morning, you may see a stranger,

You may see a stranger across a crowded Delhi University classroom.
And somehow you will know, you'll know even then,

That somewhere (actually right there) you'll see her again and again.
Some enchanted morning, you may hear her laughing,

You may hear her laughing across the crowded classroom.
And many nights in fifty years,

As strange as it seems,

The sound of her laughter will sing in your dreams.
Who can explain it? Who can tell you why?

Foolish and intrigued fellow students give you reasons,
Wise old professors never try.

Some enchanted mornings, afternoons, evenings and nights,
You may hear her calling,

You may hear her calling across many crowded and
empty spaces and many gaps in time,

Then fly to her side, (though with no wings,
and airfares being what they are, you can't),

And make her your own, (but how can you,
somebody else had already made her his own),

Or all through your life you'll always be alone
(not actually, maybe some other stranger may take her place).

Once you have found her, never let her go.

Once you have found her, never let her go
(as if you had a choice—she left and let you go long ago, you chump).

*Som Benegal*

[Som Benegal, 20 June 1994. He is also known for his direction of Aleksei Arbuzov's *The Promise*. Arbuzov was a Soviet playwright whose plays were immensely popular in the Soviet Union. His play *The Promise* was also popular in the West. A romantic drama, it featured Zarin Chowdhury, Zahoori Mohieddin, and Aftab Seth. Tinged with irony, the play was staged by Yatrik at the Defence Pavilion Theatre in 1969.]

# FOUNDING MEMORIES...
## As the Travellers Became Yatrik

*You see this creature with her kerbstone English: the English that will keep her in the gutter to the end of her days. Well, sir, in three months I could pass that girl off as a duchess at an ambassador's garden party. I could even get her a place as lady's maid or shop assistant, which requires better English.*

**Henry Higgins in *Pygmalion***
**by Bernard Shaw**

They had travelled, bonded, and experienced the initial euphoria of the world as a stage, with each one playing his part. Here we get to know them, and travel with their memories, as they did with Joy Michael.

**Kusum Haidar** has dedicated her life to theatre. One of the founder members of Yatrik, Kusum has had an outstanding career as an actress, spanning nearly five decades, working under great Indian directors and essaying important characters from classics and significant contemporary dramatic works.

A highly qualified theatre artist, Kusum was trained in mime and movement at L'Ecole Internationale de Theatre (1960–62) under the noted teacher Jacques Lecoq, the British Drama League, London (1963–64) and the School for Contemporary Dance, London (1987–91). Before joining these higher dramatic institutions abroad, she had thorough training as an actress under Ebrahim Alkazi. Still in her mid-teens, Kusum enrolled herself as a student of Theatre Unit's School of Dramatic Art, Mumbai.

She expresses her heartfelt gratitude to Mr Alkazi for his personal attention and for initiating her into the wonderful world of theatre. He helped her transform into an excellent actress in the realistic style of acting. Kusum also reflects on her totally different experience of working under the direction of Habib Tanvir, who directed a play for Hindustani Theatre, founded by Begum Qudsia Zaidi in the 1950s. She had an equally rewarding experience working in plays directed by Amal Allana.

Kusum moved to Delhi to join Miranda House, University of Delhi, as an undergraduate student. She missed the vibrant theatrical scene of Mumbai. Her observation of Delhi's theatre scene during those days was, "There was a great deal of theatre activity in Delhi and although I felt there was a genuine desire to foster theatre, the standards of quality and perfection set by Mr Alkazi were missing."

As a student of Miranda House, she was exposed to university theatre, acting in plays presented by the Shakespeare Society of St. Stephen's College. Eventually, a few people from the university and All India Radio got together and formed Unity Theatre. Kusum involved herself in many of their productions, such as Ibsen's *The Wild Duck and Ghosts*, Shaw's *Caesar and Cleopatra*, and Anouilh's *Dinner with the Family*.

And then shone forth a beacon of light on Begum Qudsia Zaidi and her Hindustani Theatre. Habib Tanvir had just returned from abroad full of new ideas, but with his eyes firmly fixed on indigenous folk forms and his Urdu roots entrenched in Indian culture. He joined the Hindustani Theatre as the director. Like many others, says Kusum, "I felt the strong pull of Begum Zaidi's vision. We did *Khalid ki Khala* and *Mitti ki Gaadi* directed by Habib Tanvir; Shama Zaidi created the costumes and M.S. Sathyu did the sets. *Mitti ki Gaadi*, the Hindi version of *Mricchakatika*, Sudraka's Sanskrit classic, was presented in folk style through dance, music, and mime, with a cast of six Adivasis and a handful of us in Delhi. The stylised speech and movements of these actors were an education for us, as we had been trained in realistic acting. It was an innovative experiment. The stage was bare, the actors wore half-masks and colourful makeup and the costumes were ultra-modern. We girls wore mini ghagras and the briefest of cholis, for which we were pelted with tomatoes and onions at a performance in Aligarh. But the performances were energetic and the play made its mark."

In and around 1960, Tom Noonan, the cultural affairs officer at the USIS, played a seminal role in the Delhi theatre scene. Unity Theatre invited him to direct *The Lark* by Jean Anouilh, a dramatic play based on the life of St. Joan, and Kusum was cast to play the lead. "I have played many challenging roles in my career," Kusum reflects, "but I still think Joan was my best. This was largely due to the Alkazi training combined with Tom Noonan's extraordinary skill as a director. It was an exacting and demanding role. Tom did not have a heavy hand; nor did he give copious instructions or talk much. His non-interfering approach to the production promoted individual creativity. He encouraged us to develop our own roles within the larger picture. Such freedom helped us to innovate and enhance the quality of our performances. We enjoyed ourselves on stage.

"My approach to Joan was basically putting in two hours of hard work before rehearsals. Since the entire play rested on me and I was on stage all the time, I had to lead the climaxes, the highs and lows, and structure in an emotional graph. I started working on further developing the range of my voice and had to change from playing a simple peasant girl who heard voices from God asking her to save France to being a soldier leading an army. My body had to transform itself and I had to muster physical strength and stamina to deal with the intense emotional variations in the trial scene and inspire soldiers in the battlefield with a complete change of personality. It was a lifetime's experience.

"When the play opened at the auditorium at the All India Fine Arts and Crafts Society (AIFACS) on Rafi Marg, with Indira Gandhi and John Galbraith, the then serving American ambassador to India, in the audience, there was a short power failure. The lights came back after 10 minutes...the play carried on smoothly. The audience had sat patiently and engrossed. Those were also the days when there was no over-the-top security. Mrs Gandhi came up to the stage and appreciated the performance. She told me that she was deeply affected by the story of Joan, and as a child, she had identified herself with Joan's mission to save her country. Being a French play, personnel from the French Embassy were represented in strength in the audience. That year I was awarded the French government scholarship for Theatre Studies in France."

Tom Noonan's experience of working with local talent led him to do *Abe Lincoln in Illinois* in 1963, which paved the way for the formation of Yatrik under the record-breaking leadership of Joy Michael, who has sustained the group for the past 50 years. Many of those who are prominent in theatre and film today and have been over the years have contributed in a big way to Yatrik, and the group, in turn, has given them the platform to display and develop their talent. Yatrik was the first group to establish and maintain weekend repertory theatre.

Acting is Kusum's first love, and she is continuing her journey uninterrupted. In 2013, she played the role of Roshanara in *Dara* under the direction of Tripurari Sharma. Although it was a minor role, with her consummate artistry, she imparted freshness to the character of Roshanara, the spinster daughter of Emperor Shah Jahan, who clamoured for the execution of Dara to support Aurangzeb in the bloody war of succession.

While working on the characters she plays, Kusum tries to fit in her director's vision and she does her homework seriously: "I read the theme of the play and its period and the social background of the action is set to feel the mood of different situations my character confronts as the play moves forward. What is most important is the grasp of different acting styles. Your emotions should be communicated through your action. Featuring external characteristics of a character is not enough; you have to discover the inner image of the character."

As a result of her devotion to her art, various cultural bodies have honoured Kusum for her contribution as an actress. She received the best actress award by the Delhi Natya Sangh (1960–61) and by Bhartiya Natya Sangh (2011). Sangeet Natak Akademi gave her the prestigious award in 2013 for her contribution to enriching Indian theatre as an actress.

As a consummate actor and director, passionately in love with theatre, having been with the group through its glorious half-century marked by achievements, she affirms her faith in the future of Yatrik as a vibrant theatre group to offer momentous moments to the audience.

Kusum has directed a number of plays for Yatrik, but in most of these she did not act. "There has to be some distance between the work of a director and an actor. As a director, I give actors enough room to use their own imagination, but that should be in tune with my scheme. My overall approach is subtlety." She has to her credit *Salom*e (1993), *Antigone* (1996), *Blood Wedding* (2005), and *Metamorphoses* by Mary Zimmerman (2012), which, by her own admission, has been her most exciting and challenging directorial venture. There was also *When Five Years Pass* by Lorca, which she did for the Spanish Cultural Centre.

**Reminiscences:** The long artistic journey with Yatrik began when I was very young, full of beautiful dreams, experiencing spring in the air. This has continued ceaselessly, empowering me to reflect on the world philosophically.

The inspiration to form the group was driven by our passion for theatre and working with like-minded people. The potential of developing our talents was further endorsed by the success we had with performances at schools and summer workshops. We worked to reach out to a higher audience and find a way to contribute to the cultural life of Delhi. The inspiration came from people like Tom Noonan and from the leadership that Joy Michael provided, which spearheaded the formation of Yatrik.

Yatrik was founded in 1964, following close at the heels of the National School of Drama under Alkazi, from where Hindi theatre and some other regional-language plays emerged. Habib Tanvir, Balwant Gargi, Begum Zaidi, and Sheila Bhatia determined our own indigenous expansion that had been somehow blotted out by the early training in colonial schools. We had to revive our sense of belonging to our own culture and, at the same time, take advantage of what we learnt from Western theatre. Sai Paranjpye also produced plays for Yatrik and her whole directorial art was subtle.

Joy transformed Yatrik into a front-ranking theatre group in the capital with several distinguishing features of its own. She worked hard to discover the world of the characters' external and internal lives and their interrelationships. She has always paid a great deal of attention to detail. The curtains have to be just right, the furniture has to be in keeping with the period, the lighting and music have to be in sync, and so on. She has always kept in mind what happens at the front of the house and ensured, for example, that the audience is ushered in properly. Her major contribution as the director of Yatrik was to inspire its members, actors, directors, designers, and backstage artists to pursue a quest for excellence. Over the years, she had built up a huge costume wardrobe, which served Yatrik for many years. It was heartbreaking when Joy and I had to reduce its volume due to a shortage of space.

Our aesthetic came from our academic backgrounds. We had knowledge about plays from all over the world and about what was coming from within the country. We travelled as a family. Joy "mothered" us and we performed with whatever we brought with us. We shared rooms and never thought of discomfort of hardships; and we were happy to have an appreciative audience. It enabled us to meet people outside our world.

The greatest hurdles were and continue to be finances. In the early days, there was a scarcity of places to perform. Theatre was more or less homeless. The back garden of Joy Michael's flat in Kidwai Nagar was the designated rehearsal space. For the performance of *Sabrina Fair*, we started in that back garden with a couple of spots provided by Mr Dhingra; furniture and costumes were gathered from our own homes. These were indeed pioneering days; if you didn't have an auditorium, you just had to create your own space for theatre.

The lack of funds is a perennial hurdle. The British Council helped us from the beginning and even donated some equipment for

Stage set for *Sabrina Fair*, in the back garden of Joy Michael's house

Kusum Haidar (left) in *Sabrina Fair*

Another scene from *Sabrina Fair*

*Sabrina Fair*—Kusum Haidar and the parakeet

lighting—and then survival was dependent on box-office sales. There was so little theatre in the 1950s and early 1960s that people were hungry for it. It was culturally enriching both for the audiences and for us. Seeing and understanding Ibsen and Chekhov, for example, was educating and entertaining. From sparse audiences of 50, they grew to 500 by the late 1960s.

I had the good fortune to receive a great deal of knowledge and experience, being trained both abroad and in India, especially with Mr Alkazi. I have applied all that I have learnt: mime in France, directing and teaching at the British Drama League, as a student of Mr Alkazi, the many years of teaching at St. Columbus School, and as a voice production teacher at Amal and Nissar's Dramatic Art and Design Academy.

But the most valuable learning experience I had was with Alkazi, whom I think is an even better teacher than a director. All the speech and voice exercises I learnt from him I use till today to apply in my teaching. My teaching experience helped, of course, not only as an actor, but even further to develop a sense and skill for direction. In the Alkazi school, we were trained not only to focus on the theme of a play, but also absorb and study characterisation and all the technical aspects of a play—lights, sets, music—that enhance its message or theme.

Yatrik is where I was able to fulfil myself as an actress. It also gave me the opportunity to develop my potential as a director over the years. The group has achieved unprecedented success, setting new standards in theatrical art, and has now completed over 50 glorious years of uninterrupted creativity. Joy Michael and I are the only founder members still here. If the old guard provides the sustainability and steadiness, with the anchor of experience, then the new talent brings in the much-needed breath of fresh air. And Yatrik is already attracting young people. We hope that some promising young talent will emerge to lead the group in this fast-changing world.

Among the directors I have known and worked with, Joy is an inspiring director, steadfast and sound in her approach, and delves deeply into the theme and meaning of plays. Having been a teacher, she makes sure that her actors get to reach their best potential. I have enjoyed working with all these directors: Alkazi, Joy, Sai Paranjpye, Habib Tanvir, and certainly Amal Allana in my later years. I learnt from them in different ways. *Erendira* with Amal Allana in 2004 was most memorable; we travelled to several places around the world, including Colombia.

A scene from *The Seagull*

*Sylvia Plath*—Prabha Tonk (front), Kusum Haidar (standing), Sabina Jaitly in the background

**Memorabilia with Yatrik**

*Abe Lincoln in Illinois*: training with the company, under the leadership of Joy; Tom Noonan's direction of Robert Penn Warren's play.

*All the King's Men*: stage version of the novel by Robert Penn Warren.

*The Seagull* by Chekhov: an unforgettable experience.

*Sylvia Plath*: a play on the life of the American poet.

*Uncle Vanya* by Chekhov: played Yelena Andreyevna

and co-acted with Bhaskar Bhattacharya, who was an outstanding actor.
*9 Jakhoo Hill* by Gurcharan Das: directed by Sunit Tandon, played the role of Amrita.
*The Wild Duck* by Henrik Ibsen: played Hedvig.

**Milestones**

*The Seagull* and *Uncle Vanya,* Anton Chekhov's two plays, are full of subtlety, lyrical beauty, gentle humour, and the muffled sighs of unfortunate people unable to cope with their harsh surroundings. Joy Michael directed these plays with remarkable sensitivity and with a feel for the Chekhovian mood and aesthetics. Kusum recalls, "When I portrayed Nina Zarechnaya, the daughter of a wealthy landowner, and Helena Andreyevna Serebrya, Professor Serebryakov's young and beautiful second wife—I felt deep down inside me a sigh of pain and tragic sense of unfulfilment of hopes and aspirations."

The consummate and sensitive actress that she is, Kusum truly lived this complex role of Nina Zarechnaya, revealing with subtlety the multiple emotional layers of the character. This is the tragedy of the slain seagull; the mockery and crudity of life. A provincial girl in love for the first time does not notice the checked trousers, the worn shoes, or the stinking cigar. Life's ugliness is realised too late, when life is broken, all sacrifices made, and love turned into a habit. New illusions are needed, for one must go on living—and Nina looks for them in zealotry.

Helena Andreyevna Serebrya, the young and beautiful second wife of Professor Serebryakov, is torn between her revulsion for her aged, pompous husband and repressed attraction for the country doctor whom her stepdaughter wants to marry. With Joy's sensitive direction, the story flowed slowly and effortlessly, capturing the pale, tender humour in the lives of the characters.

**_Blood Wedding_—A Matter of Love and Hate**

Family feud and wild passions lead to an unbroken chain of murder and intense hatred. In this barbaric act, men are killed and women are left to mourn their dead. This most shocking and tragic aspect of human destiny is revealed in Federico Garcia Lorca's *Blood Wedding*, presented by Yatrik at India Habitat Centre. Different versions of this play have been seen on the Delhi stage in the past. Yatrik's production seems to capture the tragic vision of Lorca with a poetic intensity that deeply stirs the human soul. An ambiance of doom and sombre lyricism is projected to heighten the tragic mood.

*Blood Wedding* forms parts of Lorca's trilogy; the other two are *Yerma* and *The House of Bernarda Alba*.

*Blood Wedding* is a simple tale on the surface, and unfolds the story of a bride who runs away on her wedding day with her former lover. The mother of the bridegroom provokes her son to pursue and catch hold of those who have broken the solemn conventional law of marriage and its sanctity.

He chases them deep into a dark and dense forest and a fierce knife combat ensues. The confrontation takes place against the backdrop of family feud and hatred between the family of the bridegroom and the lover of the bride.

Except for one character—Leonardo—all the characters have no names. The intense inner conflict of the characters makes this play dramatically rich and the movements and actions of the characters are powerful and convincing, characterised by a kind of spontaneity.

Director Kusum displays fine visual imagination, imbuing her production with scenic images remarkable for their symbolic meaning.

The wedding procession scene is beautifully composed. Similarly, the scene of the forest where the young lovers are frantically pursued by the bridegroom, with three woodcutters, the moon, and a beggar woman, is pervaded by gloom and haunting suspense. The characters respectively symbolise the mournful chorus, the messenger of death, and death itself.

The director aptly handles offstage sounds to create the illusion of reality on the stage, where a savage drama of murder, hate, and revenge is unfolded.

The cast gives a brilliant account of itself. Oroon Das as Leonardo, the lover who had married the cousin of the bride but passionately remembers his first love, invests his portrait with intense passion and obsession. Seema Sarin, the bride, is torn between her passion for her former lover and her loyalty for her bridegroom. Ankana Bhalla as the mother gives a penetrating revelation of her character's complex world of hatred. Ranjit Mathur as the humiliated father, Shairi Mathur as the neglected wife of Leonardo, and Nikhil Murali as the bridegroom give impressive performances.

### *Metamorphoses*—Myths and Modernity

This was first staged by Yatrik at the open-air auditorium of the India Habitat Centre in 2012, and takes the audience to the world of Greek mythology inhabited by characters that get metamorphosed by the gods. Directorial ingenuity, brilliant performances, and visual imagery captivated the audience. The play is adapted from a Latin narrative poem by the Roman poet Ovid.

Structurally, the play is not conventional. There are different stories that have no thematic connection. However, love in its various manifestations is the recurrent theme to bring into focus the inevitability of change; there is nothing static. This inherent phenomenon could be described as a "poetic bridge between myth and modernism".

One of the important aspects of the production is that it combines comedy and classic tragedy; Rajesh Singh designed highly imaginative sets and lighting. The water pond, with water enough to swim and space enough for the movements, occupies the central space. This is essential for the enactment of most of the stories—used as a swimming pool, a washbasin, the underworld, and the sea. The water is at once a destroyer and a redeemer. With subtle light and sound effects and drapery, the illusion of storms is created. Most vital and gripping scenes like the passionate sexual encounter between a father and an accursed daughter take place in this pond.

The play opens with the comments on the evolution of the world from chaos. Narrators introduce the stories to the audience and also comment on them. The first story deals with Midas and his golden touch that turns even his daughter into gold. Bacchus advises him to seek a mystic pool to return to normal. One of the stories depicts the tragic tale of the grieving husband who tries to retrieve his dead wife from the underworld. God allows him to do so, on the condition that he should not turn back to look at her until he crosses the border of the underworld. He fails to fulfil this condition and his wife is condemned to stay in the underworld. It has another version in which the husband forgets about his wife while returning from the underworld and the wife does not follow him, so they remain eternally separated.

The agonising metamorphosis a man undergoes is revealed in the story of Erysichthon, a non-believer, who cuts down a tree sacred to a goddess. In an act of revenge, the goddess transforms him into a person with eternal hunger. As a result of this insatiable hunger, he loses all his fortunes and ultimately he sells his mother to a merchant to buy food. The poor old woman prays and gets transformed into a beautiful little girl. Erysichthon dies trying to devour his own body to satiate his hunger.

In a story within the story, Vertumnus tries to woo Pomona, a female wood nymph who has rejected her suitors and is now alone. Vertumnus approaches her, disguising himself in a variety of costumes. To win her heart, Vertumnus narrates the shocking story of King Cinyras and his daughter Myrrha, who was cursed for rejecting her suitors. She is condemned to have a lust for her father as a punishment for her arrogance. The curse culminates in a shameful passionate act and her ultimate disappearance into the water when her father tries to strangle her after recognising her. The scene, imbued with emotional intensity, is artistically choreographed. Finally, Vertumnus succeeds in winning over the heart of Pomona, who asks him to take off his disguises.

A story narrated by Phaeton is about his father Apollo, who has neglected him, and Apollo's consequent guilt for his fatherly neglect. This story has a contemporary ring.

The concluding story is about Baucis and Philemon, a poor couple who receive strangers with respect, calling them the children of God. To fulfil the couple's wishes, the gods turn the two into "a pair of trees with branches intertwined to die at the same time to save each other the grief of death". The play ends on an optimistic note with Midas discovering the mystic pool to regain his original self, ecstatically embracing his daughter, who too has regained her human form.

The play is aptly cast throughout. Sunit Tandon as Midas and Phaeton acts in a spontaneous manner, establishing lively rapport with the audience. Arti Nayar, Anirudh Nair, Ashish Paliwal, Kavita Seth, Keshav Moodliar, Rueben Israel, Shena Gamat, Sonali Sharma, and Vani Vyas act in a variety of roles, impressing the audience.

Gods play the main role in the development of the plot in the stories enacted. Here, man is a mere captive in the hands of the gods and there is no escape. Defiance against the gods invites punishment. Some of the stories metaphorically reflect the dilemma of modern man and his cynicism, although the story of two gods visiting the human world appears to be naive in the context of the complexities of modernist society. The play talks about the continuity of transformation, which is illustrated through the characters that undergo metamorphosis—

this is a mythical interpretation and is obsolete. Philosophers of different schools do agree about the inexorable nature of transformation, which is brought about by a dialectical process. This view is scientific.

However, the elements of mystery, suspense, and straightforward narrative keep the audience—sitting on the three sides of the amphitheatre, enabling them to watch the vital theatrical scenes without any obstruction—engaged, offering them poignant, comic, and moving experiences.

*Metamorphoses* was judged one of the 10 best productions of the year 2012. It was staged at the Bhartendu Natya Mahotsav, 2013, organised by Sahitya Kala Parishad, Delhi. It was also featured at Bharat Rang Mahotsav in 2013, organised by the National School of Drama, Delhi. These two festivals are prestigious theatrical events. The selection of Yatrik's *Metamorphoses* for these events was a feather in the group's cap.

*Metamorphoses*—The unique water pool on the stage, with Sunit Tandon and others

*Metamorphoses*—A collage for one of the stories

**Nigam Prakash** was born and brought up in Bihar. He moved to Delhi in 1959 to join St. Stephen's College. He came in contact with Roshan Seth and joined the Shakespeare Society of the college. That was how he got initiated into the magical world of theatre. Later, he came in contact with Joy Michael and joined Unity Theatre. Nigam became an active founder member of Yatrik.

A poet, playwright, actor, and director, Nigam had the honour of playing the significant role of the professor in *All the King's Men*, the first play staged under the banner of Yatrik in 1964–65. Nigam was not only credited with giving a most appropriate name to the group, but he was also instrumental in introducing Hindi and Urdu plays in the repertoire of Yatrik. Its first production in Hindi was *The Government Inspector*, which was translated into Hindi by Rakesh Vichitr. Apart from working for Yatrik, he worked for All India Radio and Doordarshan as an artist.

Nigam finally joined the Indian Foreign Services. He served as the Indian ambassador to France, Tunisia, and Argentina. After retirement, he rejoined Yatrik. During his extensive travels Nigam never missed an opportunity to see theatre. When he was posted in Brussels, he directed Girish Karnad's *Hayavadana* in 1977 in the English version, featuring actors who appeared for the first time on the stage.

He writes both in Hindi and English. An anthology of his poems entitled *Mere Deshvaasi* was published. It appeared in French also. As a playwright, Nigam's first venture *Apni Dhapli Apna Raag* was presented by the Dramatic Society of St. Stephen's College at the College Hall in 1960. The comedy was centred on a family, and the lead character Mathur discovered how to achieve happiness. Nigam directed it, and it featured 17 students. Roshan Seth was in the lead role. Nigam was cast in the role of Shayar. Some of the participants recorded their happiness on the brochure released on the occasion of the premiere of the show. One of the comments said, "Nigam-*da* and your nature, especially your irresistibly charming smile, will always inspire me in life." Another wrote, "Niggi Bhai—I owe you so much in the field of drama." He was much loved as a director and actor by his co-performers.

**Reminiscences:** We were all part of the team and for us, all roles were important. We were all heroes and having a great time. At the same time, we earned some money as well. The ticket price in those days was 5 rupees.

Both the American and British embassies had theatre groups. It was the time that "Shakespeare Wallah" was marketing theatre. This inspired us to take our productions to Dehra Dun, Nainital, Mussoorie, and Shimla. We staged our plays at Gaiety Theatre in Shimla, which has now been renovated. In 1961–62, Tom Noonan, cultural attaché, American Embassy, directed *Abe Lincoln in Illinois*. This Pulitzer Prize-winning play was written by Robert E. Sherwood in 1938. Habib Tanvir played Abe Lincoln. We took this production to Jaipur, Jodhpur, and Calcutta. Our shows were received with great enthusiasm. Noonan's office was at Mandi House and it was our centre of activity. While enjoying ourselves as travelling performers, it dawned on us to start a permanent travelling troupe. Then the question of naming the troupe arose. It occurred to me to name it Yatrik (Traveller), and after some deliberations, it was unanimously accepted. This is how Yatrik came into being in 1964.

*Abe Lincoln in Illinois* was staged at an auditorium on Mahadev Road, near Gole Dak Khana (Gole post office). It was a small and intimate theatre. There was not enough space to use huge sets. So we used minimal sets. Since we were initially staging English plays only, we had audiences from Delhi University, the embassies and senior government officers. We used to stage a new play every month, on the weekends. The tickets were sold at a small cost. Our aim was to develop a professional theatre in the capital.

The entire team, including the actors, directors, and technical staff, were doing theatre as a hobby. Subsequently, the central government acquired this auditorium for the Films Division and we shifted to a bigger venue at Pragati Maidan, which was allotted to us by the Ministry of Defence. At Pragati Maidan, we staged another memorable play *The Italian Straw Hat,* written in 1851 by Eugène Marin Labiche and Marc-Michel and adapted by Thomas Walton. Smt. Indira Gandhi and Smt. Sonia Gandhi attended one of the shows.

We rehearsed on the huge lawns of Joy Michael's bungalow at Kaka Nagar. The best part of these rehearsals was the hospitality offered to us by Joy's mother, Ruby Christian. Sometimes she would offer us dinner. We were even paid a conveyance allowance. The atmosphere was full of excitement and camaraderie.

I have acted in and directed several plays for Yatrik. I enjoyed comedies the most. In fact, comedy is close to life. One should know to laugh at oneself. It offers to watch life and society from a

A scene from *The Italian Straw Hat*

A scene from *The Italian Straw Hat*

new perspective. We laugh at pompous, hypocritical, miserly, and ridiculous characters with inhuman features. It has a life-affirming power. Georges Feydeau's comedy *Hotel Paradiso* was directed by Tom Noonan and was one of the most memorable productions by Yatrik. I remember that an official from the French Embassy watched the show continuously for seven days just to see a particular scene. This play continues to stay with me. In fact, when I was in Paris, I was told that *Hotel Paradiso* was playing. I used to see Moliere's comedies. T.P. Jain, one of Yatrik's great actors, had much skill in creating a comic portrait. His gait, facial expressions, and style of delivery all combined to create multiple comic shades.

Tom Noonan also directed another superb comedy that we did—*The Little Hut*. This is perhaps my favourite. I played a significant role in it, and with me were Aftab Seth, Siddharth Kak, and Eileen, the highly talented British actress. She went on to America and acted in films there.

*The Little Hut*

The stage set of *The Little Hut*

A scene from *Hotel Paradiso*

Even during the student days, I used to regularly get work as an actor. When I was to appear in the MA final, I got an offer from a British filmmaker, who wanted me to play the role of an Indian farmer. But I refused the offer because, for me, my education was the first priority. My father wanted me to join a "regular" service rather than work in "nautanki". My friend Roshan advised me to keep theatre as a hobby. He believed that the moment I took up theatre full-time and tried to make it a source of my livelihood, I would lose the creative excitement. My creativity would become more mechanical.

I directed *The Government Inspector* and played one of the comic roles. Other performers included Salima Raza, T.P. Jain, Sushma Seth, Roshan Seth, and Kewal Kapoor. But the way the final script was prepared was interesting. Most of the actors changed the dialogue in their own words, which resulted in the spontaneity in the delivery of lines with comic effect. We acted as if we were playing a game and enjoyed ourselves while performing our role.

Next was *Azar Ka Khwab* in Urdu. Begum Qudsia Zaidi adapted this from Bernard Shaw's *Pygmalion* and T.P. Jain directed it. Salima Raza, Anuj Kumar, Ashok Sarin, Kulbhushan Kharbanda, Sarvar Khan, Sudesh Syal, and Kewal Kapoor were in the cast, while I played the counterpart of Professor Henry Higgins. I played a professor of phonetics who was to teach Salima Raza, the flower girl (our Eliza Doolittle), the proper Urdu accent. Salima was superb. I thoroughly enjoyed delivering the dialogue in chaste Urdu and I put in a lot of energy in my portrayal of a modern Muslim from an aristocratic family. I also loved playing the leading role in Sai Paranjpye's *Vasana Kand*. Mahesh Elkuchwar had written the dialogue with remarkable felicity. For an actor to deliver such dialogue with a poetic touch is a great joy.

What I have observed is that we in India have a vast variety of theatrical forms. Such variety and richness are not easily found elsewhere. Of course, Western countries have enough resources to introduce advanced technology in the theatre and stage architect.

*Azar Ka Khwab.* Nigam Prakash as the Urdu professor and Salima Raza as his flower-girl student

A scene from *Azar Ka Khwab*

I have always loved acting and that is the reason that I have also acted in the productions I have directed. A director has his vision about the work of a dramatist and the characters. When a director acts in his own play, he finds it an opportunity to give depth to the characterisation with felicity.

Yatrik made history in the theatre movement in the country. It has produced great productions, vastly enriching theatrical art in all aspects. It was the first group that attracted foreign diplomatic corps, who considered cultural exchanges as an important tool for good relations between nation states. Faculty members and students from Delhi University came to see Yatrik productions and were eager to become members, as it offered them hope for foreign scholarships to study theatre abroad. Many of Yatrik's members have become famous both nationally and internationally, such as Joy Michael, Kusum Haidar, Roshan Seth, Sushma Seth, and Kulbhushan Kharbanda. Many young talents have blossomed into fine artists. Yatrik has a generous, educationist, dedicated person in Joy Michael as its source of inspiration. In fact, her entire family, including her mother, selflessly devoted their time to the growth of Yatrik.

**The Memorable Plays**

***Abe Lincoln in Illinois,*** written by Robert Penn Warren, depicts the rise and fall of a politician who initially failed because of his obsession with moral values in public life. He goes to Italy and learns the tactics of dirty politics to climb the ladder of political power. Blackmailing, treachery, and brazen opportunism are his weapons, and he becomes a dominant political force, but his wife and son start despising him intensely. Roshan Seth played the lead role. Rati Bartholomew also acted in this play. Marcus Murch and R.K. Dhingra designed the lights and Peter Hadjikakou put together the music.

*Hotel Paradiso* is written by Georges Feydeau, famous for his lighthearted comedies. This is a comic exposure of the 19th-century elite living in Paris. The source of the comedy is mistaken identity and as the characters indulge in extramarital escapades, they create hilarious situations. Tom Noonan directed this play for Yatrik, and it was staged at the auditorium on Mahadev Road. The characters played by Sushma Seth and Joy Michael were having an affair with that of Nigam Prakash. The husband wanted to distract the wife so that he could continue his scandalous acts. In the process, a seductive situation was created.

Leading theatre critics observed:
*Hotel Paradiso*: Well acted...what a world of good the routine of playing constantly to a regular audience has done...each of the actors and actresses as a more confident player, the play progresses with accurately timed movements on the stage, the lighting is so efficient and the production has a clearly discernible rhythm.—*Hindustan Times*

This talented company of players excellently brings out the spirit and mood of the farce...there is hilarious action and speech, which keeps the audience roaring with laughter. To echo the last lines of the play, "What a night! What a night!"—*The Times of India*

A naughty French farce...was received with shrieks of laughter by a grateful house...Yatrik has taken a fast tempo and chosen to treat this play as a farce and not as a comedy: the result is excellent entertainment....Yatrik has done wonders with this small stage.—*The Statesman*

***The Little Hut***, written by the French writer Andre Roussin is a romantic comedy full of fun and humour.

In certain ways, *The Little Hut* offers an ebullient French style of sex enjoyed the British way, with due ceremony. The result is a vinegar and salt mixture: tart and witty and frivolously amusing, filled with the most winning suggestions a wife ever made to her husband to cure him of the pains of cuckoldry... Yatrik's production of *The Little Hut*...bears the hallmark of this most competent and versatile group. —*The Times of India*

Here is this typical thing about two men and a wife between them. It doesn't really matter whose wife... Playwright Roussin's script is indeed a pleasant exercise in both comicality and seriousness, the one dominating the surface and the other serving the script as its soul, so to say.—*Link*

No one who loves good theatrical entertainment should miss Yatrik's delightful presentation of *The Little Hut*...This amusing comedy of two good friends and the wife of one of them, cast away on a desert Island (joined by one intruding stranger) is a hilarious farce on marital life and the shakiness of morals when circumstances make conditions different from the civilized life we are accustomed to.—*The Statesman*

***The Government Inspector***, written by Nikolai Gogol, the greatest Russian satirist, has tremendous universal relevance. Professor Sergei Mashinsky, a Russian scholar, asserts that the English and the French consider it their own national play. But judging by the number of

Hindi and Urdu versions of the play staged in Delhi, it tends to be identified as Indian as well.

...a true-to-life satire on patterns of behaviour as could have been found in more than one Indian princely State before independence....Yatrik brought this off beautifully, quite above the run of the average Hindi play.—*Hindustan Times*

Nigam Prakash's direction is slick...On the stage is a talented company of players...I am now more than ever convinced that the future of the professional Hindi theatre is intimately linked with repertories of the Yatrik type.—*The Times of India*

*The Government Inspector* is hilarious....Bureaucracy with its pants down never fails to amuse. In Yatrik's production...these pants were embroidered with considerable acting gusto and then taken down in a cackle of mirth.—*The Statesman*

**Rati Bartholomew.** One of the founder members of Yatrik, she was a professor of English at Indraprastha College, University of Delhi. She has been constantly involved in the productions of Yatrik since its inception. She featured in the first two productions of Yatrik—*All the King's Men* directed by Nigam Prakash, and *Sabrina Fair* directed by Joy Michael. She herself directed Federico Garcia Lorca's *Blood Wedding* in collaboration with Kusum Haidar.

*The Statesman* commented: "The production is deeply moving and should not be missed by anyone

Sushma Seth and Rati Bartholomew at Yatrik's silver jubilee celebrations. Hugh and Joy Michael in the background

who loves the theatre. This is a great piece of work and Yatrik must be congratulated on the choice of the play, the direction, and an outstandingly good cast."

Rati used to handle all aspects of production. She conceptualised the props in Aleksei Arbuzov's *Promise in Leningrad*, directed by Som Benegal. For a media critic to give a pointed reference to the props used on stage endorses the level of commitment and focus. In the words of the *Statesman* critic, "Rati Bartholomew had devoted good care to the props right up to the matryoshka dolls on the writing desk."

Nigam Prakash is highly appreciative of her creativity. He says, "She is a valuable founder member. She has been actor, director, costume designer, and promoter, all in one."

**Roshan Seth.** He is an internationally acclaimed film and stage actor. As a student of St. Stephen's College, University of Delhi, he became actively involved in the Shakespeare Society of the college, displaying his histrionic talent. The society provided him with the opportunity to hone his skill. Subsequently, he joined Joy Michael and American and British embassies' theatre groups, USIS, and then became a founder member of Yatrik. In the late 1960s, he went to the UK to

Roshan Seth (left) in *All the King's Men*

study British repertory theatre at the London Academy of Music and Dramatic Arts at his own expense. He struggled hard to free himself from the stereotyped image of an "ethnic actor". His first break was in Peter Brook's production of *A Midsummer Night's Dream*, which toured the US in 1972.

In the early 1980s, Richard Attenborough asked Roshan to play the pivotal role of Jawaharlal Nehru in *Gandhi* (released in 1982). Roshan was nominated for the BAFTA Award for Best Actor in a supporting role for his performance in the film. He also played Jawaharlal Nehru in *Bharat Ek Khoj*, a 53-episode series shown on Doordarshan in 1988. His role in *Such a Long Journey as a Parsi* earned him his greatest acclaim to date.

He is an excellent actor and has always been committed to theatre. His English diction is impeccable. He has played roles in Hindi also. His contribution to the growth of Yatrik is significant. He used to do difficult and complex roles.

With Yatrik, he was active in the early productions *All the King's Men* and *Sabrina Fair*. In *All the King's Men*, he portrayed the leading role of a politician. The strength of his acting art is that he truly lives his character. As far as the range of his voice is concerned, Nigam Prakash compares it with that of Lata Mangeshkar.

**Reminiscences:** Nigam and I decided, in our final year at college, to become professional actors. *All the King's Men* was the first play Yatrik staged, followed by a play in Urdu in which I played a small role.

A group of committed amateur actors was brought together by Tom Noonan of the USIS to perform American plays in a few cities around Delhi. The idea that the group might stay together after Noonan left the USIS was wildly idealistic, especially in the context of a professional theatre that would pay artists' salaries. The chief idea behind Yatrik, in the beginning, was to stage plays regularly at one location only on weekends. The initial hope was that the small group of players would stay together as a troupe. Joy Michael was and still is the guiding spirit behind Yatrik. She was helped greatly by her husband Hugh when he was alive.

Yatrik's decision to stage plays written in Urdu and Hindi, in addition to those written in English, was sound. It was also inescapable, as the trend pointed in that particular direction.

I left for England to try to get into one of the drama schools. I remember my association with Yatrik with a mixture of affection and sadness. I tried to remain connected to the group, despite my involvement in films and theatre abroad.

About the future, to my knowledge, there is no established professional theatre of any merit in the NCR. The Repertory Company begun by the NSD may or may not still exist, but I am not aware of any lasting impact. Performance as entertainment requires performers that stay together and earn their livelihood from the work they do. If the standard of work falls below peoples' expectations, the group will collapse. Theatre, I'm afraid, will remain the poor relation, while TV and films are relatively richer.

**Sushma Seth** is an all-round theatre personality, and undeniably a popular and loved artist whose creations of characters on the stage, television, and films have deeply moved audiences. In the 1960s and 1970s, she was a most wanted actress who had the opportunity to work under the direction of eminent theatre directors, such as Habib Tanvir, Rajinder Nath, and Joy Michael. Excelling as a director, music composer, and choreographer, over the years she has mesmerised audiences with her portrayals of complex, intricate characters with fire, colour, vitality, and life. Old-timers still remember her performances as Champa in *Sakharam Binder* by Vijay Tendulkar, directed by Sai Paranjpye and presented by Natya Dweep, and as Rano in *Ek Chaadar*

*Maili Si* by Rajinder Singh Bedi, which he adapted as a play, and was directed by Rajinder Nath for Yatrik. Her dadi in Doordarshan's longest-running serial *Hum Log* became a favourite household character. Only an actress of her calibre can create a portrait so lovable for viewers of all age groups.

Apart from directing and acting in over 150 stage plays in Hindi, English, and Urdu for a number of theatre groups based in Delhi, Sushma has acted in more than 100 feature films, and acted in and directed many television plays and soap operas. Sushma graduated in drama from Carnegie Mellon in the US and her work to enrich Indian children's theatre has been one of her passions. She found children's theatre to be fulfilling, particularly working with the underprivileged students of Arpana's Basti Vikas Kendra. She is the honorary cultural director of Arpana—an NGO involved in addressing the problems of 40,000 people of resettlement colonies, including teaching children. She has produced ballets, featuring children from the slums. Her deep concern for the cultural and aesthetic development of children is reflected in the valuable work she has been doing under the banner of Children's Creative Theatre. "Those extremely gifted young ones respond beautifully and eagerly to creative opportunities. Creative drama workshops are the best means for empowering children with confidence and knowledge," says Sushma.

In comparing theatre with television or films, Sushma feels that television and films are a director's media; an actor has little control over the end result, and has to master the technique of emoting convincingly to absent stimuli. The basic study and analysis of the story and the character in the progression of a story as it unfolds on stage is a cathartic and satisfying experience. The feedback with a live audience is instantaneous and elating.

Sushma Seth has been the recipient of: All Excellence at Briarcliff College, New York, Founders Scholar Award from Carnegie Mellon,

Pittsburgh, Distinguished Alumni Award, Lady Irwin College, New Delhi; Best Actress Award, from the Sahitya Kala Parishad; Kalashri Award for Best Supporting Actress; Aashirvaad Award for Best Performance; Bharat Nirman Award; Lifetime Award, Bhawan Kala Mandir; and Woman Achievers Award from CPAA.

For Yatrik, she has directed and acted in more than 20 plays, which reflected her brilliant artistry both as director and actress. Here, it would be appropriate to give brief outlines of some of the productions produced by Yatrik under her direction. An example of her superb histrionic prowess reflected in her lead role of Rano. Sushma Seth's directorial venture for Yatrik that caught the attention of the discerning audience and ever-vigilant critics of the period was Eugene O' Neill's *Desire Under the Elms*.

Sushma Seth (left) in *Luv*

**Reminiscences:** I live in the present and think about the future. Nostalgic memories of the past and the exciting time I experienced with Yatrik, headed by Joy Michael, however, are touching.

When the USIS invited the Delhi actors to participate in its plays, their demand was for us to be available to travel during the next two years. Most of the working male actors were unable to fulfil this condition; therefore, college students were cast in the plays. The ladies who fitted the roles and were in jobs were perhaps able to take leave or be replaced by understudies. I was able to travel and perform in all the shows—having a doting and progressive family to support me.

We gave birth to Yatrik. So I cherish the years of experience—the continuous wonderful theatre involvement of approximately 8–10 years, acting in the choicest of lead roles which any actress could only dream of doing, such as Rano in *Ek Chaadar Maili Si*, Kate in *The Taming of the Shrew*, Susan in *The Little Hut*, Tarala in *Ayee Bala Ko Taal Tu* (Noel Coward's comedy *Blithe Spirit*), Raina in Shaw's *Arms and the*

Sushma Seth (right) in *Hotel Paradiso*

*Man*, Ellen in Murray Schisgal's *Luv*, and Sophia in Errol John's *Moon on a Rainbow Shawl.* Then directing, doing costumes, designing sets, and all the camaraderie and fun. This was a dream come true for me. To be on stage—performing every weekend, rehearsing the next play, and reading new plays for future performances. Despite the fact that during those years I was teaching speech and doing children's theatre at the Convent of Jesus and Mary, and in the evening doing rehearsals, I never felt exhausted or complained of fatigue. On the contrary, there was a feeling of elation. Our whole group shared this feeling too.

A number of amateur theatre groups surfaced during those years of the 1960s. The dedication, passion, involvement, and talent of the theatre workers were of a professional level, as were the standards of productions. The only amateur element was the absence of payment to actors, directors, and workers.

*Hotel Paradiso*—Joy Michael and Sushma Seth

It was unfortunate that Delhi was not able to make theatre-going a habit. At Yatrik, we planned a yearly programme of plays in English and Hindi, which included comedies, entertaining, dramatic plays, and two new plays or what we referred to as "experimental" productions. The maximum number of shows of the most appreciated plays never exceeded 10. With tickets priced as low as 15 rupees, the box-office intake did not even cover production costs. So payment to the cast and crew was impossible. Therefore, all of us, bitten by the theatre bug, worked during the day for sustenance and indulged our hobby of theatre in the evenings. Yatrik kept its promise of repertory of good productions every weekend for Hindi and English plays; the variety and number of plays were not offered by any other group in Delhi. Over the years, Yatrik did manage to create a theatre-going audience. We were able to lure a sizeable number of "faithfuls" who came to all the plays, but not enough to put us in a "professional" category. Many guest directors, actors, technicians, and playwrights were regularly invited to participate. The scene remains almost similar, except for NSD and META productions and festivals. Other theatre groups are still struggling passionately, hoping for ideal conditions.

Yatrik also prepared a Christmas production every year, and we all performed in and travelled with children's plays to the schools. The response was very satisfying. When we travelled to Nainital schools with my son Kavi, who was eight months old, he became the mascot of the ladies' dorm every morning as he woke up the cast with his cooing and cuddling. In the later years, my little daughters Divya and Priya would fill in for any missing actor during rehearsals at our home. The genesis of my forming Children's Creative Theatre was in involving my three children during vacations in the only subject I was equipped to teach.

As a repertory, Yatrik toured during the summer to schools in the hills—Mussoorie, Dehra Dun, Nainital, and Shimla. We travelled, rehearsed, put up sets, lights, helped with costumes, did our own make-

*Arms and the Man*—Sushma Seth and Marcus Murch

up, performed, and then brought down the sets to travel again. It was hectic but enjoyable. When we were performing *Abe Lincoln in Illinois* in Dehra Dun, there was a scene with Nigam Prakash, Roshan Seth, and Marcus Murch. Nigam was to be drunk in the scene; from the beginning, he would sit chewing and packing his cheek with some paper to get the desired slur. Marcus had an entry and the scene was between the three, but was clearly dominated by Nigam. Marcus was an excellent actor with tremendous stage presence, but uncertain with his lines. He made an entry, stood in the centre of the arch, and with great confidence and assurance, albeit with prompting, delivered all his lines and made an exit with a flourish, thus ending the scene. He received a thunderous applause from the audience. He had cut out everyone's lines and the rest of the scene—Nigam was left chewing the cud.

The annual programme, the rehearsal schedules, the allocation of duties, casting and rehearsal venues—all this and more were meticulously planned and carried out, mainly due to Joy Michael's organisational abilities and focus. Her dedication and passion overcame most of the hurdles in the half century of Yatrik's existence. Without her sensitive approach to handling the whole group, guest actors, and technicians, Yatrik could not have endured the test of time, nor maintained the quality of productions. The Michael home and all the family members gave their support to Yatrik activities. Without Joy Michael, there would have been no Yatrik.

*Ek Chaadar Maili Si* revolves around the life of Rano, forced to marry her brother-in-law, 10 years younger than her, whom she had loved as a child. The production vividly brings alive rural Punjab, its ethos, and the agony of a woman condemned to follow the outdated and inhuman feudal traditions that treat a woman as a mere commodity.

This was a milestone production of Yatrik in terms of direction and the performance of its lead female actor, Sushma Seth. The *Hindustan Times* wrote, "Being vignettes of Punjab, it has more than 30 characters. Rajinder Nath handles them deftly, giving them changes, moves and at places beautiful compositions...Sushma Mathur (Seth) as Rano electrifies some moments." *The Times of India* commented: "To assemble a cast of 25 is no easy task for any company or producer in Delhi. But Yatrik cast its net wide and assembled a group that has stood out for individual and collective talent. And at the end, when the shade of twilight deepened into night, and Rano cried out to the goddess, Sushma brought pathos, compassion, and vitality to the production."

Prof. Frank Thakurdas, former professor of political science, Delhi University, and a keen observer of and participant in Delhi theatre, had reviewed the play in *Enact 27*:

A good play is a good play and a good production is always an irresistible invitation to nearly starved lovers (at least in the metropolis) of good theatre. *Ek Chaadar Maili Si* falls undeniably in this category. Indeed, it was a rare piece. Yatrik needs to be congratulated further for successfully demolishing the myth that plays in Indian languages (so-called operas notwithstanding) do not command an audience…

…But what splendid support he (the director) got from his cast of brilliant actors. Sushma Mathur, equally at ease in English, Urdu, and Punjabi gave a memorable performance as Rano; this indeed was, in my opinion, one of her most inspired roles. She was so completely her character as the Woman—the vehicle of the life principle—that there was not a single false note that one could detect.

…If ever a play deserves to be staged again and again this is it; it has all the elements which would satisfy the most critical of audiences, as it would thrill the masses, whose play it essentially is…

*Desire Under the Elms,* set on a New England farm, is an intense drama of incestuous love, hate, and passion. Sushma's production imparted insights into the inner world of desperate characters in conflict with each other, condemned to rot in a world of consuming hatred, fatal sexual entanglement, and repentance. The set she designed was innovative and captured the ambiance in which the action took place. As director, she was able to bring out the best from the members of her cast to give stunning performances.

...Sushma Mathur's direction, which had obviously paid attention to diction, pitch, and cadence, was commendable. The play called for a great deal of coordination and orchestration of various moods, production by Joy Michael had given consummate attention to detail which added not only to atmosphere but the depth and realism of the play. Lighting by Raj Kumar was able to bring out the best of a very imaginatively designed and competently executed set.—*The Statesman*

In Yatrik's presentation that opened on Saturday evening, the three-cornered symbolic battle for the earthly possessions was fought out in an atmosphere of charged hatred and on a set beautifully designed to emphasize the controlling circumstances of the play. Sushma Mathur's direction succeeded in underlining the terrible destructive power of physical passion in a situation where opportunities for its gratification are so small.—*Indian Express*

Sushma Seth (left) as Rano in *Ek Chaadar Maili Si*

**Salima Raza** is an explorer of complexities of women characters. Along with the journey of Yatrik, five creative women continued their own journey of theatrical exploration, illuminating the world of contemporary theatre of Delhi with their illustrious contributions. These gifted women were—Joy Michael, Kusum Haidar, Sushma Seth, Rati Bartholomew, and Salima Raza. Their work was not limited to Yatrik; they were invited by leading groups to work for them in productions directed by eminent directors. Salima has excelled both in comic and tragic roles. In her acting career, spanning over 50 years, she has played many memorable characters, especially with Unity Theatre and Yatrik.

Salima came in contact with Joy Michael and her team, primarily from St. Stephen's College. Her husband was also a Stephanian. She was then deeply involved in the activities of Unity Theatre.

Since Salima's husband had foreign assignments, she left India and lived for 30 years in the Gulf countries; she stayed involved with promoting Indian culture among non-resident Indians. Salima came back to India in 1996 and continued her association with Yatrik. She joined Amal Allana's Theatre and Television Associates as an actress. Currently, Salima is the creative director of Wings Cultural Society, for which she directed *Chand Roz Aur Meri Jaan*, based on the letters of Faiz Ahmad Faiz and his wife Alys, in 2011. This production was featured at the Bharat Rang Mahotsav. Salima did one more production for Wings, *Ek Kutte Ki Kahani*, based on the life and writings of Sadat Hassan Manto. This play was chosen as one among the 10 best plays of 2012 and was staged at Bhartendu Natya Utsav, organised by Sahitya Kala Parishad, Delhi.

The most memorable role of her long career as an actress is Hajjo, the "Amrood Wali". Bernard Shaw took up the challenge of uncovering the qualities of an articulate aristocratic lady inherent in a flower girl, Eliza Doolittle. In her brilliant adaptation of *Pygmalion* in Urdu, Begum Qudsia Zaidi sought to unveil those qualities in the "Amrood Wali", Hajjo, in her adaptation *Azar Ka Khwab*.

The challenge was to make Hajjo blossom as an aristocratic Muslim lady, endowed with an impeccable Urdu accent and the highly sophisticated mannerisms of a begum. Old-timers still admire Salima's Hajjo. Sudesh Syal, who was once a director of Yatrik and stage manager, recalls that Kewal Kapoor was playing the role of

Hajjo's father. In a crucial scene, Kewal was busy backstage with the other actors and he missed his entry. Salima went to the window of the set and said in the dialect of Barabanki, "Father, where are you?" Kewal entered the scene. It was a sheer innovative act on the part of Salima, but the audience thought that it was part of the script. We were told that Alkazi used to refer to Salima's acting in this play in his class while teaching the nuances of acting.

Salima continues to retain the aura of her art and the charm of her delivery of chaste Urdu, a rare phenomenon these days. These attributes have been mesmerising her audience for several decades. She has created several portraits in Yatrik's productions that are unforgettable.

*Azar Ka Khwab,* Yatrik's Urdu production, which Begum Qudsia Zaidi adapted from Shaw's *Pygmalion*, was directed by T.P. Jain and staged at Mahadev Road in 1963. This created quite a stir in the theatre world of Delhi; it was an instant hit with both the critics and the audience. It ran for several weekends over many months. Salima played the lead role of Hajjo, brilliantly supported by Nigam Prakash, Sushma Seth, Kewal Kapoor, Ashok Sareen, Kulbhushan Kharbanda, and Sarwat Khan. The press was highly appreciative:

Yatrik has done it once again, and this time with Begum Zaidi's *Azar Ka Khwab*. More than half the battle of the theatre in India today is the lack of good stageable plays—whether original or adaptations. The histrionic talents of Yatrik have often been acknowledged in these columns, but more than anything else, the company owes its success to the intelligent choice of plays—both English and Hindi.—*The Times of India*

Like almost all Yatrik's plays, *Azar Ka Khwab* is delightfully successful. It has a well-knit theme, which blends with superb characterization—individually and collectively, the cast live their roles. The play clicks and clicks again. One experiences boisterous fits of laughter and the underlying seriousness of the original play concurrently.—*Thought*

An extremely enjoyable production, *Azar Ka Khwab* not only kept the audience roaring with laughter throughout the evening but also actually heralded a big leap forward in the capital's search for a vigorous Indian theatre. The overall production by T.P. Jain in association with Salima Raza was highly commendable.—*Shankar's Weekly*

*Azar Ka Khwab* breaks the very tongue of Shaw—With only Salima Raza's triumphant Hajjo, Yatrik's play in Urdu would still be a delightful evening of theatre: as it is, there is also Begum Zaidi's racy and astonishingly good adaptation...performances quick with merit from other members of the cast and a production that goes to work swiftly, unobtrusively, and well...The tempo was excellently sustained. The production by T.P. Jain and Salima Raza had the expert and unpretentious style, which is becoming a hallmark of Yatrik. Delhi has never been so close to sustained repertory theatre: this is it.—*The Statesman*

**Reminiscences:** My first public performance in Delhi was in 1958 with Delhi Art Theatre in a production directed by Sheila Bhatia. At the age of 19, I played the role of Bi Farzina. I received the best supporting actress award from Delhi Natya Sangh for that performance. I joined

Salima Raza and Nigam Prakash in *Azar Ka Khwab*

*Azar Ka Khwab*—Salima Raza

Salima Raza (left) in *Azar Ka Khwab*

Unity Theatre in 1960 and my first performance was in *Sabrina Fair*, which Joy directed. As they were producing plays only in English, I faced problems because I was not comfortable in delivering lines in the language. My parents were freedom fighters and they sent me to a Hindi-medium school. My father was a veteran CPI leader, Z.A. Ahmed, or Doctor Saheb, as he was popularly known. As a freedom fighter, he was interned during 1942–45, with thousands of Indian National Congress leaders, at the Deolali Transition Camp (DTC).

Initially, at Unity Theatre, I felt like a fish out of water. I had never done English theatre before and it was quite a challenge. I am eternally grateful to Joy for her encouragement; she taught me the correct English accent and explained the mannerisms of the English characters I was to play. Gradually, it became a joy to act in English plays.

At that time, Unity Theatre performed mostly in spaces around the residences of the committee members of the group. We performed *Sabrina Fair* in the back garden of Joy's Kaka Nagar Bungalow; the cast included Roshan Seth, Kusum Bahl (Haidar), Marcus Murch, Nigam Prakash, and Aftab Seth. Among my other plays with Unity were *Abe Lincoln in Illinois*, *Faust*, *The Lark*, and *Dinner with the Family*.

Joy directed *Dinner with the Family* and we staged it on the verandah of the residence of one of the actors. He was a diplomat from the British High Commission. The contribution from the audience included a delicious supper, which was cooked by the members of Unity Theatre.

Yatrik was founded as a bilingual repertory company in 1964 with the objective of providing regular, sustained performances and to build up an audience in Delhi. My fellow members were Joy Michael, Rati Bartholomew, Kusum Haidar, Sushma Seth, Marcus Murch, Roshan Seth, and Nigam Prakash.

Yatrik's first Hindi production was Gogol's *The Government Inspector*, which was directed by Nigam Prakash. The cast included T.P. Jain, Roshan Seth, Kewal Kapoor, Sushma Seth, and me. We had managed to rent the small Film Division Auditorium at Mahadev Road, behind All India Radio. The stage was narrow, hardly suitable for theatre, but somehow we managed with painted backdrops and minimal sets to create a stage for the theatrical presentations, which drew an enthusiastic audience every weekend.

*Hotel Paradiso* by Georges Feydeau, a hilarious French comedy, directed by Tom Noonan, was the next Yatrik production in which I acted with Nigam, Joy, Aftab Seth, Roshan, Sushma, Kusum, and Marcus. *The Matchmaker* was another wonderful play I acted in.

My father, Dr Z.A. Ahmed, was president of the Kisan Sabha and a leader of the Communist Party of India. Therefore, in our house, we treated everybody with respect and a sense of equality. I had come across working women who used to speak like I, as Hajjo, needed to in *Azar Ka Khwab*. Then the transformation into a great aristocratic lady of a ruling feudal family was almost spontaneous, because my mother belonged to Rampur's Muslim ruling class. I was aware of their mannerisms, their style of conversation in chaste Urdu, and their aesthetic dress sense—I feel these factors enabled me to create a most memorable character.

In 1970, I played the central character of a blind woman in the Hindi translation of Frederick's *Wait Until Dark*, titled *Andhera Hone*

Salima Raza as the blind girl in *Andhera Hone Do*

*Do*. Himanshu Bhaduri, B.K. Giri, and Chaman Bagga were with me on stage.

To make my characterisation convincing, I studied the emotional, psychological, and social background of the character. I went to a blind school for several days. Interestingly, I learnt that blind people tilt their heads and turn their ears towards the sound when they converse. I concentrated intensely on my character. In a show of *Sabrina Fair* at Nainital, I was playing the role of a mother and Roshan Seth played my son. The action was set in a park. He was smoking a cigarette and then he put his hand on his shoulder, still holding the lit cigarette. I came up silently from behind, looking at the audience. Without noticing it, I placed my hand on the cigarette. Controlling the excruciating pain, I continued to concentrate on my performance. After the show, Joy Michael, who directed the play, congratulated me for my performance. I narrated to her what happened to me in the park scene. We both laughed and I forgot my pain.

Once I met Naseeruddin Shah in a party. I told him that I was a great fan of his. He replied that he had seen my performance as Hajjo two or three times and that he greatly admired me for it. He told me that Alkazi wanted him to write a thesis on her interpretation of Hajjo. Naseeruddin has talked about various great performances in his autobiography. He writes in his memoirs:

These performances from the 1970s, for me, touched perfection and demonstrated the level it is possible for an actor on stage to achieve. I still consider them the greatest performances I have seen anywhere in the world: Mohan Agashe in *Ghasiram Kotwal*, Chandrakant Kale in *Begum Barve*, Shriram Lagoo in *Adhe Adhure*, Om Puri in the Kabuki Play *Ibaragi*, Sudha Shivpuri in *Billi Chali Pehen ke Joota*, Sulabha Deshpande in *Shantla! Court Chaalu Aahe*, Bhakti Bharve in *Ajab Nyaya Vartulacha*, and Salima Raza in *Azar Ka Khwab*.

What more can an actor aspire for?

**Marcus Murch.** "Irrepressible" is perhaps the best one-word description of this Delhi theatre icon. He did not mince his words, was flamboyant in gestures and expressions, and yes, irrepressible.

After completing his schooling at Sherwood College, Nainital, in 1953, Marcus joined Geoffrey Kendal's Shakespearean theatre company. He was also associated with the Royal Festive Ballet, assisting as lighting director. In 1964, the band of six founded Yatrik. From acting, directing, painting sets, controlling lights, and being involved with all aspects of staging a play, Marcus stretched himself in all directions.

But, on stage, he could often be the cause of grave anxiety for his co-actors! As Meriel Michael recalls, Marcus never learnt his lines properly. In *Arms and the Man*, while he was playing the role of a visitor to the house seeking the hand of the daughter in marriage, the audience couldn't understand why he kept going to the writing desk and reading the personal correspondence of the owner. He had hidden his script there and was checking his next line. The persons playing opposite him had to be pretty nimble with the ad-libs, as you could never tell if he had forgotten the line, and gone forward or backward in the play. On one memorable occasion when I had to prompt, he dropped a whole scene, leaving the prompter and his fellow actors frantically ad-libbing to get the play back on track.

In 1973, he started freelancing, directing plays for schools and colleges, and in 1974 he started his own theatre company, Stagedoor. Marcus left the stage of life rather early, but continues to be remembered for his contribution to English theatre.

The irrepressible Marcus Murch (right)

Marcus Murch in *Our Town*

*The Fantasticks*—Marcus Murch

# SILVER AND RUBY
## THE LANDMARKS

*The life of a play begins and ends in the moment of performance. This is where author, actors, and directors express all they have to say. If the event has a future, this can only lie in the memories of those who were present and who retained a trace in their hearts.*

**Rendition of *A Midsummer Night's Dream***
**Peter Brook**

Celebrations, accolades and sharing of good will are part of the journey...after the turbulent and challenging "beginning" years came some landmarks...the silver jubilee celebrations in 1989, and the big year-round celebration of Yatrik at 40 in 2003–04!

Silver jubilee celebrations

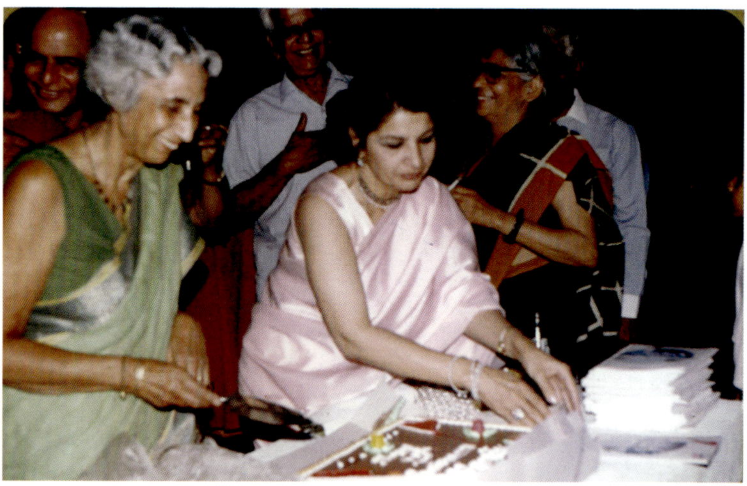

Lola Chatterji and Sushma Seth getting things ready.
Hugh Michael and Rati Bartholomew in the background

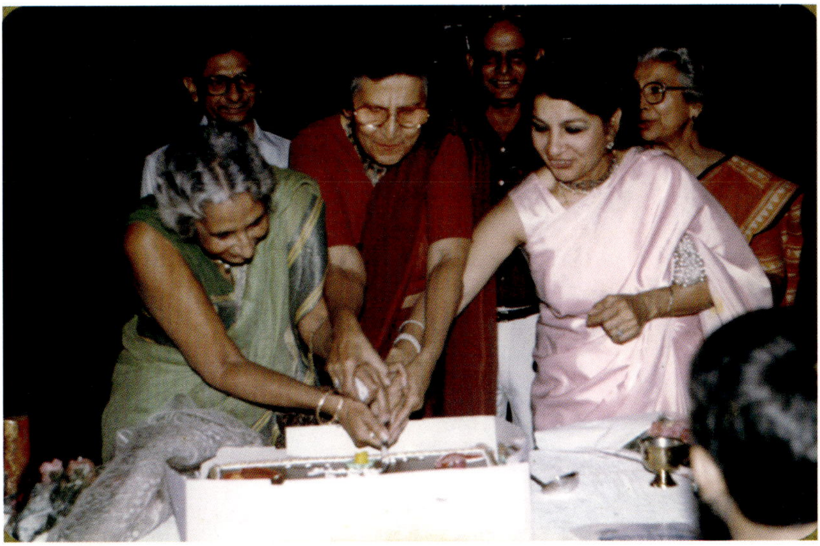

Happy birthday, Yatrik—25 years

Singing and rejoicing

Old friends and new

# *Yatrik Completes Forty Years*

*The brochure that was brought out on the occasion captures the highlights of the year-long celebrations and 40 years of Yatrik's history is reproduced in facsimile here in its entirety.*

THE PIONEER ✦ TUESDAY SEPTEMBER 17, 2002

ARTS — Vivacity 3

## THE STAGE HOLDS HER VERY DEAR

Forty years the director of Yatrik Theatre, **JOY MICHAEL** readies for celebration with revival of old favourites, says **Utpal K Banerjee**

When Yatrik stages *Educating Rita* at the British Council on September 28 and 29, it will be one more revival of the play that builds around the no-nonsense attitude to life of a disillusioned middle-age professor and his explosive encounter with an infinitely inquisitive young thing out to find meaning in her life. If you've seen it already, then here's another slice of information. It's the 200th stagepiece by Delhi's first semi-professional repertory theatre, Yatrik, which will soon be celebrating forty years of existence.

Now Emeritus Theatre-Director under Ministry of Culture, Joy Michael has been heading the group from the very beginning. Michael, who has crossed the age of three score and ten, protests, "Theatre was never in my genes." She could still shame anyone half her age with her disciplined demeanour, enthusiasm and steely resolve to maintain a sterling performance.

As a student of St. Stephen's college during the late 1940s, Joy was the only woman secretary of its Shakespeare Society from 1943. "I played parts like Lady Macbeth in *Macbeth*, Desdemona in *Othello* and Rosalind in *As You Like It*. The college gave me the rare honour of directing the Bard's *Winter's Tale* during its centenary celebrations. To repay my gratitude, I will be donating my entire theatre collection to the Shakespeare Society", she tells us. Her stage career began when she joined Unity Theatre in the 1950s after college. Then she got a British Council scholarship during 1959-60 to study direction in British Drama League and an advanced course in acting at the London Academy of Music and Dramatic Arts.

"This taught basics of direction and allowed me to observe many repertory productions. Back in India, USIS asked us to produce Abe Lincoln in Illinois and tour universities and colleges of north India as part of their college-contact programme. The response was magnificent, emboldening us to establish Yatrik. The name is a takeoff from Yatra, the Bengali folk-theatre, and Yatri, the Sanskrit word for traveller."

Their first theatre season began in July-August, 1964, with many problems like finding an inexpensive hall, choosing right plays and searching talent. "We were also anxious whether we would ever be able to fulfil our commitment to perform every weekend with a new play each month", relates Joy. But in the end they would triumph. Yatrik secured a 140-seat assembly hall on Mahadev Road, adding a forestage, converting adjoining space into greenrooms, installing back-projection facility and converting the lawn into an open-air cafeteria. "By 1965-66, we shifted to the Defence Pavilion in Pragati Maidan", continues Joy. "This had props and rehearsal space. We were there till 1971, producing some of our best works—Moliere's *Tartuff* under Ebrahim Alkazi, who played lead opposite me; Adya Rangacharya's *Rahoon-Ki-Na-Rahoon* under B V Karanth; Louis Carroll's *Alice in Wonderland* for children; Anton Chekhov's *Seagull* with Bhaskar Ghosh and Kusum Haidar as protagonists."

In 1971-72, Yatrik and Indian National Theatre (INT) merged to set up the Centre for Performing Arts. "INT, under Sheela Bharat Ram, shared our objective. Together we hoped to revitalise performing arts, integrating them with people's life in post-Independence India. We had the world premiere of *Goa* by Asif Curimbhoy, starring Zarine Chowdhury and Sai Paranjpye in 1972. Marcus March was stage manager; Barry John his assistant. Kulbhushan Kharbanda was one of the actors. Prema Karanth was costume designer. Marcus and Barry used to live in what is now Shri Ram Centre for Art and Culture."

In 1972, Joy left for New York under a Rockefeller grant for professional theatre. On her return she found the ensemble disintegrated. Max Mueller Bhawan at Connaught Place offered their rooftop for theatre in 1973. By 1975, Joy was principal of a school and everything fell in order: with stage and space till 1989. Yatrik continued, mainly with English, intermingling with Hindi and regional language theatre.

Plans for Yatrik's 40-year anniversary are afoot. "We have been promised support by British Council and Habitat World to hold an exhibition of photos, slides and reviews; and perform one-hour excerpts of old favourites by Rati Bartholomew, Sushma Seth, Kusum Hyder, Roshan Seth, Salim Raza and myself: all from the original old guard," concludes Joy.

***Main photo by Alwin Singh features Bhaskar Ghosh and Shyama Haldar enacting a scene from Yatrik's forthcoming production,* Educating Rita**

### ALMANAC

*Siddhartha Sengupta is showing his works at the Fescoes Gallery, Lalit Kala Akademi till September 19. "His paintings reveal an eternal quest for the unknown, an endless journey towards an undefined goal...Even when he dwells on traditional topics like Krishna-Chaitanya, his mode of representation is contemporary," goes one critical appraisal.*

■**Embassy of Japan:** As part of the Japanese film show, enjoy movies like *Disaster Prevention, Home Village* (Furusato), *Beijing Watermelon* (Peking Teki Suika), *Homes*, every Friday at 6 pm.

■**British Council:** Between September 21-28, there will be a special screening of the *Great Writers* series of documentaries at 10am. Begins with Douglas Adams' profile, *The Man who Blew Up the Earth*.

■**IIC:** Sanjib Bhattacharya, disciple of Guru Bipin Singh and Smt Kalavati Devi, presents choreographic works by his Guru on September 19 at 6:30 pm in the Centre's Auditorium. Sanjib

In an interview with *Pioneer* in 2002, Joy Michael announces the year-long celebrations for Yatrik's 40th anniversary planned for 2003–04

40
MEMORABLE YEARS
YATRIK
THEATRE
Our grateful thanks to
Govt. of National Capital Territory of Delhi
BRITISH COUNCIL
HABITAT WORLD

YATRIK
THEATRE
40th
Anniversary Festival
1964 - 2003

p r o g r a m m e

**At British Council**

Friday August 8th
Inauguration of Festival and Retrospective Exhibition.
'Interview with Roshan Seth and collage of recent Yatrik plays', a video film by Avijit Dutt

Saturday August 9th
'Scenes from Shakespeare' Video film of excerpts from Macbeth, Hamlet, Taming of the Shrew, Othello, Merchant of Venice presented by Arjun Raina

Tuesday August 12th
'Gitanjali' directed by Joy Michael, originally produced in 1988-89

Wednesday August 13th
Video of 'A Wilde Evening'. This will include excerpts from Lady Windermere's Fan and Salome, presented by Lola Chatterji, Avijit Dutt and Kusum Haidar

Thursday 14th
'Mangalam' by Poile Sen-Gupta and directed by Bhaskar Ghose, originally produced in 2000- 2001

Please collect your passes from the reception of the venues before the dates of the performances.

**At Habitat Centre Main Auditorium**

Friday August 29th
'Ek Aur Dronacharya' by Shankar Shesh directed by Prakash Bhatia, originally produced in 1988-89

Saturday August 30th
'Mangalam' by Poile Sen-Gupta and directed by Bhaskar Ghose

Sunday August 31st
Scenes from 'Azar Ka Khwab' by Begam Zaidi originally produced in 1964 -65 presented by Salima Raza (with several of the original cast)

Friday September 12th
'Death And The Maiden' readings by Sabina Jaitly, originally produced in 1995-96

Saturday September 13th
'Bombay-Bosnia' by Avijit Dutt originally produced in 1996-97

Sunday September 14th
'Come As You Were' by Nicholas Khargonkar directed by Sunit Tandon, originally produced in 2002

## Yatrik's 40 Years Onstage

*By Lola Chatterji*

YATRIK was founded as a bilingual repertory company in 1964 with the objectives of projecting the arts as a dynamic, living force in our times by providing regular sustained performances of theatre and other arts and building up an audience for them.

One of its founder members, Joy Michael Director of Yatrik, for over 40 years, has carried on in spite of many vicissitudes, with courage, determination and commitment.

*Our Town with Sushma Seth, Joy Michael and Monica Tanvir*

*[illegible] with Habib Tanvir and Joy Michael*

**TOM NOONAN** was an unusual Cultural Affairs Officer at the United States Information Services, New Delhi during the early 60s. He was a trained puppet-maker and had some experience of Broadway. Roshan Seth has said of him, 'He was our Stanislavsky, our director/mentor/teacher'.

We are proud to say that she was recognized and felicitated for her lifelong contribution and service to theatre at the Asian Women's Directors'Conference in Delhi in January. Apart from Marcus March who passed away twenty years ago, the other founder Members are still around, though not necessarily as active in the group as they were.They are Rati Bartholomew, Kusum Haidar (nèe Bahl) Sneih Dass, Sushma Mehra (now Seth) Nigam Prakash and Roshan Seth. Salima Raza was among the first members.

*Sabrina Fair with Kusum Haidar*

*Hotel Paradiso with Roshan Seth, Joy Michael and Nigam Prakash*

## THE FIRST DECADE (1964 - 74)

**1964-65**

**ALL THE KINGS MEN** by Robert Penn Warren directed by Nigam Prakash with Roshan Seth, Rati Bartholomew.

**SABRINA FAIR** BY Samuel Taylor directed by Joy Michael with Salima Raza, Rati Bartholomew, Roshan Seth, Marcus Murch, Nigam Prakash, Raghu Sudon, Aftab Seth, Sushma Mehra, Ena Nadar.

**OUR TOWN** by Thornton Wilder directed by Tom Noonan with Nigam Prakash, Syeda Saiyidain, Joy Michael, Sushma Seth, Monica Tanvir, Shivendra Sinha, Marcus Murch.

**THE GOVERNMENT INSPECTOR** by Gogol in Hindi directed by Nigam Prakash with Kewal Kapoor, T.P.Jain.

**HOTEL PARADISO** by Georges Feydeau directed by Tom Noonan with Nigam Prakash, Joy Michael, Aftab Seth, Sushma Mehra, Kusum Bahl, Roshan Seth, Rajni Mathar, Ena Nadar, Raghu Sudon, Marcus Murch.

**WHO'S AFRAID OF VIRGINIA WOOLF** by Edward Albee.

**AZAR-KA-KHWAB** adapted from Pygmalion by Begum Zaidi directed by T.P. Jain with Salima Raza, Nigam Prakash, Anju Kumar, Ashok Serin, Kulbhushan Kharbanda, Sarvat Khan, Sudesh Syal, Kewal Kapoor.

**THE MATCHMAKER** by Thornton Wilder.

**FIVE FINGER EXERCISE** by Peter Shaffer directed by John Pitman with Ajit Poolai, Joy Michael, Raghu Sudon and Prakash Mirchandani.

**1965-66**

**KHYAL HAI DEMAGH KA** adapted into Hindi from Axelrod's The Seven Year Itch.

**DIAL M FOR MURDER** in Hindi by Frederick Knott.

**A TASTE OF HONEY** by Shelagh Delaney directed by Harbhajan Virdi with Kabir Bedi, Vinanti Sarkar, Prakash Mirchandani, Prabha D'Rosario.

**THE LITTLE HUT** by Andre Roussin.

**AFTER THE FALL** by Arthur Miller.

**THE KNACK** by Ann Jellicoe.

**1966-67**

**TARTUFFE** by Moliere directed by E. Alkazi with Joy Michael, Malti Nehru, Indira Joshi and Prakash Mirchandani.

**RAHOON-KE-NA-RAHOON** by Adya Rangacharya.

**THE THEBAN PLAYS** by Sophocles-an adaptation.

**ALICE IN WONDERLAND** an adaptation by Lewis Carroll.

**THE SEAGULL** by Anton Chekov directed by Joy Michael with Kusum Haidar, Bhaskar Ghose, Nirmala Mathan, Jai Chandiram.

## ROSHAN SETH REMEMBERS

If you want to know if there was a sign, precise, astronomical date when Yatrik was born, I can't tell you. A phone call confirmed that it was early August 1964. So I wish you a HAPPY 40th BIRTHDAY. I wish it survives another 40 years. Will it survive that long? I don't know. Theatre will go on. It is a form of self expression. So long as there is imagination, creativity and the desire to interact with others, there will be the desire to be on stage and do a play. The desire continues whether it is in Yatrik, in me or in you

I remember clearly saying to myself "Etch this moment in your brain because its important and you need it" Sometime early in 1962 we were preparing for our BA exams. Nigam said to me " what do you do after the exam, I could become an actor" . I said, "so will I" and the cat was out of the bag. I said something that was deeply said and also deeply veiled but having brought it out into the open light, then I knew what I was working toward. I went back to College to do my MA, that is really when I spent all my available time doing plays at St.Stephen's and Unity Theatre as well. Something happened before Yatrik was born. There were two institutions at that time that supported the English language theatre, one was the British Council and the other was USIS which was not active theatre-wise, until Tom Noonan, the Cultural Affairs Officer arrived. He was a Kentuckian, very laid back, relaxed, liked saying 'aacha', smoking Salem cigarettes in a soft package. Noonan got Galbraith ,the Ambassador in those days, to put money aside for American plays and ABE LINCOLN was the first. The play attracted actors from various groups, like Habib Tanvir because it was secular and did not subscribe to any particular group. USIS in those days was in Bawalpur House where they had the entire building long before the NSD. It was very central and convenient for us from the University North Campus. They had a small auditorium. So that is the genesis of Yatrik.

After we had done several performances for USIS, I remember we were traveling back by train and I remember Joy saying we have gained so much traveling around as a group of players, we should not waste this valuable experience. Nigam sitting in the compartment said "I know we will call ourselves YATRIK" This is quite specifically Joy's baby. Why do I say that? I don't know because the question is this. Would there be a YATRIK without Joy?

Our first production was *Abe Lincoln in Illinois* by Robert Sherwood and *Our Town* by Thornton Wilder directed by Tom Noonan. Yatrik's beginnings are closely bound up with these plays.

The production was skilfully mounted on a three-level stage with the players sitting on either side of it, from where they made their entries in the folk theatre tradition.

The show was a tremendous success. For more than a year, the production toured various universities and colleges. Everywhere it was received with great enthusiasm. Such

**THE MERCHANT OF VENICE** by William Shakespeare directed by Elizabeth Hicks with Prakash Mirchandani,Pankaj Mohan,Malti Nehru,Nigam Prakash and Bunny Kapadia.

1967-68

**LUV** by Murray Schisgal directed by Minnie Boga with Sushma Mehra,Ludwig Rudel, Kenneth Stevenson.

**EVAM INDERJIT** by Badal Sarkar in a Hindi translation by Bharat Bhushan Agarwal and Ram Gopal Bajaj directed by Mohan Maharishi with Om & Sudha Shivpuri, Sudesh Syal ,R.G. Bajaj,Bandev Sinha.

**SALEEB PER MARIAM** by Kishwar Zaidi.

**TAMBAKU KA NUKSANAT** by Chekhov translated into Urdu.

**MOON ON A RAINBOW SHAWL** by Errol John directed by Joy Michael with Indira Kohli,Sushma Mehra,Sant Juneja, Meriel Michael and Nigam Prakash.

**AAI BALA KO TAL TU** translated in Hindi from Noel Coward's Blithe Spirit directed by Sushma Seth with Kavita Nagpal, Kewal Kapoor,and Sushma Seth.

Azar Ka Khwab with Salima Raza and Anju Kumar

**THE LAND OF CARDS** by Sai Paranjpye directed by Sai Paranjpye with Meriel Michael, Pablo Bartholomew, Chandrika Grover, Kristine Michael, Janice Darbari, Sohail Chander, Vijay Verghese, Yusuf Mehta, Kabir Seth.

**VICTIMS OF DUTY** by Errol John.

**BLOOD WEDDING** by Frederico Garcia Lorca.

**THE ITALIAN STRAW HAT** by Eugene Labiche.

**KAISI YEH JODI MILAI MORE RAM** based on Neil Simon's The Odd Couple.

1968-69

**DESIRE UNDER THE ELMS** by Eugene O'Neill.

**NEXT TIME I'll SING TO YOU** by James Saunders.

**GANDHIJI'S SADHANA** by K. S. Rangappa.

**NAYAK-VINAYAK** by Adya Rangacharya.

**THE FOUR SEASONS** by Arnold Wesker directed by Joy Michael with Jai Chandiram, Phil Harvey.

**AWAJ-KA-RAZ** adapted and translated into Hindi from William Fairchild's The Sound of Murder.

excellence, critics said, had never been witnessed on Delhi's stage before -- and that by an amateur company. And so the idea of setting up a repertory company was born and Yatrik was registered in August 1964.

One of Yatrik's aims has been to promote theatre in education by holding workshops in schools and colleges and staging performances in educational institutions, which we still continue to do. In that first year, Yatrik produced seven plays, some comedy -- black and white, and the famous *Azar-ka-Khwab* an Urdu translation by Begum Qudsia Zaidi of G.B. Shaw's Pygmalion. Our programmes, well saved, and on view at the exhibition, show how all members of the group were ready to function backstage and on stage on a shoestring budget. To a certain extent, this is still true, and in our workshops we try to inculcate the idea that theatre doesn't just mean taking a star role on stage!

*Tartuffe with E. Alkazi, Joy Michael and Prakash Mirchandani*

*Giddh with B V Karanth*

*Promise in Leningrad with Zarin Chaudhary and Aftab Seth*

**AN EVENING OF MIME** with Zarin Choudhary.

**PROMISE IN LENINGRAD** by Alexei Arbazov directed by Som Benegal with Zarin Chaudhary, Aftab Seth, Zahoori Mohiuddin.

**THE SLEEPING BEAUTY.**

**EK CHAADAR MAILI SI** by Rajinder Singh Bedi directed by Rajinder Nath with Sushma Seth, Shyam Arora, Kulbhushan Kharbanda, Ashok Sarin, Mohini Mathur, Madhu Raja ,Veena Khanna.

**A FLEA IN HER EAR** by Georges Feydeau.

1969-70

**ANDHERA HONE DO** Hindi translation of Frederick's Wait Untill Dark with Salima Raza.

### JOY MICHAEL

Professional theatre training in the UK at London Academy of Music and Dramatic Art. Travelled widely abroad. Directed and lectured in some American colleges. Received many awards. Educationist. Developed Creative Drama in Schools. Emeritus Theatre Director Govt. of India.

### WEEKEND & REPERTORY

YATRIK has many 'firsts' to its credit. It was the first to establish and maintain week-end repertory theatre. From 1964-72 for 6-7 months in the year, there were regular performances every Saturday and Sunday, first at the mini-theatre on Mahadeo Road, and then at the bat-and-pigeon ridden Defence Pavilion auditorium in exhibition grounds which are now Pragati Maidan.

Brochures listing the season's programmes were issued in September, and theatre-lovers were invited to become members and buy season

*Goa with Sai Paranjpye and Raghu Sudan*

**A DELICATE BALANCE** by Edward Albee directed by Joy Michael with Zarin Chaudhuri, Ram Hingorani, Sriiata Swaminadhan, Prabha Tonk Rati Bartholomew and George Henry.

**THE BALD SOPRANO** and **THE CHAIRS** by by Eugene Ionesco directed by Zarin Chaudhuri with Pankaj Mohan, Shailaja Dhume.

**HEDDA GABLER** by Ibsen directed by Sushma Seth with Joy Michael, Zahoori Mohiuddin, Santosh Kapila, Peter Moss, Manorama Kankalil.

**GIDDH** by Vijay Tendulkar translated from Marathi in Hindi by Meena Williams with Sai Paranjpye, Shyam Arora & B. V. Karanth.

**THE UNGRATEFUL MAN** by David Horsburgh directed by Sai Paranjpye.

1970-71

**GOA** by Asif Currimbhoy directed by Joy Michael with Zarin Chaudhary, Sai Paranjpye, Raghu Sudan, Trevor Page.

**SHRIMANT** by Vijay Tendulkar.

**THE SNOW QUEEN** directed by Barry John.

Gandhiji's Sadhana with Santosh Kapila

tickets at a reduced rate. The emphasis was on variety, quality and experimentation.

Wherever possible, plays mounted in the winter were taken on tour in the summer to schools and colleges, or cities like Lucknow and Chandigarh. *Cactus Flower* (1970-71) and a musical *The Fantasticks* (1976-77) were great successes.

## THE YOUNG STAGERS CLUB

YATRIK was the first to start producing plays for children and teenagers. *Abe Lincoln* appealed to school children and *Sabrina Fair* to a slightly older age group. This play was most attractively produced in the garden of the Michael's house in Kaka Nagar when a young enchanting Kusum Bahl played the star role. Subsequent productions had Sushma Mehra in this role supported by stalwarts Marcus Murch, Roshan Seth and Salima Raza.

But in addition to plays like these, the really little ones were initiated into the fun of teamwork with the founding of the Young Stagers Club which met regularly. The club enjoyed playing in *The Land of Cards* produced by Sai Paranjype, David Horsburgh's *Ungrateful Man*, *The Dancing Donkey* and *The Sleeping Beauty* which was a pantomime for Christmas. Barry John produced some delightful plays for children,

*The Land of Cards* with Chandrika Grover, Rashid Kuswal, Rahul and Vijay Verghese, Pablo Bartholomeus, Kristine Michael and Vikram Crishna

**ARMS AND THE MAN** by Bernard Shaw directed by Marcus Murch.

**CACTUS FLOWER** by Pierre Barillet and Jean-Pierre Gredy directed by Barry John.

**DANCING DONKEY.**

**AIK TAMASHA ACHA KHASA** by Sai Paranjpye directed by Sai Paranjpye and Arun Joglekar with Madhu Raja, Champak Jain, Govind Deshpande, Channi Beddi.

**MEDEA** by Euripides directed by Alyque Padamsee with Joy Michael and Raghu Sudan.

### 1971-72

**TRUDI AND THE MINSTREL** by Allen Cullen directed by Barry John with Janice Darbari, Mukul Kesawan, Gautam Paintal, Feisal Alkazi, Ranjit Ratnakar, Meera Anand, Rachael Thomas, Reena Helms.

**ROOM SERVICE.**

**ASHADH-KA-EK-DIN** by Mohan Rakesh.

**TANGO** by Mrozeck.

**FESTIVAL OF HINDI PLAYS.**

### 1972-73

**AN ENEMY OF THE PEOPLE** by Ibsen directed by Shankar Suhail with Sham Arora, Romesh Chopra, Manoj Bhatnagar, Sharna Kaul.

**INQUILAB** by Asif Currimbhoy directed by Joy Michael with Kanwal Krishan, Chaman Bagga, Chitra Narain, Pankaj Tandon, Sunil Sethi, Santosh Kapila.

**THE SERVANT OF TWO MASTERS** by Carlo Goldoni directed by Barry John with Siddharta Basu, Sabina Mehta, Nigam Prakash, Prabha Tonk, Anurag Mathur, Cecil Qadir.

**LOK KATHA AAJ KI** in Nautanki style by Chaman Bagga.

**KRANTI AND PARTEN** by P. Lankesh.

**THE EXCEPTION AND THE RULE** by Brecht.

### 1973-74

**LOWER DEPTHS** by M. Gorky in Hindi directed by M. K. Raina with Suresh Kulkarni, Kamini Gupta , Mona Chawla, Arun Virmani, Ramesh Manchanda.

**THE SHOEMAKER'S PRODIGIOUS WIFE** by Federico Lorca directed by Joy Michael.

**GASLIGHT** by Patrick Hamilton directed by Marcus Murch with Sabina Mehta,Pradeep Pant and Sheela Bajaj.

*The Snow Queen*, *Trudi and the Minstrel*. Apart from Sai, others working with children were Meena Swaminathan and Feisal Alkazi (who continues to do so). Hugh Michael, was a tower of strength and both Joy's daughters, Meriel and Kristine, cheerfully took on a variety of tasks connected with the theatre, from appearing in the early plays and taking on leading roles.

A glance at the credits of these plays brings a big smile as one thinks of the serious professional adults who once rollicked on the stage as monkeys, tigers, fairies and elves!

*Lok Katha Aaj Ki* with Ram Gopal Bajaj & Chaman Bagga

*Trudi and the Minstrel*

*The Good Woman of Setzuan*

**OLIVER** a Musical by Lionel Bart directed by Joy Michael for St. Xavier's School ,with Hugh Michael, Jamila Verghese , Marcus Murch, Sharon Lowen, Hutokshi Tayabji, Frankie Gardner, Nirath Perakath, Jon Ramsay, Varun Sharma.

## SUMMER THEATRE WORKSHOPS

In 1971 when YATRIK ran into difficulties in finding space for our work, Max Mueller Bhawan with accommodation in Connaught Circus lent us their premises, and our first summer workshop was held there. We called ourselves "The Rooftop Theatre". The graduates from the National School of Drama helped with our course productions. *The Shoemaker's Prodigious Wife* by Lorca was produced by Joy in English, and Gorky's *Lower Depths* by M.K. Raina in Hindusthani. With this venture several budding talents were launched on their dramatic careers. We pay special tribute to Max Mueller Bhawan for their support and encouragement over many years which has been the venue for rehearsals, visual enactments and productions of plays. Irpinder Puri wrote a play based on the life of Max Mueller which was presented in 1982

*Cause Celebre with Chloe Greaves and Dayanita Singh*

**MARCUS MURCH**
Was an irrepressible thespian gaining his early experience touring India and Asia with Geoffrey Kendal's 'Shakespeareana'. His best-known roles were in 'Abe Lincoln in Illinois', 'Sabrina Fair', 'Arms and The Man', Fagin in 'Oliver'. He was a full-time Stage Manager for Yatrik.

as *Ek Roshan Awaaz* in Hindi. Upto this year YATRIK continues with the summer theatre workshops. For the last several years, the India Habitat Centre in Lodi Road has sponsored our work, and we are most grateful to them.

## READINGS AND VISUAL ENACTMENTS

Another activity in which YATRIK has tried to arouse and sustain interest in theatre has been presenting visual enactments and readings. In this way new works can be introduced; unusual and experimental plays given a hearing and those brief lulls in full-scale theatrical activity made good use of – apart from the need to economise.

We have also been able to design poetry readings on themes for special occasions like Christmas. Among the many examples of such intimate theatre one can name just a few: *Suddenly Last Summer* by Tennessee Williams; Albee's searing *Who's Afraid of Virginia Woolf? Principia Scriptoria, The Good Doctor* by Chekhov in which Ramesh Thakur delighted audiences and *The Chute* by Sarah Ann Lawrence; and very recently, Bhaskar Ghosh's arrangement of readings from Shakespeare, Ibsen's *Doll's House* and Arthur Miller's *Crucible*.

*The Crucible with Bhaskar Ghose, Surinder Dugal, Dilip Sarkar*

# THE SECOND DECADE (1974 - 84)

**1974-75**

**THE WHITE LIARS** and **BLACK COMEDY** by Peter Shaffer directed by Joy Michael with Leda and Joan Hodgson, Madhoor Kapur, Marcus Murch and Jai Sen Gupta.

**THE MOTHER** in Hindi by Brecht.

**VYAKTIGAT** by Dr. Laxmi Narain Lal in Hindi.

**1975-76**

**SIX CHARACTERS IN SEARCH OF AN AUTHOR** by Luigi Pirandello directed by Joy Michael and Joan Hodgson with Nuala Kirby, Nicholas Tucker, Vani Subbanna and Amit Jayaram.

**A SHAKESPEARE EVENING** with Ravi Baswani, Peter Hiscock, Laxmi Krishnamurty, Joy Michael, Nigam Prakash, Sushma Seth, Barry John, Kusum Haidar, M. K. Raina.

**SINBAD THE SAILOR.**

**THE PRODIGIOUS SNOB** by Moliere.

**KADI BAABE DIAN** in Punjabi adapted from Moliere's Scapin.

**1976-77**

**THE FANTASTICKS** a musical directed by Joy Michael with Jo Burton, Ray Orley, Lewie Gonsalves, Kristine Michael, Harold Carver, Hugh Michael, Eric Helms.

**SUDDENLY LAST SUMMER** by Tennessee Williams directed by Joy Michael.

**1977-78**

**THE BROKEN JUG** by Heinrich Von Kleist directed by Joy Michael with Sabina Mehta, Paul de Bernier.

**MODERN BRITISH THEATRE.**

**THE GERMAN EXPRESSIONIST PLAYS.**

**1978-79**

**THE DEVIL'S ADVOCATE** by Dore Schary.

**THE GOOD WOMAN OF SETZUAN** by Brecht directed by Sabina Mehta, Vinay Capila Bhaskar Ghose , Surinder Dugal, Dhroov Saikia, Ajay Balram, Hugh Michael, Lewie Gonsalves, Madhuri Bhatia, Meriel Michael, Jai Pathak.

**CACTUS FLOWER** by Abe Burrows directed by Barry John. with Prabha Tonk, Lewie Gonsalves, Meriel Michael.

**1979-80**

**CAUSE CELEBRE** by Terance Rattigan directed by Joy Michael with Chloe Greaves, Sant Juneja, Dayanita Singh, Lena Acharya, Lewie Gonsalves, Ajay Balram, Sunit Tandon, Bindu and Vivek Tandon, Bhaskar Ghose.

**VENUS OBSERVED** by Christopher Fry directed by Bhaskar Ghose with Preeti Batra, Dayanita Singh, Jai Pathak, Ramesh Thakur, Vivek Tandon.

**BEDROOM FARCE** by Alan Ayckbourn directed by Bhaskar Ghose with Deepa Grover, Ramesh Thakur, Jillian Larkins, Sunit Tandon, Surinder Jain, Jai Pathak, Lewis Gonsalves, Madhuri Bhatia.

## MUSICALS

YATRIK was among the very first to enter the formidable field of musicals. The requisite musical talent combined with acting and mime, plus the challenges of staging, sets and costumes for a large cast, has proved a deterrent to amateur theatre groups. Only very generous sponsorships make musicals possible. However, despite these drawbacks, YATRIK staged *Oliver* in the 1973-74 season with the help of St. Xavier's School Delhi, boys ably trained by Paramjit Singh. Adult roles were taken on by our old-timers who proved that they could not only act but also sing! Sadly, our music director, Harold Joseph, passed away soon after the performances. Other musicals presented were *The Fantasticks, The Happiest Days of Your Life* and *South Pacific*, which was an overwhelming success and played to packed houses with Madhuri Bhatia in the lead.

*The Fantasticks with Jo Burton and Ray Orley*

*The Happiest Days Of Your Life*

*Three Penny Opera with Arjun Raina, Tanvi Nagpal, Kristine Michael and Yashwant Singh*

## AND THE CLASSICS

Catering to different tastes in Delhi's cosmopolitan society is enjoyable and important. Thrillers and light-hearted comedies give place to well-worn classics every now and then. As a discriminating audience is bound to be critical if they are not really well presented, amateur groups have to

*South Pacific*

*The Good Woman of Setzuan with Lewie Gonsalves and Madhuri Bhatia*

*Don't Drink the Water with Bhaskar Bhattacharji, Deepa Grover, Jai Pathak and Madhuri Bhatia*

**TAMASHA** directed by Deepak Kejriwal with Madhuri Kamath, Surinder Dugal, Ramesh Thakur.

**1980-81**

**THE NIGHT THOREAU SPENT IN JAIL** by Jerome Lawrence and Robert E. Lee directed by Tejeshwar Singh with Sunit Tandon, Vinay Capila, Bhaskar Bhattacharji.

**THE GREAT DENUNCIATION AT THE TOWN WALL** and **THE CURVE** in Hindi by Tankred Dorst directed by Deepak Kejriwal with Irpinder Puri, Dhroova Saikia, Hemant Misra, Anurag Bisaria.

**JAI BABA GOPINATH** by J. N. Kaushal directed by Deepak Kejriwal with Vinod Verma, Hemant Mishra and Surender Duggal.

**DON'T DRINK THE WATER** by Woody Allen directed by Ajay Balram with Bhaskar Bhattacharji, Deepa Grover, Madhuri Bhatia, Sunit Tandon, Raghu Sudon, Vinay Capila, Jai Pathak, Ajay Balram, Tejeshwar Singh.

**1981-82**

**THE CRUCIBLE** by Arthur Miller directed by Joy Michael with Bhaskar Ghose, Surinder Jain, Dilip Sarkar, Bhaskar Bhattacharji, Ajay Balram, Jai Pathak, Rajiv Chandran, Smita Nirula, Bindu and Vivek Tandon.

**BEEJAN TEEJAN** dramatised and directed by Deepak Kejriwal with Irpinder Puri, Smita Nirula, Deepa Grover, Ayisha Abraham, Deepa Sahi.

**THE HAPPY MARRIAGE** by Jean Bernard Luc directed by Deepak Kejriwal with Anand Pathak, Vinay Capila, Komal Singh, Aiyasha Abraham, Deepa Grover.

**THE MAIDS** and **DEATHWATCH** by Jean Genet directed by Joy Michael and Dilip Sarkar with Surinder Dugal, Deepa Grover, Sunit Tandon, Bhaskar Bhattacharji and Vinay Capila.

**1982-83**

**THE CURLEW'S CRY** by Kamal Kapur directed by Bhaskar Ghose with Renuka Narayanan, Kumud Kapur, Bhaskar Bhattacharji, Chitra Ramachandran, Sunit Tandon.

**RUFFIAN ON THE STAIR.**

**TOO TRUE TO BE GOOD** by George Bernard Shaw directed by Joy Michael with Nerath Perakath, Kristine Michael, Ajay Balram and Sunit Tandon.

**EK ROSHAN AWAAZ** written and directed by Irpinder Puri with Bhaskar Ghose, Mala Kumar, Shiv Kumar, Kusum Prasad, Deepak Kejriwal, V M. Badola.

think twice before attempting Shakespeare, the Greeks, Molière.

We did the *Theban Plays* (1966-67) and separately *Medea* (1971), *Phaedra*, *Antigone* and very recently, *Hippolytos*. Shakespeare's *The Merchant of Venice*, *A Midsummer Night's Dream* and *The Tempest* have been performed with varying degrees of success; but perhaps we now need to take a look at the contemporary handling of the bard in the west. Adaptations, condensations, lampoon have all been tried and we have the example of the Indian film to show us how to metamorphose Shakespeare into a credible setting of our own.

*The Curfew Cry with Bhaskar Bhattacharji and Chitra Ramachandran*

*Cactus Flower with Surinder Dugal, Lewis Gonsalves, Muriel Michael*

**UNCLE VANYA** by Chekov directed by Joy Michael with Kusum Haidar, Bhaskar Ghose, Bhaskar Bhattacharya, Sunit Tandon and Kristine Michael.

1983-84

**THE MATCHMAKER.**

**THE ELEPHANT MAN** by Bernard Pomerance directed by Vinay Capila with Arjun Raina, Dhroov Saikia, Ramesh Thakur, Tejeshwar Singh, Janaki Bahadur.

**THE REAL INSPECTOR HOUND.**

**A SEPARATE PEACE** and **THE REAL INSPECTOR HOUND** by Tom Stoppard directed by Sunit Tandon with Ranabir Basu, Arjun Raina, Ranjyoti Barooah, Divya Seth, Bhaskar Ghose, Sagarika Ghose.

**A MIDSUMMER NIGHTS DREAM** by Shakespeare directed by Bhaskar Ghose with Arun Banerji, Keith Shepherd, Anand Pathak, Nirath Perakath, Ishita Das, Nandika Jaitly, Joya Chatterji, Bhaskar Bhattacharji, Sagarika Ghose.

*[illegible] Bhaskar Ghose and Surinder Dugal*

## NEW PLAYWRIGHTS – NEW TRANSLATIONS AND ADAPTATIONS

YATRIK has always been ready to sponsor original plays despite the inevitable financial risks involved. Badal Sircar's now famous *Evam Indrajit* was first presented to Delhi audiences in Bharat Bhushan Agarwal and R.G. Bajaj's Hindi translation. Om and Sudha Shivpuri, Mohan and Anjala Maharishi, Bajaj himself, Sudesh Syal, V.M. Badola as Indrajit were all involved in a very successful production of an epoch-making work.

*Azar Ka Khwab*

YATRIK like other dramatic groups in the country is keen to use good translations, and has been fortunate in having practicing theatre people giving their talents to this demanding task. One of our very earliest productions, *Azar-ka-Khwab* which set Salima Raza on an outstanding dramatic career, used a well-known translation of Shaw's *Pygmalion* by Begum Qudsia Zaidi. Habib Tanvir rendered a short story of Chekhov's about the harmful effects of tobacco into a playlet *Tambaku-ke-Nuksanat*. Meena Williams translated Vijay Tendulkar's explosive family drama from Marathi into Hindi as *Giddh*, and also Gogol's *The Government Inspector*. As this is the only way in which regional theatre can cross the language barriers we hope to be using this kind of translation designed for the theatre.

Among original plays apart from the above, Irpinder Puri Bhatia has

## THE THIRD DECADE (1984 - 94)

1984 - 85

**THE QUEEN & THE REBELS** by Ugo Betti directed by Bhaskar Ghose with Prabha Tonk, Avijit Dutt, Kristine Michael, Arjun Raina.

**BLUES FOR MR CHARLIE** by James Baldwin directed by Joy Michael with Arjun Raina, Ajay Balram, Janaki Bahadur, Vinay Capila, Surinder Jain and Nirath Perakath.

**A GOWN FOR HIS MISTRESS** by Georges Feydeau directed by Tejeshwar Singh with Arjun Raina, Ajay Balram, Prabha Tonk, Bhaskar Bhattacharji, Sagarika Ghose and Neil Chatterjee.

**A CHRISTMAS CAROL.**

**BALAMJI TUM AAGEY MEIN PEECHEY** by Irpinder Puri with Kusum Prasad, Anjali Capila, Kamini Gupta.

**BHASKAR BHATTACHARJI**

Greatly talented, versatile, a brilliant and outstanding actor and media personality. Started his acting career while at St.Stephen's College where his rendering of Macbeth is remembered. He distinguished himself in many important leading roles in the theatre to which he brought great sensitivity, understanding and distinction. Bhaskar was our "Man for all Seasons" greatly loved and respected.

dramatized contemporary themes. Realising the importance of the theme of gender and class inequality, she has given us *Baalam Ji Tum Aage Mein Peechey* , a farcical piece about a woman endlessly waiting for a husband who had deserted her, and *Karva Chautha* set in a household where the three generations of women are preparing for the puja,with the dhoban as the only rebel. She also undertook to write and direct a play on the life of Max Mueller, *Ek Roshan Awaaz*. Her next production *Kucch Door To Kissa Jayega* was based on a real life incident of an inter communal love affair and the havoc it caused in two families.

Avijit Dutt, another of Yatrik's many sided theatrical talents, has written

1985 - 86

**SAMJHAUTA** and **PEHLU** in Hindi translation of Harold Pinter's The Lovers and The Collection directed by Sabina Mehta with Sanjeev Manchanda, Arjun Raina, Suneeta Singh

**THREE PENNY OPERA** by Berthold Brecht directed by Avijit Dutt with Avijit Dutt, Arjun Raina, Kristine Michael, Tanvi Nagpal, Nilima Das, Yashwant Singh, Saganka Ghose, Vinay Capila.

**RING AROUND THE MOON** by Jean Anouilh directed by Joy Michael with Vinay Capila Yashwant Singh, Safina Uberoi, Sagarika Ghose, Bhaskar Bhattacharji.

**KUCH DOOR TO KISSA JAYEGA** written and directed by Irpinder Puri with Shakun Saxena, Palminder Singh, Abha Shrivastava, Salim Arif, Surinder Jain.

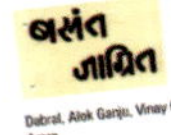

**SPRING AWAKENING** in Hindi by Sindhu Bhagya directed by Avijit Dutt with Sonal Dabral, Alok Ganju, Vinay Capila, Malvika Arora.

**SYLVIA PLATH** directed by Joy Michael with Sabina Mehta, Kusum Haidar, Prabha Tonk.

1986-87

**ABOUT FACE** by Dario Fo directed by Avijit Dutt with Vidhu Singh, Kristine Michael, Sajai Singh, Avijit Dutt.

**TAKING STEPS** by Alan Ayckbourn directed by Vinay Capila with Prabha Tonk, Avijit Dutt, Ranjit Kaul, and Kristine Michael.

two original plays. *Bamboo Flower* or Kismat Ya based on an Assamese folk tale, about every twenty years when the Bamboo flower blossoms in the village, creating a web of magic which is flung across the valley. Old loves are re-united, new loves are formed, the Bihu drums are more ecstatic and the Mahua sweeter.*Bombay Bosnia*, deals with a very contemporary theme – communal riots and their effect on the ordinary citizen faced with difficult decisions. Avijit is also versatile actor, producer and lighting expert.

Joy Michael undertook the production of an unusual new play, Manjula Padmanabhan's award- winning *Harvest* in which not – so –young seasoned actress and film star Zohra Sehgal played an exacting part. *Harvest* is not an easy play, set in 2010 with its futuristic and high-tech projections, it could be daunting to many. It is a deeply disturbing,

*The Virtuous Burglar* with Avijit Dutt and Swaroopa Ghosh

*Drums In The Night* with Deepak, Ramesh, Indu, Pia & Avijit Dutt

*Musibat Mara Murari* with Sanjeev Popley and Ratu

*Bombay Bosnia* with Avijit and Pia Dutt, Ritu & Vinod

**HUGH MICHAEL**

Nurtured and sustained Yatrik over many years, his strength, support and vision was a source of encouragement. He will always be remembered by audiences as someone who greeted them with warmth and friendship at the box office and foyer. He loved the theatre and was our "Man behind the Scenes". His caring for others, his sense of humour, dedication and rich baritone voice in our musicals will be remembered.

thought-provoking, evocative play where the characters project a searing world of human relations in the not-so-distant future. The characters are finely etched, the situation real and identifiable, the plot ingenuously developed and the visuals, a challenge. The play places questions before us- how strong are we to face the challenges of exploitation, political, economic, social, at every level of human society. When we are faced with difficult alternatives, what are our choices , what happens to our ideals, our pride, our desire for

*Harvest* with Zohra Sehgal and Tanishta Roy Choudhury

**THE HAPPIEST DAYS OF YOUR LIFE** - A Musical by John Dighton directed by Joy Michael with Avijit Dutt, Kristine Michael, Dorothy Tressler, Vinay Capila.

**OF MICE AND MEN** in Hindi.

**PLAY IT AGAIN SAM** by Woody Allen directed by Ajay Balram with Arjun Raina, Sagarika Ghosa, Avijit Dutt, Bhaskar Bhattacharji, Prabha Tonk , Janaki Bahadur, Nandika Jaitly.

**1987-88**

**THE DAILY TRUTH** from Pravda - adapted from Brenton and Hare's Pravda and directed by Tejeshwar Singh with Jasbir Malik, Bhaskar Bhattacharji, Devakna Kohli, Dilip Sarkar.

The Daily Truth

**PRINCIPIA SCRIPTORIA** by Richard Nelson directed by Prabha Tonk.

**APPROACHING LAVENDER.**

**CLOSET MADNESS.**

**THE TEMPEST** by Shakespeare direceted by Joy Michael with Tejeshwar Singh, Sunit Tandon, Rominika Dey.

**1988-89**

**ARSENIC AND OLD LACE** by Joseph Kesselring directed by Prabha Tonk with Jackie Garewal, Indu Vachani, Deepak Mukerji, Rupin Jayal, Sunit Tandon, Ranjit Mathur, Ajay Balram, Sridhar Rajan, Vinay Capila, Jasbir Malik.

**DRUMS IN THE NIGHT** in Hindi.

**MAHABHOJ** by Mannu Bhandari directed by Prakash Bhatia with Avijit Dutt, Deepak Sinha, Ajay Balram, Vinay Capila, A.K. Kaviraj, Ajay Kishnoi, Sonal Dabral, Ramesh Chand, Tarannum Ahmed.

**GITANJALI IN FIVE TIMES** directed by Joy Michael with Sita Raina, Prabha Tonk, Jacqy Garewal, Meera Oberoi.

**AIK AUR DHRONCHARYA** by Shankar Sesh directed by Prakash Bhatia with Manoj Gupta, Rewa Bhandarik, Jayashree Raman, Basab Bhattacharya, Neeraj Yadav, Vijay Manocha, Sidharth Khanna and Amitabh.

freedom? Can there be a new definition for winning. Winning by losing.

Another first for YATRIK was Asif Currimbhoy's *Inquilab* staged in 1972 in the small Max Mueller auditorium of those days. Maya Rao's choreography and the use of realistic slides suggested the social and political implications of the play. Just two years earlier in 1970, the inauguration of the Sri Ram Centre Theatre was marked by a first performance in India of Currimbhoy's *Goa* which had made its debut in the West but had been proscribed in India. Like the Indo-Anglian novel, Indo-Anglian drama had begun tentatively and has had to overcome many prejudices before it was accepted. Kamal Kapur's *The Curlew's Cry* was an interesting experiment in this genre, and produced by Bhaskar Ghosh in the 1982-3 season. The play explores intimate relationships between a group of contemporary middle-class Indians, the kind of theme introduced in Hindi by Manu Bhandari and Mohan Rakesh.

The use of English for Indian plays has come to stay, as exemplified in the popular contemporary work of Mahesh Dattani. An enormously successful original play has been 9 *Jhakhoo Hill* by Gurcharan Das, which has been skilfully directed by Sunit Tandon with a star cast which toured Bombay, Calcutta, Dubai and Shimla, where it was originally set and received much acclaim. Sunit started working with Yatrik after leaving St Stephens College and is a brilliant and versatile actor.

Another recent trend in dramatic writing has been the use of two languages in one dramatic work – a practice also used successfully in film. Plays in Hindi, Bengali and Marathi especially have lent themselves to this. Avijit Dutt's adaptation of *I'm Not Rappaport* by Herb Gardner into *I'm Not Sheikh Chilli* which has done exceedingly well in the past year, and toured India and taken to Dubai, uses English, Hindi and Punjabi. Also, *America Here I Come* by Brian Friel has been adapted by Jagat Rathore from the original *Philadelphia Here I Come* The play is about love and yearning and particularly suited for a young Indian audience who are vacillating between leaving home, family, friends in pursuit of a glamorous career in another country. A widowed father and his son find it difficult to communicate. The son has an alter ego who expresses his real feelings. Both are two views of the same man. *Gitanjali* from the original Canadian play *Albertine In Five Times* was adapted and directed by Joy Michael.

*The Tempest* with Tejeshwar Singh

*America Here I Come* with Jagat Rathore, Sudama Ramaswami and Oroon Das

YATRIK has produced other original plays using two languages. Poile Sengupta's *Mangalam* used English and Tamil and was imaginatively directed by Bhaskar Ghosh, who is an outstanding director and actor.

*Come As You Were* is an original play by Nicholas Khargonkar of Manipur. Five school friends meet after ten years at a hunting lodge. But what begins as a happy reunion quickly turns , as the old jokes and funny incidents they recount suddenly take on a serious note. Everything they shared in happy innocence is now seen in a new malignant light. As things worsen, explosive secrets about each other come hurtling out that will change their relationships forever. As the situation turns dangerously volatile, they have nowhere to hide from each other. Audiences found the play gripping, shocking and funny.

Among other talents one must mention Sabina Jaitly, Surinder Dugal, Madhuri Bhatia, Ranjit Mathur, Vivek Mansukhani, Jasbir Malik, Dilip Sarkar, Tejeshwar Singh, Prabha Tonk, Santosh Kapila, Shyama Haldar, Swaroopa Ghosh, and Oroon Das.

*9 Jakhoo Hill* with Shyama Haldar and Rupin Jayal

**1989-90**

**A TOMB WITH A VIEW** by Norman Robbins directed by Prabha Tonk and Sunit Tandon with Ranjit Mathur, Deepak Mukharji, Indu Vachani and Rupin Jayal.

**MUSEEBAT MARA MURARI** in Hindi translation by Vinod Verma directed by Avijit Dutt with Ramesh Thakur, Vinnil Markan, Sandeep Prabhakar, Sanjiv Popley, Dawan, Vinod Verma, Asha Rishi, Amar Talwar.

**SOUTH PACIFIC** a Musical by Rodgers and Hammerstein directed by Joy Michael with Madhuri Bhatia, Amar Talwar, Frances Groser, Vijay Bhushan, Deepak Castlino, Bhaveen Gosain, Arnold Harvey, Moira Meyer, Rachna Kohli.

**THE MAN WHO CAME TO DINNER** by Moss Hart and George Kaufman directed by Irene Das with Audrey Prasad, Vinnil Markan, Pradeep Kapur, Indu Vachani, Ramesh Thakur, Amar Talwar.

**CHRISTMAS CAROLS AND READINGS.**

**1990-91**

**ALL MY SONS** by Arthur Miller directed by Joy Michael with Renee Pagnon, Deepak Mukerji, Sita Raina, Jasbir Malik, Avijit Dutt, Meriel Michael, Ramesh Thakur, Anjana Kapoor

**LETTICE AND LOVAGE** by Peter Shaffer directed by Joy Michael with Prabha Tonk, Deepa Grover, Audrey Prasad and Jasbir Malik.

**TOWARDS ZERO.**

**MAHABHOJ** by Mannu Bhandari directed by Prakash Bhatia with Avijit Dutt, Deepak Sinha, A. K. Kaviraj, Vinay Capila, Sonal Dabral and Inderjit Kanojia.

**GOVERNMENT BABU.**

**BEDROOM FARCE** by Alan Ayckbourn directed by Bhaskar Ghose with Deepa Grover, Ramesh Thakur, Sunit Tandon, Lewie Gonsalves.

**1991-92**

**THE GOOD DOCTOR** by Anton Chekov

**MAHATMA MAR GAYA.**

**THE LAST OF THE RED HOT LOVERS** by Neil Simon directed by Sunit Tandon with Deepak Mukharji, Jacqy Garewal, Shibani Lulla and Indu Vacham.

**EK KISHORE KI DASTAAN.**

**1992-93**

**DANCING AT LUGHNASA** by Brian Friel directed by Joy Michael with Swaroopa Ghose.

*9 Jhakhoo Hill with Ajay Balram and Surinder Dugal*

## AJAY BALRAM REMEMBERS

### When Things Go Wrong

Even in the best of worlds, there can be goof-ups.

The St.Stephen's College centenary celebrations included a production of Shakespeare's 'Winter's Tale' directed by Joy Michael. The cast consisted of past and present Stephanians. In Act IV, scene 4, the old shepherd (Tejeshwar Singh) and his son (Sunit Tandon) meet the wily Autolycus (Dilip Sircar). They are on their way to offer a gift to the King. Autolycus persuades them to give him the bag of gold and let him do the talking. They agree, and the old man puts his hand in his left pocket, takes it out empty, puts his hand in his right pocket, takes it out empty, and then cursing the props under his beard, brightly tells his son to hand over the gold. Sunit wanders round looking for the prop. Not finding it, he picks up one of the sandbags used for chasing away flies in the Sri Ram Centre, and hands it to Dilip. Dilip, undeterred by the heavy bag, continues singing accompanied by his guitar. Then suddenly, he makes a dive to the left, picks up what looks like a brilliant slip catch at ankle level, then clapping his hand to his mouth, continues with his song. When he came off, we asked him if he were trying to impress the cricket captain. He replied, 'Guys, my false front teeth flew out as I hit a high note. I had to catch them before I could sing on'. Then when the peddler (Vinay Capila) comes on to describe his wares, his memory fails him, and he says,'I have such beautiful wares to sell, I have no words to describe them'.

On this occasion, a young 'current' Steph comes up to Ajay and asks him, 'What years were you in college?' Ajay tells her, '53-56'. A few minutes later he overhears her telling a current Steph in the play, 'Do you see that old grey-headed guy over there? He was in college in the 50s! That is not 'old Stephanian - that covers people like Sunit Tandon and Bhaskar Bhattacharjee who were in college in the 70s. He should be termed 'Ancient Stephanian'!

When Ajay was directing Woody Allen's 'Play it Again, Sam', he was suffering the usual problem of the director of an amateur group —cast members missing rehearsals. As the show dates approached, the problem was worsening. He finally pinned a large poster outside the rehearsal hall, reading 'Why get an ulcer, when you can direct a play and get a whole nervous break-down?' That seemed to do the trick. He had full attendance from that day on.

Let us pray that our current directors are saved from nervous disorders.

*Salvia Patil with Prama Tesk, Kusum Haidar and Sabina Mehta*

**A BETROTHAL.**

**PHAEDRA** by Racine directed by Sunit Tandon with Ashwin Juneja, Rupin Jayal, Indira Kohli, Prabha Tonk, Jasbir Malik and Indu Vachani.

**THE ROAD TO MECCA** directed by Joy Michael with Smita Vats, Ramesh Thakur and Kristine Michael.

**BLIND DATE.**

**THE LADY'S NOT FOR BURNING.**

**A WALK IN THE WOODS.**

**KISMET YA** written and directed by Avijit Dutt with Dilip Shankar, Mukul Nag, Swaroopa Ghose, Vinnil Markan, Shayama Haldar and Tanishta Chakravaty.

1993-94

**RISHTEY HI RISHTEY** adaptation of Thornton Wilder's The Matchmaker in Hindi by Prakash Bhatia with Swaroopa Ghosh, K. D. Pathak, Sandeep Kaviraj and Ramesh Chand.

**BOMBAY BOSNIA** written and directed by Avijit Dutt.

**A WILDE EVENING** with Roshan Seth, Avijit Dutt, Kusum Haidar, Sabina Mehta, Bhaskar Bhattachaji.

**SALOME** by Oscar Wilde directed by Kusum Haidar with Soumitra Bhagat, Bhaskar Bhattacharji, Oroon Kumar, Subhasini Sood, Dilip Shankar.

Apart from the great names YATRIK has also taken up plays from other historical periods – the Scandinavians – Ibsen, *Hedda Gabler*, Chekhov, *TheSeagull Uncle Vanya*, Shaw, *Arms and the Man*, Brecht, *The Good Woman of Setzuan*, *Three Penny Opera*. The German Expressionists, Lorca *Blood Wedding*, Pirandello, *Six Characters in Search of an Author* – dramatists whose names recall the university's Honours and Masters degree courses.

*Antigone with Sumitra Bhagat and Dilip Shankar*

*The Match Maker with Bhaskar Ghose & Surinder Jain*

## THE FOURTH DECADE (1994 - 2003)

1994-95

**SIX DEGREES OF SEPARATION** by John Guare directed by Joy Michael with Sabina Mehta,Bhaveen Gosain, Surajit Nandy, Indira Kohli, Vivek Mansukhani, Pradeep Kapoor, Oroon Kumar, Sumitra Bhagat, Jasbir Malik, Amarjeet Singh, Dilip Shankar.

**A CHRISTMAS CAROL AND POEMS.**

**ANTIGONE** directed by Bhaskar Ghose with Sumitra Bhagat, Amarjit Singh, Dilip Shankar.

**RISHTEY- HI- RISHTEY** Hindi adaptation of Thornton Wilder's The Matchmaker directed by Prakash Bhatia with K.D. Pathak, Sanjeev Popley, Manzoor Raiz, Reena Chadha, Nalini Kamal, Swaroopa Ghosh, Sandeep Kaviraj.

**THE DUMB DANCER** by Asif Currimbhoy directed by Avijit Dutt.

1995-96

**DEATH & THE MAIDEN** by Ariel Dorfman directed by Sabina Mehta with Bhaskar Ghose, Avijit Dutt.

**VERDICT** by Agatha Christie directed by Joy Michael with Oroon Kumar, Swaroopa Ghosh, Bhaveen Gosain, Piu Dutt, Vivek Mansukhani, Amarjit Singh.

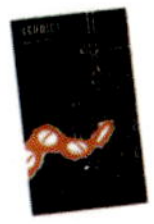

**LET US GO THEN...** Poems About Journeys : In Three Parts with Vivek Mansukhani, Sunit Tandon, Tejeshwar Singh, Salima Raza, Kusum Haidar.

The list of those who have worked with YATRIK over the years, some of whom are still with us, is very impressive. Indispensable backstagers have been our carpenter Sardar Chanan Singh, well-known lights experts R.K. Dhingra and V. Ramamurthy, who has made lighting history all over auditoria in India, and Sudesh Syal. Vinay Capila, man of many parts, being actor, director, lightsman and magical creator of moveable sets has been recently honoured by the Chaman Lal Award.

Our directors, often on as well as off the stage, are also innumerable. To mention some of them, Joy Michael of course heads the list, closely followed by Bhaskar Ghosh, Avijit Dutt, Sunit Tandon, Ajay Balram, Sabina Jaitly and Kusum Haidar. Prominent among our directors is Prakash Bhatia who has done a magnificent job in giving a new impetus and bringing

*Mangalam with Pradeep Kapoor and Renuka Narayanan*

*Don't Dress For Dinner with Surinder Dugal, Ramneeka Lobo, Shyama Haldar, Vivek Mansukhani, Deepak Mukharji and Ramesh Thakur*

**DON'T DRESS FOR DINNER** by March Camolletti directed by Vivek Mansukhani with Ramesh Thakur, Surinder Jain, Ramneeka Dhillon Lobo, Shyama Haldar, Rupin Jayal.

**THE MATCHMAKER** in Hindi.

**9 JAKHOO HILL** written by Gurcharan Das directed by Sunit Tandon with Bhaskar Ghose, Surinder Jain, Ajay Balram, Kusum Haidar and Shyama Haldar.

9, JAKHOO HILL

1996-97

**BOMBAY BOSNIA** written and directed by Avijit Dutt with K.D. Pathak, Reena Chadha , Piu Dutt, Swaroopa Ghosh, Vinnil Markan, Prakash Bhatia, Pradeep Kapoor,Mr. Rice and others.

**A WALK IN THE WOODS.**

**UNBEATABLE SHAKESPEARE.**

**BORDERLINE** by Hanif Kureshi deected by Avijit Dutt with Prakash Bhatia, Tanuja Roy Chowdhary, Oorun Kumar Das, Avijit Dutt.

**LOVE IN THE TIME OF PROTEST** with Joy Michael, Kusum Haidar, Bhaskar Ghose, Sabina Mehta, Sunit Tandon.

1997-98

**THE BROTHERS KARAMAZOV** in Hindi directed by Prakash Bhatia.

alive our Hindi theatre productions, among some of his productions are *Of Mice and Men, Mahabhoj, Ek Aur Dhronacharya, Bhalabhpur Ka Roop Katha*. Earlier directors include Rati Bartholemew, Habib Tanvir, Alyque and Pearl Padamsee, Barry John, Nigam Prakash, T.P. Jain, B.V. Karanth, Sai Paranjpye, Mohan Maharishi, M K Raina, Ramgopal Bajaj, Rajinder Nath, Som Benegal, Sushma Seth E. Alkazi, Zarin Chaudhuri, John Pitman, Philip Henderson .... and so the list goes on. We mourn the early loss of Marcus Murch, and more recently, Bhaskar Bhattacharji.

Yatrik has won numerous awards. *Kismet Yah* and *Bombay Bosnia* at the National Theatre Festival, *I'm Not Sheikh Chilli, Mangalam* and *Educating Rita* by the Sahitya Kala Parishad in 2003.

*I am not Shaikh Chilli with Avijit Dutt and Omkar Goswami*

Now looking back on our theatres's long history, we realise how much has changed. Auditoria, rehearsal space, sound and lighting technology, competition from mass media and perhaps, most of all – our audiences. We now cater to a much wider spectrum of age

*Six Degrees of Seperation with Sabina Mehta*

**HARVEST** by Manjula Padmanabhan directed by Joy Michael with Vikramjeet Sinha, Tannishtha Chatterji, Zohra Sehgal, Monsoon Bissel, Jaydeep Sarkar, Rajesh Thanikan, Bhrigupati Singh, Jai Chandiram.

**THE VIRTUOUS BURGLAR** by Dario Fo directed by Avijit Dutt with Swaroopa Ghosh, Sunit Tandon, Vandana Ranganathan, Vinnil Markan.

**1998-99**

**THE HERBAL BED** by Peter Whelan directed by Joy Michael with Malvika Rajkotia, Rajat Seth, Radhica Ganapathy, Sunit Tandon, Sant Juneja, Jasbir Malik, Pradeep Kapoor, Damini Ralleigh.

**EK SAPNE KI MAUT.**

**VIRASAT.**

**1999-2000**

**THE VIRTUOUS BURGLAR** by Dario Fo directed by Avijit Dutt.

**BOMBAY BOSNIA** written and directed by Avijit Dutt.

**9 JAKHOO HILL** directed by Sunit Tandon.

**2000-01**

**MANGALAM** by Poile Sengupta directed by Bhaskar Ghose with Surinder Jain, Sunit Tandon, Pradeep Kapoor, Renuka Narayanan, Suhel Seth, Smriti Kishna, Priyanka Jhajaria.

**LOLA CHATTERJI**

Is Yatrik's chronicler. She has helped in an advisory capacity and backstage for many years. She has taught English in Calcutta and Delhi universities, retiring as a senior Lecturer from Miranda House. She writes articles and reviews and undertakes editing commissions.

groups and interests. Much has been achieved due to the help, support and encouragement of a wonderful, dedicated executive Committee, and the enthusiasm of its youngest member, Amarjit Singh. A small dedicated group of theatregoers exists, but finding new plays both in English and Hindi has become more challenging than ever. We look forward to the 21st century, building on our past and being prepared to face the future with its many challenges.

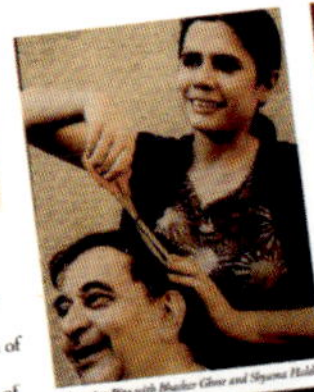

*Educating Rita with Bhaskar Ghose and Shyama Haldar*

*Balabpur Ki Roop Katha*

*Mangalam with Suhel Seth*

**GETTING AWAY WITH MURDER.**

**BALABPUR KI ROOP KATHA** directed by Prakash Bhatia.

**I AM NOT SHEIKH CHILLI** based on Herb Gardner's I am not Rappaport directed by Avijit Dutt with Omkar Goswami, Piu Dutt, Jagat Rathor.

**2001-02**

**AMERICA HERE I COME** adapted from Brian Friel directed by Joy Michael with Jagat Rathore, Oorun Kumar, Swaroopa Ghosh, Pradeep Kapoor, Sushma Ramswami, Sant Juneja, Nayantara Sood, Ranjit Mathur.

**HYPPOLYTOS.**

**COME AS YOU WERE.**

**EDUCATING RITA** by Willy Russell directed by Joy Michael with Bhaskar Ghose and Shyama Haldar.

**2002-03**

**EK AUR DRONACHARYA** by Shankar Shesh directed by Prakash Bhatia with Sonal Dabral, Tarannum Ahmed, Vidya Bhushan, Naved Zahur Ansari and Inderjit Kanojia.

YATRIK THEATRE

Executive Committee of Yatrik

Joy Michael
Director

Amarjit Singh
Secretary

Pradip Kapoor
Jt. Secretary

Sushma Ramswami
Treasurer

Executive Members

Ajay Balram
Prakash Bhatia
Vinay Capila
Lola Chatterji
Avijit Dutt
Bhaskar Ghose
Kusum Haidar
Sabina Jaitly
Sant Juneja
Sunit Tandon

We offer our grateful thanks to the following for their assistance:

R. K. Dhingra of Modern Stage Service
Lolita & Anando Dutta
Rajeev Ralleigh
Kristine Michael
Teamwork Films
Edmund Marsden, Chandrika Grover & the Arts team of British Council
Programme Staff of India Habitat Centre

Photo credits: Madan Mehta and Richard Bartholomew for the first two decades
Opposite page: Avinash Pasricha

*Rati Bartholomew, Kusum Haidar, Sushma Seth and Joy Michael*

# THE PILLARS OF YATRIK...
## AS THE STORY CONTINUES

*There are actors whose skill inspires one with an infinite love of the theatre. The magical power of their impact on the audience is so irresistible that the theatre becomes the raison d'être for many young men and women.*

**Boris Tilippov**

*There are so many people who have made invaluable contributions and kept this journey going. From the founders to those who worked closely with them over the first decade or two are those who have continued since then. Many have been drawn to the group and happily joined the bandwagon, focused on the common platform of the stage. This movement of vibrant personalities has kept Yatrik dynamic and active. Meet some members of the widely spread Yatrik family.*

**Ajay Balram,** a man of few but significant words. I am as bad at writing as I was at learning lines. In fact my main role and activity in Yatrik was learning my lines, preferably prior to opening night. I was good at remembering my opening lines from my previous plays, but that somehow did not satisfy the director.

How did I join Yatrik? That in itself is memorable in its own way—in 1965, I came on holiday from Mumbai to Delhi. When I got home, I asked for Vinay (my brother, Vinay Capila) and I was told he had gone to the hall for a rehearsal of *The Matchmaker.* I went across there and Joy Michael was pleased to see me because one of the lead actors was unwell. She asked me to read in for him, which I did. At the end of the rehearsal, she asked if I could also come the next day, opening night, in case the actor was still unwell. He was, so I played the role, well prompted in my lines by all the other actors, both on and off stage. That went off well. Thereafter, I tried replicating that "success" each time Yatrik asked me to act in a play. Thus ended my thespian career.

All I manage now is to lisp. All lisp and no thesp makes Ajay a dull actor.

*South Pacific*—Ajay Balram (centre) as the "commanding" Naval Officer

*The Tempest*—Ajay Balram (left) and Sunit Tandon (right) with Sonjoy Kant and Rominika Dey in the centre

**Amar Talwar.** At age 39, I got back to theatre after 20 years. As luck would have it, I got my first break as a "lead", and that too in a musical. Yatrik was celebrating its 25th anniversary, and as part of the celebrations, the group decided to stage *South Pacific*, the musical. Madhuri Bhatia had already been cast to play Nellie, the female lead, but the male lead was up for grabs. Well, I was the one they selected for that job.

What an experience, what a high that was for me! And after that, it was all up and up for me as an actor: before I knew it, I found myself in Bollywood playing a lead in India's first daily soap, *Shanti*.

I have many people to thank for pushing me, guiding me along this way, but among the two or three on top of the list comes Joy Michael, who had the confidence in me to cast me, a newcomer, as the lead

Indira Kohli and Amar Talwar in *Bedroom Farce*

in what was for her and Yatrik a prestigious project. After that, I had the chance to be part of many Yatrik productions, including *Bedroom Farce* and *The Man Who Came to Dinner*, both enjoyable experiences. In fact, I enjoyed being part of all the plays I was in. Thank you, ma'am, and thank you to all at Yatrik who enriched my life in the 1990s—and continue to do so to this day.

**Amarjit Singh,** or A.J., as everyone who has anything to do with Yatrik knows him, joined Yatrik in 1994, when Kusum Haidar's daughter Navina asked him to read for *Six Degrees of Separation*, a play to be directed by Joy Michael.

Over 23 years since then, A.J.'s office conference room has served as the venue for the initial rehearsals

Sumitra Bhagat (left) as Antigone and Amarjit Singh seated in front (right) in a scene from *Antigone*

for most of the plays. The conference table has served as the round table for committee meetings, with several cups of tea being readily served. A.J. has played a pivotal role as a member of the Yatrik Executive Committee, and has also served as the secretary of the group for several years.

As A.J. recalls: I acted in a few more plays, including *Antigone* after that first play. Because of time constraints and work commitments, I then went on to doing sound for plays and then producing them. I produced a bunch of plays, including *Come As You Were* by Nicholas Kharkongor, which Sunit Tandon directed. My association and friendship with Nicholas Kharkongor recently led me to co-produce his first movie *Mantra*, starring Kalki Koechlin and Rajat Kapoor, among others.

I had the opportunity to tour many cities and countries, including Dubai and South Africa, with various Yatrik plays, particularly *9 Jakhoo Hill*. Easily, my two favourite plays are *Six Degrees of Separation*, which had my first stage appearance, and *9 Jakhoo Hill*, one of Yatrik's landmark productions as directed by Sunit Tandon.

**Avijit Dutt.** A versatile theatre artist, Avijit Dutt has directed and acted in more than 70 productions in English, Bengali, and Hindi over the years. He moved to Delhi from Calcutta in 1983. And in the decades that followed, Avijit worked actively both as a director and an actor. Productions such as Bertolt Brecht's *Three Penny Opera*, Dario Fo's *About Face* and *The Virtuous Burglar*, Hanif Qureshi's *Borderline*,

Avijit Dutt and Sita Raina in *All My Sons*

and Peter Weiss' *Museebat Mara Murari*, were memorable. His roles in *Mahabhoj*, *Death and the Maiden*, Arthur Miller's *All My Sons*, and in all Dario Fo's plays are equally unforgettable. His ability to work both in Hindi and English has given him special versatility.

A multifaceted creative personality, a stage actor, director, playwright, film actor, and documentary maker, Avijit plays leading males in the productions that he writes and directs. His directional art and his productions are neat and realistic, and the lighting, which he himself designs, is subtle—all these elements are synthesised and fine-tuned. His competence as a director handling plays belonging to different genres is reflected in most of his plays, especially in comedies.

Yatrik played a pioneering role in conducting theatre workshops in Delhi. Avijit contributed much in making these workshops meaningful. At the end of each workshop, Yatrik would stage a play created in the course of the workshop. In 1995, under the guidance of Yatrik, he produced *Mahatma Mar Gaya*, which is a critical

Avijit Dutt in *The Virtuous Burglar*

commentary on politicians exploiting people's sentiments in the name of religion, denouncing the forces of fascism that intend to destroy the social fabric of communal harmony. This was the only time that Yatrik presented a street play, and the group performed in all low-lying colonies of Seemapuri, Trilokpuri, Jama Masjid, and Turkman

Gate. Yatrik collected 42,000 rupees, which was donated to Rice Rais, an actor whose shop was destroyed in communal riots.

A versatile artist, Avijit has many memories still fresh in his mind of his working experience with various groups, though his association with Yatrik has been the longest one. He co-dramatised and directed *Hazaar Chaurasi Ki Maa* with Shyamanand Jalan and did theatre workshops countrywide, along with Badal Sircar. In *Hazaar Chaurasi Ki Maa*, he played the role of Brati Chatterjee, a Naxalite who was brutally killed by goons in collaboration with the police. Padatik Theatre staged it. Mahasweta Devi was in the auditorium when it was staged, but she remained seated quietly. She was visibly moved. She said, "I didn't ever believe this could be done as a play; my heartiest congratulations." It was a great and most unforgettable moment for the cast and crew. The production was brought to Delhi for the discerning audience of Delhi. The Padatik production was one of the best productions among several versions of the play seen on the Delhi stage.

Avijit wrote and directed *Bombay Bosnia* for Yatrik in 1993–94. It was an attempt to analyse the cause of the Mumbai riots. Avijit has depicted the agony of the people forced to leave their homes by religious fanatics with searing poignancy. He has also projected the insensitivity and partisan attitude of the police. This was one of the bold and original productions of Yatrik that indicted communal forces. The Sangeet Natak Akademi refused to present this play at North Zone Culture Centre Festival in Amritsar.

Bamboo Flower or *kismet ya chakrant* is an allegory. Every 50–60 years, the bamboo flower blossoms. It spins its web of magic across the Brahmaputra valley. Old loves are reunited, new loves are formed, and the mahua tastes sweeter. But the fragrance also brings down thousands of rats, which eat the standing crops to a stubble; invariably spreading hunger and pestilence. The Mizo National Front was formed around one such incident.

*Bombay Bosnia* and *Bamboo Flower* featured at the prestigious national theatre festival—Bharat Rang Mahotsav—organised by the National School of Drama in Delhi in 2003 and 2005, respectively.

**Memorabilia**

Important plays directed and acted in: *Three Penny Opera, Museebat Mara Murari, Twelfth Night, Drums in the Night, About Face, The Virtuous Burglar, Abducting Diana, I am not Sheikh Chilli.*

Scripted and directed: *Bombay Bosnia, Bamboo Flower, Breaking News.*

Adapted for theatre: *Hazaar Chaurasi Ki Maa.*

Acted in: *All My Sons, Otherwise Engaged, Mahabhoj, Principia Scriptoria, Death and the Maiden.*

*Drums in the Night*—Ramesh Thakur and Indu Ramchandani (seated), and Avijit Dutt (standing right)

Yatrik is perhaps the only amateur group in the country that has taken several of its productions abroad. This started in the 1990s, when Yatrik was invited to Dubai with Dario Fo's *The Virtuous Burglar*. The work was appreciated and subsequent invitations for Avijit's other Dario Fo plays followed. Joy and Avijit are registered as artists with the Indian Council for Cultural Relations (ICCR) and that has also helped with three tours.

**Yatrik's Highlights Overseas**

1994: *The Virtuous Burglar*—Dubai: performed at the Indian Consulate, celebrated and had to do additional shows.

1998: *9 Jakhoo Hill*—Dubai.

2003: *I Am Not Sheikh Chilli*—Dubai: three shows to full houses.

2004: *Mirza Bagh*—Lahore: well received, played to a full house.

2004: *9 Jakhoo Hill*—five cities in South Africa. Assisted by ICCR.

2007: *Pushkin's Last Poem*—Moscow and St. Petersburg: well received in Moscow; standing ovation in St. Petersburg. Sponsored by ICCR.

2015: *Comedy About the End of the World*—Slovenia, Italy, Austria; well received. Sponsored by ICCR.

**Reminiscences:** My first play with Yatrik was *The Queen and the Rebels*, directed by Bhaskar Ghose. I played the male lead. *All My Sons*, directed by Joy Michael, came later, wherein I played the younger son.

I have written three full-length plays. What was the inspiration to write these plays? As a playwright, I respond to situations that move me. The phenomenon of the the bamboo flower and the rise of the Mizo National Front inspired the play *Bamboo Flower*. The first time I went to the Federal Republic of Germany (West Germany) was

*The Virtuous Burglar*—Avijit Dutt, Swaroopa Ghosh, Vandana Kilim Datta, Shibani Bedi, and Sunit Tandon

*The Virtuous Burglar*—Pranay Manchanda and Avijit Dutt

*The Virtuous Burglar*—Shibani Bedi, Pranay Manchanda, and Avijit Dutt

in 1987 to study German theatre. On a Goethe Fellowship, I went to Germany for the second time in 1994. The Berlin Wall was now demolished. The people of GDR and FGR have united emotionally, politically, and psychologically. It was a different Germany, a different world. The German Democratic Republic (East Germany) had formally ceased to exist. The catchphrase was "us" and "them". The internationally renowned director of the Berliner Ensemble, Heiner Mueller, was being questioned for his political views.

Suddenly, I conceived of the idea of *Bombay Bosnia* against the backdrop of the ethnic cleansing of the Bosnia Muslims. The focus would be the devastating communal riots in Mumbai in 1992–93. The script of *Bombay Bosnia* was my outcry against fanaticism and the rise of the majoritarianism in our country. It is my agonised manifestation of the traumatic experience that radio broadcaster Ameen Sayani went through when his house was burnt down in communal violence. The communal carnage described in *Bombay Bosnia* is based on the carnage that followed a series of bomb explosions in 1993, perpetrated by criminals and underworld gangsters. The play was banned in Mumbai. Keeping in view the highly encouraging response from the audiences, however, Yatrik revived its production and it was staged in Delhi in 1996–97 at the India Habitat Centre.

*Breaking News* is a reaction to media and its need to manufacture eye-grabbing events.

> *Bombay Bosnia:* The action takes place in the house of Rishab. The family members are terrified by the impending danger to their lives, as the city is possessed by madness. The family members are receiving threats about their factory, which could be burned by the criminals if they are not paid "protection money". Then the action transfers to a waiting room of first-class railway passengers with Muthu, a lumpen, who declares

the waiting room as "the security zone". He collects money from those who come for safety in this waiting room. Although he is trading in human suffering, he retains some humanity. He rescues a young girl who is just in her petticoat and brings her to "the safety zone" and does everything possible to save Saeed. The action now shifts to a deserted road. The street-smart Muthu has managed to secure a temporary pass and he is accompanied by Saeed and the young girl, feigning to be a rape victim, being taken to the hospital.
They are confronted by a police inspector, who orders them to reveal their names:

Muthu: Muthu Krishna Swamy,
s/o Ms Doraiswamy resident of…
Girl: Asha...Sharma
Inspector: *Aur aapka*?
Saeed: S...Sa...Sir?
Muthu: Ajay Khanna s/o, Rajesh Khanna

Saeed thanks Muthu for saving his life. But suddenly, they are encircled by a mob, being asked to identify their religion in a crude and humiliating manner. As Muthu is removing his trousers, Saeed runs for his life. The play portrays with telling effect Rishab's state of mind when the family is determined to escape from their house with essential belongings to protect themselves from mob fury, and the quandary is: What can they carry? He says, "Just wounds, injuries, and abuses." His wife Tehmina reacts: "We have lived all our lives in this city. We've always known everybody who was anybody. We thought we owned this place. But we obviously didn't know the people of consequence. There was a time when people who mattered came up to Rishab and congratulated him on his programme. And now, there was no one around even to make polite sounds."

Looking out from his window, he describes the city on fire, "...Purgatory is here, Reshma, the flames are lit. Now nothing will douse them. They are fuelled by hatred and fanned by greed. I've walked that way to get to school. Everyone used to know me and had a special message for me...Now...you can put the fire off. But the flames will never die."

Avijit played the role of Rishab and Prakash Bhatia acted as Advani, who migrated from Pakistan in the wake of the Partition. Both these senior artists of Yatrik have excellent chemistry, which was discernible in this prestigious production.

*Breaking News* made news, as it evoked rave reviews for its remarkable contemporary relevance. Using all elements of multimedia, the play shows the inner workings of television news. With biting humour and sarcasm, the play depicts how our imaginations are held captive by TV, and in search of eyeballs and TRPs how they stop at nothing. Strangely, the farce becomes reality when political fates are decided based on the maps laid out on TV. Dhruv Jagasiya as the minister, Neeraj Yadav as the politician, Prakash Bhatia as the chief of police, Abhay Manas as the journalist, and Avijit as the failed writer were impressive. Of the women, Simriti Kalra as the anchor and new find Priyanka Jhijaria were outstanding.

A scene from *Abducting Diana*—Diana (Kriti Vij) and her kidnappers

*Abducting Diana* by Dario Fo, internationally renowned Italian satirist, playwright, actor, and director, presented by Yatrik at the Natyotsav, offered a hilarious experience. Exposing media exploitation, the play opens with a young woman claiming to be an actress playing the role of a media magnate, instructing a clumsy young man to kidnap her for ulterior motives. Another twist takes place. She is actually kidnapped by three kidnappers. The woman claiming to be an actress is forced to reveal her identity. It turns out that she herself is Diana. Through the interactions between the kidnapped and the kidnappers, a number of awkward situations take place, which are hilariously funny. Because of her cunning manoeuvring, the kidnapped becomes the boss, exploiting the utter ignorance of the kidnappers about their profession. Dutt has created a satirical theatrical piece that makes for entertaining viewing.

Avijit Dutt played the role of a gun-toting priest. His stage presence was impressive and his delivery distinct for its clarity and dramatic force. His entry reinforced the element of suspense. Kriti Vij as Diana and Vani Vyas as Diana's mother performed admirably. The play was in collaboration with the Italian Cultural Centre and Mr Fo was to come, but his health didn't permit it; instead, his designer Luca Ruzza came.

*Comedy About the End of the World* was written by Evald Flisar, a Slovene novelist, playwright, essayist, and editor. It was first staged in Delhi at the Shri Ram Centre in 2014. The play was then invited to the Kranj Annual Theatre Festival, Slovenia, where it was well received. The play was taken to European countries under the aegis of the ICCR and received critical acclaim. The team travelled overland to Trieste, Italy, where the play had a good run; finally, they went to Graz, Austria, where they performed at a traditional theatre owned by a group that had state sponsorship.

The script is structurally highly innovative. Every scene begins with a report announcing the dismal world situation caused by greenhouse effects, large-scale devastation as a result of drought, and finally, a warning of catastrophes that will destroy the world. Against this grim, pessimistic, and dreadful background, the play begins with the conversations of three characters who interact in an ambiance that is "faded", "disordered", and "neglected". The characters are Joe Orton, 25, a chronically addicted pot smoker who claims to be a playwright; Elvira, 48, the owner of the lodge, a nymphomaniac and worried about her advancing age; and Majerhold, 55, an inventor and a fugitive. Konjevic, 50, a swindler, joins up later.

All the characters have false identities. In the course of their interactions, their various identities are revealed. These characters are morally nihilistic. Majerhold's several identities come to the fore, a genius who is out of tune with the established social order. One of the characters says, "...considering the times we live in, dying for your principles, which are no more than momentary urges, would be an anachronism. I appeal to you not to surrender to such childish desire for heroism." Gradually, the narrative moves towards a climax.

The situations in the play are absurd. The play is a severe indictment of a world on the verge of extinction because the forces it has created are out to destroy it. Pretensions and reality keep on merging. The faded world of these characters is a web of conspiracy and scheming. Avijit has treated his production with remarkable ingenuity, bringing to the fore the serious intent of the play, combining various elements of realism, comedy, and satire to create a gripping production—one that tends to be a metaphor to warn humanity about the impending dangers for survival.

Avijit in the lead role of Majerhold gives an outstanding performance. Pranay Manchanda, a graduate of LAMDA as Joe Orton, Vidhushi Mehra as Elvira, a woman with a shady past, and Oroon Das as Konjevic give convincing performances.

Why *Comedy About the End of the World*? Well, I met Evald Flisar virtually; he had seen a short film of mine. I was interested in this peripatetic writer who had lived in many countries and whose plays have been translated into 30 languages, including Bengali and Hindi. I chose this play because of what it talked about and its closeness to me—both the environmental issue and the debate of commerce over research. These matters are as pertinent for India as they are for the world over.

Being both the director and actor in a production, I experience complete freedom of expression and interpretation. As a director, I grapple to understand a given play and its interpretation in terms of its relevance to our time. When I project my vision as a director, and act it out as a performer, I interpret a greater dimension to the characterisation. The vision of the director and the interpretation of the actor combine to reinforce the meaning of a play.

I believe Yatrik has a future only if it embraces the bilingual staging principle. I have done over 50 plays and conducted summer workshops, which were the cradles for new actors. There is a need for active groups to attract audiences who are keen on watching television and films. The National School of Drama has set a bad example: students are trained with government funding to be theatre artists. But the graduates run to Mumbai for any small roles in films or on TV. This is a huge problem for theatre. This is a reflection of society. We have to sustain theatre.

I want to restart the theatre workshops for Yatrik. We did this in the past with tremendous success. It is the "honey" that attracts artists into the group. Yatrik's production of *Mahabhoj* was produced in the course of a workshop and was a great success.

Some amusing incidents flash through my mind. In my first play for Yatrik, I was rushing to get to rehearsal on my motorcycle and I had an accident. I managed to get a lift to rehearsal. I was about 10 minutes late. I apologised and was about to begin when Bhaskar noticed I was bleeding. They sent me to a doctor, who gave me seven stitches. As a result, I had to play the character hobbling and with a stick.

Narayana Murthy of Infosys had sponsored our Bangalore production of *I Am Not Sheikh Chilli*. Nandan Nilekani, Sudha Murthy, and all were backstage, watching us warming up, wondering why we couldn't come to Infosys to do a workshop. Then they avidly watched us. Young Rohan Murthy came shyly at the end of the production to congratulate us.

We performed the street play *Mahatma Mar Gaya* at Jama Masjid; when we looked up, there was Imam Bukhari watching the play. He invited us to dinner afterwards. The beggars at Jama Masjid who had watched the play pooled in and wanted to make a contribution to us. And we accepted it gracefully.

I am one of the few theatre practitioners who has had the opportunity of working with great Indian theatre personalities such as Badal Sircar, Shyamanand Jalan, Sheila Bhatia, and Joy Michael. I went to Berliner Ensemble to meet Heiner Muller and see the ensemble first-hand. The Brechtian Verfremdung style of acting is a typical necessity for certain plays. But it is Stanislavsky who has been a constant inspiration. I think work experience then builds your special method that works for you. Habib Tanvir, Shyamanand Jalan, Sombhu Mitra, and Badal *da* have been constant inspirations. Last but not the least, a word about Joy—she always had the means to pull out every glitch and determinedly move forward. Every hiccup the group had, she would assemble all the forces and continue the climb to new peaks. She is to me "Mother Courage".

**B.V. Karanth,** another stalwart of the Hindi theatre, translated and directed a play of Kannada playwright Adya Rangacharya (or Sriranga, as he was known) as *Rahoon ke na Rahoon.* Yatrik produced the play, and it was staged in 1966 at the Defence Pavilion, Pragati

Maidan. It was considered a bold attempt to stage a regional play on its platform—an admirable attempt to enrich Hindi theatre in Delhi. Most of the cast and crew were graduates from NSD. The cast included Karanth himself, V. Ramamurthy, Anjala Maharishi, Harjeet, Sudesh Syal, Dinesh, M.S. Azad, Tilak Raj Ahluwalia, and O.P. Kohli.

This experimental play tried to bring about a series of images of our true selves as to what we really are amidst the maze of our hectic lives, confused ideals, and more often, artificial, meaningless human relations. At another level, the play reflects the defiance of young people against obsolete values.

In fact, Sriranga's celebrated play *Kelu Janamajay* was first staged in Hindi as *Suno Janamajay* by NSD students, before the original play in Kannada was staged in Karnataka in 1965.

**Bhaskar Ghose.** A consummate actor and director, Bhaskar is endowed with a talent that enables him to portray characters of a wide range, from serious to light-hearted, from tragic to comic. In all these characters from classic to contemporary, he displays a sensitivity and emotional depth remarkable for artistry and profundity. He is not a professional actor; nor has he been trained in any dramatic institution. It is his sheer passion that drives him irresistibly to the magic of the theatre.

As an IAS officer, Bhaskar Ghose had reached high echelons of administrative apparatus. He served as director general, Doordarshan; secretary, Department of Culture in the Ministry of Human Resource Development; and secretary, Ministry of Information and Broadcasting. A writer and columnist, Ghose had the opportunity to act in various Shakespeare plays as a student of St. Stephen's College. The turning point in his life to take theatre seriously came when he moved from West Bengal to Delhi and joined Yatrik in 1965. His journey into the fascinating world of theatre is closely linked with the artistic journey of Yatrik itself.

Bhaskar's acting career with Yatrik began with Joy Michael casting him in the role of Kostya Treplov, or Konstantin Treplov, the son of Irina Arkadina, an actress. This production of *The Seagull* was a fine production that sensitively and laconically captured the Chekhovian mood and his lyrical philosophical vision of a world where true love culminates in tragedy—Joy captured the deep inner turmoil of characters vividly, intensely, and with restraint.

Bhaskar has devoted over 60 years to theatre both as an actor and director. He started his artistic journey when he was 16. His art became more profound and deep as Yatrik strived to produce plays that pulsated with life and vitality, reflecting social forces that affected both art and society.

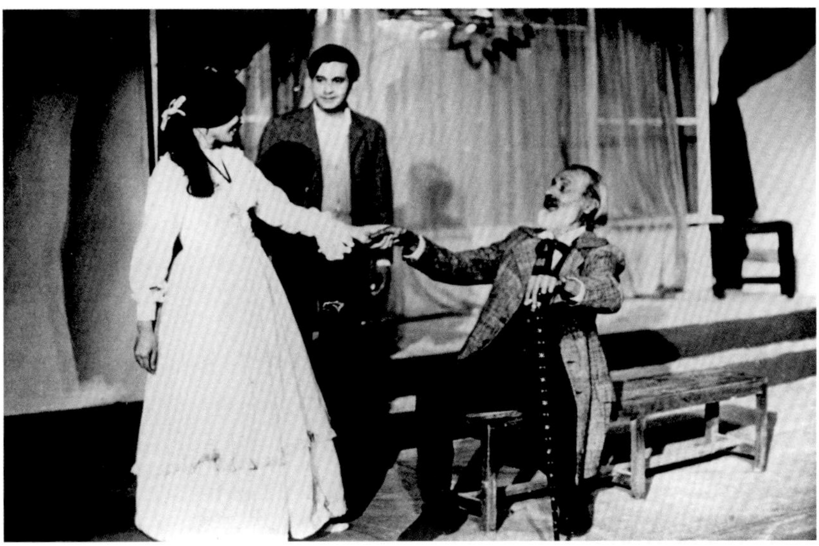

Kusum Haidar (left) and Bhaskar Ghose (centre) in *The Seagull*

Kusum Haidar and Bhaskar Ghose in *The Seagull*

**Reminiscences:** I joined Yatrik because of my commitment to and involvement with theatre since college. Yatrik was the only group then doing serious theatre, and Joy persuaded me to join. Yes, Yatrik does pursue a distinct credo: the staging of meaningful and outstanding plays, those that enrich as well as entertain. This was a time when most other plays being staged were salacious, vulgar, and attracted crowds who wanted that kind of "entertainment". We, on the contrary, wanted to choose the finest plays of the time, which would entertain, and yet be dignified with finesse.

During most of the 1970s, I was not in Delhi. When I returned in 1978, I started working with Yatrik again, and at that time it was a small, close-knit group of committed persons who staged new and challenging plays. I was involved, for example, right after I came back, with the staging of three German expressionist plays directed by Sabina Mehta Jaitly—I acted in one of them. The other actors were even more committed to theatre than I was. Among them were Madhuri Bhatia, Lewie Gonsalves, and Deepak Kejriwal (now Qazir). Soon after that, Joy directed two major plays, *The Devil's Advocate*, a dramatised version of Morris West's novel of the same name, and Terence Rattigan's *Cause Celebre*, in both of which I had substantial parts.

At around that time, thanks in no small measure to the interest in theatre stimulated by Yatrik and other groups, newer theatre groups came up and NSD also expanded its work through its repertory company. Yatrik continued to rely on British and American plays in English, the audience of which was not growing fast. Money was a major problem as well; sponsors were reluctant to put money into English plays of this kind, while the bawdy comedies that were being staged continued to be popular. Nonetheless, we managed, and our plays, both in English and Hindi, drew large enough audiences.

Yatrik was regarded as a major group in the theatre world; plays staged by us made a difference in terms of standards of acting and production and were immediately commented on in journals and by theatre aficionados. Deepak Kejriwal's staging of *Beejan-Teejan*, based on a folk tale retold by Vijay Dan Detha, stirred up considerable interest and commentary because it reflected the love of two women for each other, something that was a topic entirely tabooed at that time.

I was by this time firmly committed to theatre, while taking care to see that it never interfered with my work as a civil servant. This was possible because of the extraordinary generosity that Joy showed, and the truly admirable cooperation of my fellow actors. They willingly accepted my late arrivals for rehearsals—I could never get to them

Bhaskar Ghose in *Beejan-Teejan*

before 7:30 pm every evening, and we rehearsed till almost 11 pm on some days. But Delhi was a much safer place in those years; autos and taxis were reliable, and we never had an incident of any of the women acting in the plays being subjected to objectionable treatment when they returned from late rehearsals. Some of us, including me, had cars, and we dropped as many of them as we could to their homes.

I had a role in virtually all the plays that were staged by Yatrik in the early 1980s; if I wasn't acting in one I was directing another. In fact, when we did Christopher Fry's *Venus Observed,* I played the main role and directed the play—not a wise thing to do. That play was most remarkable for its sets, created by Ajay Balram. Ajay had two complete and separate sets—the Duke's observatory and the outdoor garden leading to the stables. To change the sets, Ajay "flew" one set up, immensely heavy though it was, right up beyond the proscenium. All of us had to bend our backs and haul on the ropes that he had tied the observatory to securely, and lift the set up. It was a tribute to his practical sense of what could be done and what couldn't that it worked every night. There was never a mishap.

The play was also notable for one other thing—the debut of Dayanita Singh, now a celebrated photographer, as an actor.

I directed Alan Ayckbourn's *Bedroom Farce* with a fine cast: Madhuri Bhatia, Lewie Gonsalves, Ramesh Thakur, and Sinia Dugal, among others. Then the hilarious *Cactus Flower,* which I directed by default—Joy was to have directed it, but had to leave town on unavoidable work, and left the play to me, still a novice, to direct. But it was a great success, thanks to the wonderful cast, which featured a brilliant performance by Sinia Dugal and a delectable cameo by Sara Adhikari, who was with Yatrik briefly, playing Botticelli's Springtime, a rather colourful character in the play.

In 1981, I played the lead role of John Proctor in Arthur Miller's *The Crucible,* one of the most difficult yet satisfying roles I have ever done, running a close second to Hamlet in *Hamlet*, which I did in St. Stephen's in the years before Yatrik was founded. *The Crucible* was directed by Joy, and had a superb performance by the late Bhaskar Bhattacharji as Reverend Hale, the passionate yet discerning and principled pastor; a memorably evil performance by the beautiful Bindu Tandon as Abigail Williams, who virtually starts the mass hysteria leading to the hangings; finely presented performances by the late Dilip Sirkar and by Ajay Balram; and a wonderfully subdued, yet intense performance by Sinia Dugal as Proctor's wife. The play drew packed houses for all the shows we did—I know if we had done more, they would have been sold out.

I remember this play for one special reason: Dilip, God bless his soul, always forgot his lines, and would fly into a rage if someone told him that. Joy got around that by having the large number of girls in the cast learn his lines, which they did, especially one who had a photographic memory. It so happened that in the play one or the other of the girls—usually two or three—would be on stage when Dilip was on, as the judge, and if he forgot his lines, they would whisper it loudly as if they were talking to themselves, and Dilip, the true thespian, took it smoothly from there. The audience never noticed.

I ventured into Hindi theatre with a fairly major role in *Beejan-Teejan*, which Deepak Kejriwal directed. I was apprehensive, as my Hindi was rudimentary, and, what was worse, it had, according to the other actors, a foreign accent to it that made it comic. Deepak said he wanted me for the part of the Bhooton ka Sardar for precisely this reason, but it actually led to more laughter than the quality of strangeness Deepak wanted. I have Madhuri Bhatia to thank for spending hours and hours with me when we weren't rehearsing, patiently correcting my Hindi pronunciation, and it worked: no one laughed and I was complimented by several people on being a convincing sardar of ghosts.

I then played the lead, if you please, in another Hindi play: Max Mueller in *Ek Roshan Awaaz*, written and directed by Irpinder Puri.

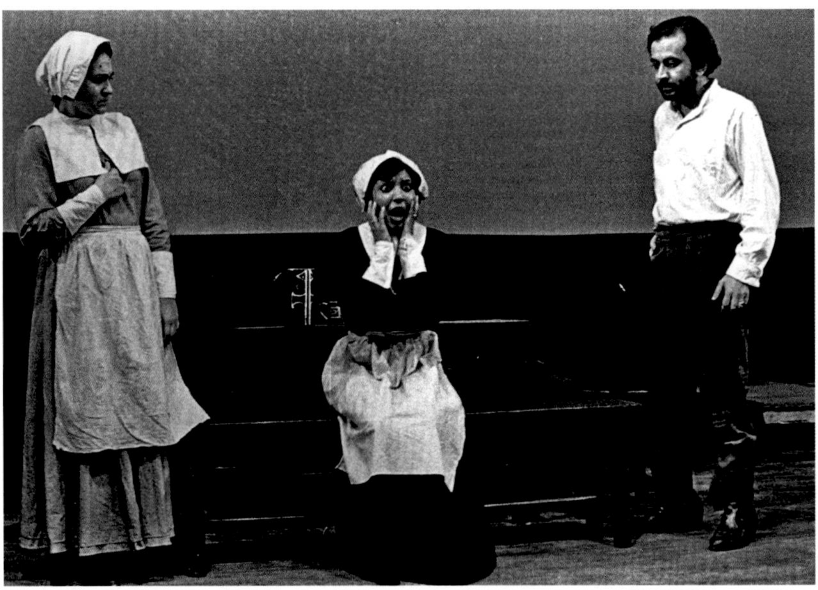

Sinia Dugal, Suniya Luther, and Bhaskar Ghose in a scene from *The Crucible*

Not only was I on stage for most of the play, I also had to recite Sanskrit slokas, as if speaking in Hindi wasn't tough enough. But that was all I ever did in Hindi. I found the tension of working in it to be too great. One of the mainstays of actors—which all actors will endorse—is the ability to ad-lib, that is, make up lines which approximate the ones that one may have forgotten. I was not able to do this in Hindi, and that added unbearably to the tension of working in a language I was not good at speaking in the first place.

*Uncle Vanya*, directed by Joy Michael, was another high point, in which I played Vanya to a finely delineated performance of Bhaskar Bhattacharji's Doctor Astrov and Kusum Haidar's Yelena. But the performance that was poignant and sensitive, and in a real sense embodied the situation Chekhov delineated so memorably, was the delicate and vulnerable presentation of Sonya by Kristine Michael. Her hopeless, unrequited love for Astrov, which she quietly accepted, and her eloquent words of compassion to Uncle Vanya at the end of the play, themselves so full of pain, had the audience in tears.

The 1990s brought with them more plays. A fine staging of Anouilh's *Antigone*, directed by Kusum Haidar, in which I played Creon to a spirited and eventually triumphant Antigone, played by the immensely talented Sumitra Bhagat, is something I will not forget.

Another memorable, brilliantly presented play was Ariel Dorfman's *Death and the Maiden*, directed by Sabina Mehta Jaitly, who also played Paulina, the main role, with brilliance. I played her husband, and Avijit Dutt was the doctor whom she accused of being her torturer.

And then there was the one play that has had the longest run of any play in Yatrik's colourful history through the decades—Gurcharan Das' *9 Jakhoo Hill*, first presented in 1996, and then at different times right up to 2004, at such diverse places as Dubai, the Grahamstown Festival, Johannesburg, Pretoria, Cape Town, Mumbai, Calcutta, the

Kusum Haidar and Bhaskar Ghose in *9 Jakhoo Hill*

Hindu Theatre Festival in Chennai, Shimla, where the play is set, and Delhi. I played the role of Karanchand, who is both the narrator and a participant in the action, and revelled in the role, though it was at some points in the play a terribly difficult task to switch immediately from the intense melancholy, and even grief, of the one to the detached informality of the other. Any actor will tell you what a wrench it is mentally to do that. Sunit Tandon directed the play with truly admirable skill. He also played a major role in the play, the ardent young lover who turns out to be weak-willed and so completely in his mother's power that he gives up his love and what could have been great happiness because she demands it. Sinia Dugal was absolutely magnificent as the mother. In fact, the play had a "star" cast with those I've already mentioned, and Kusum Haidar and Ajay Balram. Shyama Haldar acted as the spirited Ansuya, the girl who is rejected but is determined to make a life for herself on her own, and she does.

*Antigone*—Sumitra Bhagat and Bhaskar Ghose

What's even more amazing and gratifying is that whenever and wherever the play was presented, it was to packed halls and it received great acclamation after every show. Vinay Capila devised a wonderful Lego kind of set for our South African tour, which we never got to use, tragically. No plane would take it as cargo on account of its shape and size and we had to leave it behind in Johannesburg. Despite our repeated appeals to the ICCR to get it out of customs, where it was after being sent back by the consulate general in Johannesburg, it stayed there and was, I believe, auctioned off by the customs authorities.

Then I turned more and more to plays written in English by Indian playwrights, set in India with Indian characters. I had directed *The Curlew's Cry* by Kamal Kapur in 1982, and I was astonished at the warm response the play got from the audience. "It's so like our own place, just like something that could happen next door," was the general refrain, and it was that, really, that showed me the value of

A scene from *Antigone*

looking for plays by Indian playwrights. Unfortunately, I couldn't find any suitable ones right then, and owing to Yatrik's desperate financial situation at the time, couldn't afford to stage Mahesh Dattani's *Bravely Fought the Queen*, even though Mahesh had agreed to our doing it.

Fortunately though, I came across the fine plays of Poile Sengupta, actor, director, and playwright. I directed her *Mangalam* first, which played to a delighted audience; then two one-hour plays as a double bill, *Alipha* and *Thus Spake Shoorpanakha*; *So Said Shakuni*; and finally *Keats was a Tuber*. *Mangalam* was presented again as a part of Yatrik's 40th anniversary celebrations, and I was lucky to get the same wonderful cast, except for Suhel Seth. His replacement was a total disaster—in fact, that, oddly, is what I remember of these shows more than anything else. But, on the whole, these were received with great acclaim by the audience, owing to a large extent the fact that they related to situations or characters with which they were familiar, and more particularly because of Poile Sengupta's wonderfully expressive dialogue and her brilliant craftsmanship as a playwright.

Yatrik has done other plays written in English by Indian playwrights. Aside from the ones I have already talked about, we have done dramatised readings of Anuvab Pal's plays, and many years ago, Yatrik staged Asif Currimbhoy's plays, and *Harvest,* a play by

Manjula Padmanabhan. That had won an international award. One of our members, Avijit Dutt, is a prolific playwright as well, and Yatrik has presented a number of his plays, which have been mentioned elsewhere in this book.

But while I was discovering Indian plays and the pleasure of presenting them, Joy persuaded me to act in Willy Russell's *Educating Rita* with Shyama Haldar. While casting, Joy looked primarily for suitability in terms of ability to portray the character the way she wanted it to be done. She insisted I do the role of the alcoholic lecturer of English literature, even though I felt and told her that someone younger would be more suited. I was 64 when she cast me in the play, and the character was clearly 40-something. Shyama was superb as the working-class girl, desperate for an education through a correspondence course, and I enjoyed the part of the boozy tutor to whom she had to come from time to time. I must confess I had my doubts about doing this play, because I did not want to do another "foreign" play again, but Joy's persuasive powers prevailed. She wouldn't hear of any change and got me to do it as written. It was a play she'd always wanted to do, and she insisted that the fact that it was "foreign" did not, in the end, matter. She was right: this was the only Yatrik play to be selected for the NSD Festival, the Sangeet Natak Akademi Festival, and the Sahitya Kala Parishad Festival, all in the same season.

I made another exception, if it is that, in directing Euripides' *Hippolytos* in an outstanding translation by David Lan, wherein he is true to the Greek text but uses contemporary English to convey the sense of the dialogue and action. Once again, I had to play unwillingly a role in the play—that of Theseus. I need not have worried, though; the play was lifted to admirable heights by riveting performances by Malavika Rajkotia as Phaedra and Suhel Seth as Hippolytos, with a lively performance by Shyama Haldar as one of the two washerwomen who represented the chorus. A tour de force, truly—it was a pity that it could be performed just twice for financial reasons.

Although I was neck-deep in the immense task I had been given by the speaker of the Lok Sabha to start Lok Sabha Television, I did find time to stage a play written by my former colleague and now good friend Achala Moulik on the Russian poet Pushkin called *Pushkin's Last Poem*. The play needed a good deal of rewriting, which Achala willingly did, though at some points she gently put her foot down. I knew when to stop pressurising her and quietly accepted whatever she wanted at those points. The tribulations of being a director were what I remember most about this play, of having to do everything from getting police permission, hiring the hall, settling with the entertainment tax authorities, and everything else. Vinay Capila was one of the few who helped with a wonderful set, and Achala herself managed to get sponsors who paid for the staging. Later, this play was taken with changes made by the new director Avijit Dutt to Russia, about which there is an account elsewhere in this book.

In 2011, I directed a play by a person who had never written for theatre, but who produced an interesting script. This was Nilanjan Mukhopadhyay, and his play *Everything Personal* made clever use of the kind of reality shows that are popular on television and even on radio. The relatively large cast had a great amount of energy and played together seamlessly and convincingly. Staging for me was a satisfying experience, and underscored once again the bonding that theatre brings with it between persons from different professions and of widely varying ages.

I believe that Yatrik has been one of the groups responsible for the present interest in English-language theatre. Today, a number of youngsters are performing such plays, because a whole lot of young people enjoy English-language theatre. They don't have any hang-ups over the language; in fact, many of their plays are a mix of English and Hindi or Punjabi, or all three. I know in Chennai, plays have English mixed with Tamil, and in Calcutta, English merged with Hindi and Bengali. Whatever reaches out to the audiences is what matters.

Yatrik productions always showcase some artistic merit. Because that is what the directors and actors and backstage crews have striven for. That has in itself inspired so many youngsters to come to our performances, and is the reason they want to take part in Yatrik plays. That is why our summer theatre workshops are packed, whenever we hold them. From these workshops have emerged young, talented, and dedicated theatre people, whom you see performing in our plays and in others.

The importance of a director's perspective cannot be overlooked. And this has been one of Joy's greatest strengths; she was an exacting director. She wanted, and still wants, I imagine, the play to move and progress in the way she imagined and worked out. Joy's rehearsals were always marked by one feature, which was dominant, apart from all the others—discipline. She insisted everyone needed to be there, be totally involved and, above all, on time. She was also uncompromising and would do a bit over and over till she was satisfied with it.

She also left a great deal to the individual actors; that's the way we grew, actually. She would discuss the characters with us, the situations, the interrelationships, but she would leave a great deal to us to develop. She often had improvisations: that meant taking the thread of a scene, but improvising different situations that helped us "find" the character, so to speak. In 1965, Joy directed Chekhov's *The Seagull.* I played Konstatin, a young poet and dramatist, with the greatly talented Nirmala Matthan playing the key role of Irina Arkadina, my mother (even though she was a good bit younger than me). Joy would leave us to work with each other while watching and intervening, if she thought it necessary, as we played to each other.

The part I played had some momentous scenes. I remember one improvisation with Nirmala where we were so involved with our characters and the situation that we were both, at one time, in tears—angry, yet loving each other as mother and son—and that intimacy was what we got out of that session and kept, I remember, during the shows.

*The Seagull*—Bhaskar Ghose and Nirmala Matthan

It moved the audience greatly; one can tell from the stage, as you know, when you have got across to the audience and when you haven't. And at that time, we had. Thanks to Joy's nurturing us to play to each other, yet keeping us within the strict discipline of her own vision of the play.

> An interesting and memorable feature of the production of *The Seagull* was that it was presented on a stage with no cyclorama and no wings; there was a flat wall at the back and steps on either side to get on stage. All our entrances had, therefore, to be timed carefully, as we had our green rooms and "preparation" area behind the audience. We had to go down quietly past the audience, just in time to make our entrance. And, being the perfectionist that she was, Joy would not have us arrive even a second too early; it had to be just at the moment we had to make our entrance—not a second early, not a second late. This was in the grounds of what was then called the Defence Pavilion, a dilapidated, bat-filled structure, owned by the Ministry of Defence in what is now Pragati Maidan.

Joy intervened much less in *Uncle Vanya* because, I think, she knew that most of us—Kusum, the late Bhaskar Bhattacharji, I, and the others—had had 20 years of experience after *The Seagull*, and she could let us develop scenes and situations with just a few directions from her. But we did have long discussions on the characters and the situations. She encouraged us to think for ourselves, not wait to be told what to do by her. What she was concerned with, in both plays, was the overall feel, the pace, and the atmosphere, which are so important for Chekhov plays.

Yatrik's single most enduring factor has been Joy Michael. It would have been nothing without her. She has steadfastly nurtured it through bad times and good times. Whatever it has achieved as a group has been because she set the standards and got Yatrik where it is now. It exists because of her, because of her total, unswerving dedication to theatre of the finest quality. She has put it before everything else, and is in the true sense one of the great pioneers of theatre in Delhi, indeed in the country. Her immense energy, strong determination, imaginative ways of organising plays and sponsors, and getting people involved are legendary.

All the directors that I have worked with, in fact, have shown the same kind of understanding, discipline, and commitment. They also have the competence to reflect contemporary realities to the extent the play requires. Sunit Tandon, for instance, was sensitive to it when he directed *9 Jakhoo Hill*; Kusum Haidar was sensitive to it when she directed *Antigone*; Irpinder Puri was equally so when directing *Ek Roshan Awaaz*, her play on Max Mueller.

Directors like Sunit Tandon, Kusum Haidar, Avijit Dutt, and Prakash Bhatia do an excellent job of encouraging youngsters to act; Avijit enthused some of them to direct dramatised readings of plays. That did wonders in creating enthusiasm and confidence in the younger members, who will one day soon take Yatrik forward in the way they want to.

**Memorabilia:**
Bhaskar has vivid memories of playing the young man in Chekhov's *The Seagull* in 1965. But the roles that gave him the greatest satisfaction were:
John Proctor in Arthur Miller's *The Crucible* (1981).
Uncle Vanya in Chekhov's *Uncle Vanya* (1983).
*Creon* in Jean Anouilh's *Antigone* (1994).
Karanchand in Gurcharan Das' *9 Jakhoo Hill* (1996).
Among his directorial ventures is Poile Sengupta's *Mangalam*, which was staged twice, the second time for Yatrik's 40th anniversary in 2004, and *A Midsummer Night's Dream* in 1983.

Shakespeare's *A Midsummer Night's Dream* has been criticised by Jan Kott, a Polish scholar of international repute, who, in his book *Shakespeare Our Contemporary* (1966) has described this particular play as "a defiance of parental authority and state laws…the most erotic of Shakespeare's plays." Jan Kott further refers to the *Dream* as "the one full of allusions to contemporary life."

What was Bhaskar Ghose's approach to and interpretation of the *Dream*? "I must confess I never had any intention of doing anything other than present the play as it has been written. I wanted to let Shakespeare communicate to the audience whatever social significance and relevance he had written into the play. What interested me was something quite different; I had a young cast, and I wanted to let them bring their youthful energy to the play, which they did, and that, I think, made it as enjoyable as it was. And I think that's what Shakespeare wanted to do as well; all this scholarly jargon about eroticism is, to me, all right in a lecture room or a finely researched treatise, but not in a theatre. *A Midsummer Night's Dream* is not the most erotic of Shakespeare's plays, whatever anyone may say. Haven't people read *Hamlet*? *Othello*? Every play of Shakespeare is 'erotic'! From *Romeo and Juliet, The Merchant of Venice,* to *The Tempest*. Eroticism in Shakespeare is a subject that is infinitely more complex than we have time to discuss here."

**Deepak (Qazir) Kejriwal.** Delhi theatre's talented young director joined Yatrik in 1972 and left for Mumbai in 1980. He then charted his acting career to become a well-known character actor in Bollywood films and television serials. He recalls:

When I joined Yatrik, I was doing backstage work initially. In those days, Yatrik was mainly staging English plays. Max Mueller Bhavan had permitted Yatrik to use the terrace at their office in Connaught

Place. Then Joy Michael asked me to do Hindi plays. I directed one play in English and five plays in Hindi. I don't recall much about the English play, but two plays that I directed for Yatrik remain vividly in my mind despite the lapse of more than three decades. These two productions, *Tamasha* and *Beejan-Teejan*, were musicals, which were considered milestone theatrical productions in the history of musical plays staged in the capital. I was impressed with *Kaanch Ghar*, a novel by Ram Kumar Bhramar, which exposes politicians sexually exploiting the traditional performers of the Tamasha theatre form.

Madhuri Bhatia and I went to Maharashtra to study the art form, interact with the artists, and observe their social and economic environment. Madhuri did the choreography and the lead role was played by Sinia (Jain) Dugal, who created magic on the stage.

Another memorable production with Yatrik was *Beejan-Teejan* in the form of a musical. I adapted it from a Rajasthani folk tale by Vijaydan Detha, an eminent reteller of Rajasthani folk tales. The story depicts the deep emotional bonds between two young women who decide to live together, defying the norms of a conventional society. It featured Deepa Sahi, now a prominent personality of Bollywood, Irpinder Puri, and Bhaskar Ghose, among others. I also directed a comedy *Jai Baba Gopinath*, an adaptation from Moliere's *Tartuffe*.

Yatrik encourages its members to write original plays. Avijit wrote two plays in English. Young, talented, and charming Irpinder Puri wrote two full-length plays in Hindi. In *Ek Roshan Awaaz,* she tried to dramatise the life, work, and time of Max Mueller, the German philologist, orientalist, and Indologist. The play had a large cast, with Bhaskar Ghose playing the lead role of Max Mueller.

I loved working with Yatrik. Those were good days. Joy Michael was affectionate and treated me like a son.

**Indu Ramchandani, nee Vachani,** was almost a founder member of Yatrik herself. As she recalls: While I was in Indraprastha College (IP College), Delhi University, I was brought on to the stage by none other than Rati Bartholomew. I was keen on acting, having participated in school plays. She encouraged me and I became a regular actor in all the college plays. In 1962, in my third year, the annual college show was being planned…Kaufman and Hart's well-known play, *The Man Who Came to Dinner*. At IP, boys were not allowed to come and act with us, as used to happen at Miranda House, so girls used to do the male roles. I was selected to play the lead male role of Sheridan Whiteside. Joy Michael was the visiting advisory director to the college for that production, and that was my first experience of the "Yatrik-to-be"…the honour of being directed by both Rati Bartholomew and Joy Michael. Roshan Seth was doing his Master's at St. Stephen's College, and I was really drawn into the "actors" group, so to say.

Roshan and I acted in *A Phoenix Too Frequent*, at a show "by invitation only" staged at the Town Hall, in 1963. But, soon after that, I got married, lost touch, and left Delhi.

While I might have left theatre, it had not left me. When I was back in Delhi in the late 1970s, I met up with Joy again…and in 1981, I was back with Yatrik. But with family commitments, I did not get back to acting for the first few years. Joy said, "Indu, we need you…we need reliable, responsible people to work on production and backstage." And that is how I stayed involved for the first few years… props, makeup, costumes, and even standing in to manage music a couple of times. I started being known as the "reliable right hand". Both Tejeshwar Singh and Bhaskar Bhattacharji had me assisting them in direction. I met Jasbir Malik when he was working with Tejeshwar on *Daily Truth* and I was the production manager and assistant director for that play. We all remember these three great theatre people.

Backstage work is exacting and demands focused attention to detail. In the initial years, I learnt a lot from Joy Michael, Lola

Chatterji, and Vinay Capila and his magical stagecraft. I recall, the set for the first show of Joseph Kesselring's play *Arsenic and Old Lace* was incredibly crafted by Vinay, as it created the ambiance for the setting of the story. The innocent-looking and elegant "window seat" was central to the action; it had a box into which the corpses of the victims were temporarily stored, and into which tumbled the corpse of a "stranger", as Jonathan and Einstein tried to bring it in from the window behind it.

*Arsenic and Old Lace*: It was at the end of the 1980s that Prabha Tonk caught hold of me and said, "It's time you came on stage from backstage!" So I played one of two "crazy" sisters, Martha Brewster, to Jacqui Garewal's Abby Brewster in *Arsenic and Old Lace*. The two sweet, charming, and lovable elderly ladies were focused on "humanitarian work", poisoning old single men with their special brew of elderberry wine laced with arsenic and other deadly ingredients to add "taste". This work of "charity", as they asserted, was to relieve the poor souls of their miserable lonely lives; and once they had been lulled into the hospitality of tasting the delicious wine, the sisters buried them in their cellar. During the first show, Lola did our makeup and had to whiten Jacqui's and my hair. That was such a great experience, working with Sunit Tandon as the psychotic and menacing Jonathan Brewster, the murderous nephew, and Ranjit Mathur playing the German doctor, Einstein. Jasbir Malik, the absent-minded Police Inspector, Rupin Jayal, who believed he was Teddy Roosevelt, and Sridhar Rajan, among the many others, were the first cast. We went on to stage *Arsenic* several times thereafter. Prabha insisted that I would continue as Martha whenever she staged the play, even if other characters were to be changed…which they did, due to their non-availability. Sinia Dugal came in as Abby at some point, and a new Jonathan was played by Ramesh Thakur. There were many new members in the cast with every show, but Dr Einstein and Martha Brewster stayed put through the 26 years…We last staged this play in 2012; Jacqui came back as Abby, and Vinay Capila was our final "victim"…this time our hair was naturally grey. This show was staged just a few months before dear Prabha passed away.

The other productions I have acted in include, most interestingly, *The Man Who Came to Dinner*. This time, I was the secretary to Sherry Whiteside, played by Ramesh Thakur. Other memorable plays in which I have acted include Bertolt Brecht's *Drums in the*

*Arsenic and Old Lace*—Jacqui Garewal, Deepak Mukarji, and Indu Ramchandani

*The Man Who Came to Dinner*—Indu Ramchandani and Sridhar Rajan (left), with Ramesh Thakur (right)

*Night*, directed by Avijit Dutt, and *A Tomb with a View* with Ramesh Thakur, directed by Prabha Tonk and Sunit Tandon. Sunit directed Jacqui Garewal, Rahat Raza, and me, playing the three ladies who are propositioned, in turn, in Neil Simon's *The Last of the Red Hot Lovers*—a hilarious comedy where Deepak Mukarji played the title role. Sunit Tandon's production of *Phaedra* was very special. Acting in this classical verse-tragedy was a new experience for me after a series of comedy roles, and the entire production with the music, sets, and costumes was fascinating. Apart from, once again, enjoying being directed by Sunit, the play is all the more memorable for me as I shared the stage with Prabha Tonk and Jasbir (Bunny) Malik.

During the 40th anniversary celebrations, I thoroughly loved being directed by Joy again in *Gitanjali in Five Times*, the story of a woman in five different stages of her life, with me playing Gitanjali at age 50, Prabha as Gitanjali at 60, and Jacqui at 70. Later, again under Joy's direction, in Poile Sengupta's *Inner Laws*—I was a "terrorised" mother-in-law, with Sonali Sharma playing my "military" daughter-

Indu Ramchandani in *Phaedra*

Deepak Mukarji and Indu Ramchandani as "The Defenceless Creature" in *The Good Doctor*

in-law. This is a hilarious take on five pairs of mothers-in-law and daughters-in-law.

There have been many productions that I was involved with, both on stage and off stage, through all these years, *The Tempest, Principia Scriptoria*, and *Everything Personal* among them. I continued as the deadly sister with Sinia Dugal in *Zehrila Nehla Meetha Dehla*, the Hindi version of *Arsenic and Old Lace*, staged as a private show for a charitable cause. In 2006, working as the production manager for *Mirza Bagh* and travelling with the play was exciting. From 2008 through to 2016, I was first joint treasurer, then treasurer in the Yatrik Executive Committee.

Working with Joy Michael, Prabha Tonk, Tejeshwar Singh, Bhaskar Bhattacharji, and Sunit Tandon, among others, was an incredible experience and made for tremendous learning. Handling backstage work for Bhaskar Ghose and Sabina Jaitly was equally rewarding.

There have been some memorable and amusing incidents as well. I was the prompter for Shakespeare's *The Tempest*, directed by Joy. Only because it was a Shakespeare play, Joy reluctantly agreed to have a prompter available. Ajay Balram, in the middle of a scene, suddenly added this incredible line to the Bard's script: "Me thinks I shall slumber in yonder nook". And he walked across the stage to get the cue from me, sitting crouched behind the curtain. The others stood frozen on stage, wondering what was to transpire next, but sure enough, Ajay turned around dramatically to deliver his next dialogue with great aplomb.

Jasbir Malik, during *Arsenic*, looked at me as we stood on stage for him to deliver his lines, and said, "I know I am here for something important, but for the life of me, I don't know what it is!"

With a straight face, and rather coyly, I said to him, "Would you by any chance be wanting to go down to our cellar?"

"Ah yes, of course! That is exactly why I am here!" said Jasbir most joyously…and the play rolled on. In both cases, the directors, Joy and Prabha, respectively, were not amused.

The freedom that Yatrik gives to work with other groups adds so much to one's growth as an actor. In the earlier years, *Rumours*, a farcical play by Neil Simon, was staged by TAG, which Sunit Tandon directed. One frightening experience, however, occurred when Bhaskar Bhattacharji was directing *The Butler Episode*, also for TAG, and I was the stage and production manager. Jasbir Malik (Bunny) was playing the lead role of the narrator. We were just two days away from show day. As I walked in during rehearsal, I saw Jasbir and screamed, "Guys! Come quick!" While the others thought he was grabbing 40 winks during his offstage stint, I saw that he was unconscious. Some of us rushed him to hospital; he had suffered a major cardiac attack and the doctor said, "If you had come a few minutes late, he might not have made it!" I had sort of lost my voice in the tension, as we had driven at breakneck speed to the hospital, but I managed to call Bhaskar Bhattacharji and say, "Start learning the lines!" Bunny recovered well and was with us for another couple of decades.

My unforgettable association with Mahesh Dattani and acting in his two plays, *Tara* and *Bravely Fought the Queen*, are quite the landmarks for me. A cameo scene with Tejeshwar Singh and Sinia Dugal in *Chai Pani etc.* (1994), a film by Manu Rewal, and a 10-minute role as the dadi in Tanuj Bhramar's debut directorial venture of the film *Dear Dad* (2016) are equally memorable experiences. For me, being part of a play or a show has been meaningful if it has managed to bond everyone in a spirit of "togetherness".

In the early days, because I lived in a large bungalow in South Delhi, we often rehearsed plays in my house, as hiring rehearsal space was always a problem. The living room was completely "dismantled" and the space emptied out for movements. My parents, as long as they were alive (till the late 1990s), and whose home it really was, were sporting. Mother even monitored the snacks "backstage". Till 2004, that house in Mayfair Gardens was the hub for many a late-night rehearsal, and equal focus was directed to the refreshments.

While my professional career as an editor and publisher blossomed with a national award in book production, my hobby with theatre also thrived. It has been a great innings over the past 36 years…And hopefully, one can continue to be part of this Yatrik family for many more.

**Irpinder Puri.** Deepak Kejriwal introduced me to Yatrik. Earlier, I had worked with Sheila Bhatia and acted in *Mitro Marjani* under the direction of B.M. Shah, who had adapted it from Krishna Sobti's novel of the same title. I had also acted in a teleplay written by Dayanand Anant, also directed by B.M. Shah, which explores the life of a young working girl who is forced to remain unmarried to support her father's family. I wrote and directed *Ek Roshan Awaaz* under the Yatrik banner. The play tries to capture a segment of history and therefore the presentation takes the form of a collage of simultaneous events, conflicting attitudes, clashing values, and the confrontation of vested interests, which altogether shaped the sum total of Friedrich Max Mueller's tangible work and which reflected the mental, emotional, and spiritual odyssey of the man.

The second play that I directed for Yatrik was *Balamji Tum Aagey Mein Peechey*. This appeared to have immediacy with the audience. It reflected the social reality of the condition of women in a patriarchal society in which they are condemned to live like second-class citizens. The inferior status of women is celebrated in a number of rituals, mostly performed with slavishness. Karva Chauth is one of these, in which women fast and pray to the moon for granting a long life to their husbands. The story of the deserted woman unfolds in the background of the Karva Chauth pooja. Even when her husband divorces her and remarries, she continues to believe that he will finally come back to her.

The play also reflects on the social structures of Hindu society. The working-class women have liberated themselves from hypocritical and orthodox rituals. There was nothing abstract and stylised, as the message was unambiguously communicated. The value of the production was enhanced, as it featured seasoned actresses—Suchitra Gupta, Amita Udgata, and Neera Sehgal.

I am no longer associated with Yatrik because I live far away from the hub of theatre. I miss Yatrik. It is the only professional theatre group I know of. I am grateful to Joy Michael, who, despite her high status in the world of theatre and in the social field, gave me full freedom to direct and write. Yatrik has cultivated a professional culture in theatre and especially promoted the cause of meaningful and artistic Hindi theatre in Delhi. Under Joy's guidance, Yatrik has developed and honed the skills of many actors, who have made great names for themselves in the world of theatre and film.

Now based in Mumbai, **Kulbhushan Kharbanda** said, "Yatrik was planning to start its Hindi theatre wing. I was working with it as a full-time paid worker, looking after lighting, props, and accounts. Other workers were Barry John, Sudesh Syal, and Marcus Murch. At that time, Yatrik was doing English theatre. So I was not acting. When Hindi plays were staged, I got the opportunity to act. The response of the audience was tremendous. Soon thereafter, I shifted to Mumbai."

Kharbanda's portrayal of characters in Hindi plays evoked critical acclaim. In Sudhir Tandon's translation of Vijay Tendulkar's *Giddh*, directed by Sai Paranjpye and presented by Yatrik at Defence Pavilion, Pragati Maidan, he played the role of a poet who is an

Kulbhushan Kharbanda (standing) in *Awaz ka Raaz*

A scene from *Giddh*

illegitimate son. The performance won him laurels. A critic commented, "Kulbhushan Kharbanda has given a brilliant performance as the sensitive poet. He is the illegitimate son and lives in the garage. He gives the play dramatic force through sheer contrast. His language is different. So is his thinking. His sense of tension and torture festers under his casual airs and everything explodes in an intensely emotional scene with Rama, his brother's wife..."

In Delhi, as an actor on the Hindi stage, he gave several memorable performances in productions by Abhiyan. Although a successful character actor in Bollywood, he continues to work on stage. In recent years, he worked for Padatik Theatre, Calcutta, playing the role of an aged professor, revealing his tangled personal life. The play was seen in Delhi, Calcutta, and Bhopal. "I remember my days with Yatrik with warm feelings. I joined it when I was a student of Kirori Mal College, University of Delhi."

**Madhuri Bhatia** is a well-known actor in the film industry, Mumbai. She is an actor both in English and Hindi, an accomplished Indian classical dancer in the Mayurbhanj Chhaau dance of Odisha, and a great singer of jazz and folk rock, including Indian and Western musical theatre material. She graduated in the Performing Arts and acquired a diploma in Hatha Yoga and Pranayama from Shriram Bharatiya Kala Kendra, New Delhi.

Madhuri joined Yatrik in 1975. She continued to work with Yatrik, playing several roles in Hindi and English plays till 1981. Later, she was a resident of Canada from 1987 till 2002 and was a member of ACTRA and EQUITY. After relocating to Mumbai in 2002, her film and TV career took off.

She has toured independently and also under the auspices of The Indian Council of Cultural Relations through India, South East Asia, Australia, England, and Europe as an actor, singer, dancer, choreographer, and costume designer. She is a member of CINTAA and AVA.

Madhuri conducts workshops in improvisation, scene and character study, movement and voice. She also does voice-overs on a regular basis, with Disney and E-learning, for a variety of narrations, both in Hindi and English. Her widely acclaimed talents and successes include: co-writer, choreographer, dancer, singer, and actor for *Peacocks and Bandaids* for Carousel Players.

As a radio artist, she has been heard in assorted plays, short stories, poems, and several narrations for CBC Radio. Madhuri was the principal actor and singer in Alyque Padamsee's *Unspoke Dialogue*. In the multilingual (English, Hindi, and Urdu) stage show, *Chugaad Dhaam* by Chandan Roy Sanyal, Madhuri played the role of Lady Begbick.

Avijit Dutt refers to Madhuri as actor, jazz singer, voice-over artist, yoga practitioner, danseuse, choreographer, and most importantly, an unassuming and interesting personality. Madhuri Bhatia is all this and much more. Her artistically designed and meticulously maintained abode in Andheri, Mumbai, reflects her personality.

**Reminiscences:** Joy Michael introduced me to Yatrik, while I was teaching dance at St. Thomas School, during her tenure as principal. I enjoyed participating in Yatrik productions because it provided a platform for professional and amateur artists from varied backgrounds to work together and explore the options of communication for the purposes of elucidations and entertainment via dramatic idiom.

Joy Michael's *Stree*, the incredible play that she conceived of and directed, was a joy to choreograph. The play was based on

Madhuri Bhatia with Ramesh Thakur in *Bedroom Farce*

A scene from *The Good Woman of Szechuan*

interviews with Aruna Asaf Ali and Kamaladevi Chattopadhyay. This presentation by St. Thomas was a theatrical masterpiece.

In those early years with Yatrik, I travelled to Maharashtra with Deepak Kejriwal to study the Tamasha theatre form, and went on to choreograph the dance-drama, *Tamasha*.

Joy Michael has been my teacher, adviser, critic, supporter, mentor, friend, and ultimate guru in the most complete sense of the term.

**Memorabilia**

Among the films and TV shows in which Madhuri has acted: *Pardes*, *Kites*, *My Bollywood Bride*, *Masala*, *Dreams of the Night Cleaners* and *The Kalani of Shiva*.

TV shows: Vasundhara of *Kahin to Hogaa,* and Devika of *Kuch Is Tarah*, *Harry Case*, *Relic Hunter Traders*, *Highlander*, *The City*, *My Father's Shadow*, *Harry's Case*, *ENG*, *Spoken Art*, *Missing Treasures*, *La Femme Nikita*, *Relic Hunter*.

With Yatrik, Madhuri played key roles as dancer, choreographer and/or actor in several productions: *Tamasha*, *The Curve*, *Albertine In Five Times*, *The Chute*, *Antigone*, *Bedroom Farce*, *The Sound of Music*, *The Good Woman of Szechuan*, *The Mass of St. Francis.*

Other than Yatrik, memorable are the three productions in English with Troy Ribeiro—*Red Hot Mamas*, *Apples and Walnuts*, and *Maureen, He and Me.*

**M.K. Raina** had just graduated from NSD and met Joy Michael, who recognised the creative talent in the young man and gave him the challenging assignment of directing Maxim Gorky's *Lower Depths* in Hindi.

While talking about Yatrik, Raina's face brightens up and there is a thrill in his voice as he recalls: During those days I was reading a great deal of Russian literature, especially plays by Anton Chekhov and Maxim Gorky. I was delighted when Joy gave me an assignment to direct *Lower Depths*. The production process started with discussing the play at a theatre workshop held in Connaught Place. A large number of young people, including Suresh Kulkarni, Kamini Gupta, Mona Chawla, Arun Virmani, and Ramesh Manchanda participated in the workshop that V. Ramamurthy, Ranbir, and I conducted. It was a wonderful workshop, exuding enthusiasm and youthful energy. Joy was always there to guide the young people.

The production of *Lower Depths* was uniquely remarkable for its ingenuity. The set was designed out of the heaps of the scraps that lay around near the Defence Pavilion, the venue of the play.

It was watched by the discerning audiences of the capital. Among them was P.L. Deshpande, the eminent Marathi playwright. He was overwhelmed to see the production and said to me, "Are you able to make ends meet as a theatre practitioner? In any case, if you have any problem, contact me." We became close friends, exchanging our ideas about arts and culture.

Raina is known for his interpretation of classics. Here is the world of the dregs of society who have lost everything they had, including their dignity; they live in appalling conditions in a dingy and dilapidated inn. They have no future. In the words of Gorky, "The main question I wanted to ask in my play was: what is better, compassion or the crude truth? What do you have more need of? Does compassion serve any end if a man begins to resort to lies, like Luka? This is not a subjective matter: it is a question of philosophical import." There is another character Satin, a romantic dreamer who talks of lofty ideas about man. But all the characters have no will to protest.

Later, I directed the *Lower Depths* for the students of NSD. But I experienced a great creativity while working with Yatrik.

A scene from *Ek Chaadar Maili Si*

Joy Michael was producing *The Shoemaker's Prodigious Wife* by Federico Lorca and I attended another workshop for that. I was asked to direct *The Mother* by Bertolt Brecht in a Hindi translation. The workshop accommodated a large number of actors. It was a great creative experience. In the crowd scenes, I cast 75 performers. The audience had not yet seen anything quite like that on the Delhi stage. Yatrik did it for the first time. From that day, I became famous for composing crowd scenes. The Defence Pavilion, the venue for Yatrik's productions, was the hub for Delhi's theatre practitioners. It was known as "Theatre Wala Ghar". I saw several Yatrik productions there. I still remember *Ek Chaadar Maili Si* by Rajinder Singh Bedi, directed by Rajinder Nath, with Sushma Seth in the lead role.

Yatrik has contributed immensely to the growth of artistic and socially relevant Hindi theatre in the capital. Most of those who participated in Yatrik's theatre workshops became famous in Hindi theatre and some went on to join Bollywood. The workshops were a great source of inspiration and a place for serious training in various aspects of theatrical art.

Young, talented, and passionately committed to theatre, **Mohan Maharishi,** who had just completed his graduation from the National School of Drama with flying colours, was invited by Yatrik in 1967–68 to direct Badal Sircar's *Ebong Indrajit* in a Hindi version. It was translated into Hindi by Bharat Bhushan Agarwal, a great name in the world of Hindi literature and culture, as *Evam Indrajit*.

Reminiscing about those exciting days, Mohan Maharishi said, "I had the privilege to direct this great dramatic work for the first time in the country. I was young and worked with passion. I would go on foot from Bengali Market to Pragati Maidan, the venue of rehearsal and staging, because those were the days of hardship for theatre artists. But it did not dampen our spirit and we were determined to do nothing but theatre. I had a dedicated team of young artists, including Ram Gopal Bajaj, Om Shivpuri, Sudha Shivpuri, Anjala Maharishi, Sudesh Syal, Bandev Sinha, Dinesh Thakur, Ram Murti, and V.M. Badola. The production turned out to be historical. Eminent critic Charles Fabri gave a rave review. Then I went to the German Democratic Republic and joined the Berliner Ensemble and received a letter from Alkazi, profusely praising my production of *Evam Indrajit*."

The play broke new ground in the realm of contemporary play writing through the confrontation of two characters—the playwright and Indrajit—the alienated world of the middle class, its hypocrisy, and its vision of a world which considers human existence as futile. It also deals with the dilemma of the playwright in search of form, context, and language and was considered highly innovative. No wonder this remains one of the most widely translated Bengali plays, having been translated into a large number of Indian languages.

**Poile Sengupta** is an award-winning playwright, poet, novelist, and acclaimed author of children's books. She wrote her full-length play *Mangalam* in 1993, and it was staged the next year. Her other plays include *Inner Laws* (1994), *A Pretty Business* (1995), *Keats was a Tuber* (1996), *Collages* (1998), *Alipha*, *Thus Spake Shoorpanakha* and *So Said Shakuni* (2001), and *Samara's Song* (2007).

*Mangalam* won a special award at The Hindu-Madras Players play scripts competition in 1993. *Keats was a Tuber* was shortlisted and received a special mention in the 1996 British Council International New Playwriting Competition. *Samara's Song* was one of three plays in the final shortlist of The Metroplus Playscripts Competition, 2008. Six of her plays were published in 2010 in a book titled *Women Centre Stage*. Her first novel for adults *Inga* was published in October 2014 and received critical acclaim. The DNA Mumbai called it Booker-worthy.

Poile Sengupta is also a well-known writer for children. She received a Senior Fellowship of the Department of Culture, Government of India in 1999–2000 for Literature to write plays for children. Puffin published a set of seven one-act plays for children—*Good Heavens!* Poile has also written a musical for children, *Yavamajakka!*, which has been performed to much acclaim in Bangalore and Delhi. Her stories have been included in important anthologies such as *The Puffin Treasury of Modern Indian Stories* and others. Poile Sengupta has been on the governing body of the National School of Drama.

**Association with Yatrik:** Poile Sengupta says: it was Bhaskar *da* (Bhaskar Ghose) who wanted to stage *Mangalam*, and brought me into the Yatrik fold. He and Joy have been so supportive of my work and I am deeply grateful to them. While my husband Abhijit (who retired as Secretary Ministry of Culture) and I were in Delhi, we held a series of readings of my plays at the IIC Annexe and were excited to work with Yatrik. The group has performed several of my plays, including *Mangalam, Inner Laws, Keats was a Tuber*, *Alipha*, and *Thus Spake Shoorpanakha*.

**Pradeep Kapoor.** In 1984 when I was on leave from the Army, I heard of the shooting of the film *Gandhi* and that the casting director Joy Michael was looking for an actor to play the ADC to Lord Mountbatten. I wanted to do that role, although I had no acting experience. My hesitation in coming forward to enquire about the role resulted in my missing that opportunity. In 1987, I was again on leave in New Delhi and I sought out the same Joy Michael and discovered Yatrik. This time, I was determined to learn how to act. Yatrik was conducting a workshop and I joined with great enthusiasm. Joy and Avijit were the gurus. Three plays followed the workshop—*Towards Zero*, *A Husband for Breakfast*, and *Relatively Yours*.

*Relatively Yours* was performed at the Shri Ram Centre basement theatre. The audience was seated on cushions on the floor, at the same level as the stage. One night, I had my children come in to watch the performance. They were seated up front. In one scene, a woman had to strike me on the head to murder me. That night, as usual, I was struck and I collapsed on the floor, playing dead. There was pin-drop silence in the auditorium. Just then, I heard a whisper from the audience, "Dad, Dad, are you okay?"

I was nervous, but I had become an actor. Soon, I went on to take the responsibility of stage manager for *Lettice and Lovage*, directed by Prabha Tonk. This was followed by a role in *The Man Who Came to*

*Six Degrees of Separation*—Pradeep Kapoor, Sabina Jaitly, and Bhaveen Gosain

*Dinner*. I watched in awe as Kristine Michael, a young actress, played a slinky, svelte, and glamorous person to perfection on stage.

In 1989–90, Joy Michael directed a musical, *South Pacific*. I was a naval officer with the background of World War II. I watched with fascination the intricate weaving together of music, costumes, and character roles to produce something that was the talk of the town. This was an outstanding production.

Yatrik staged *The Good Doctor*, written by Neil Simon, at the Taj Hotel coffee shop in 1992. These were several one-act pieces put together one after the other in rapid succession. I played a nervous bank manager to Indu Ramchandani's portrayal of the "Defenceless Creature". I had become far more confident and could put in nuances into the acting. We had quite a hilarious time together. All the short plays were incredibly amusing. We loved doing them just as much as the audience enjoyed watching them. We rehearsed through the night, as we could not get the coffee shop during the day.

In 1994, I left the Army and had more time for the stage. Joy directed *Six Degrees of Separation*, which was a great hit. The Lalit Kala Akademi declared it the best play of the year. It was written about and acclaimed by the press.

After the terrible 1993 riots in Mumbai, Avijit Dutt decided to write and direct *Bombay Bosnia*. Initially, I was assigned the character role of a Malayali and I began diction training to speak like one. However, Avijit felt the risk was too great and changed my role to a different one. I was in awe of Swaroopa Ghosh, who could burst into tears at the desired moment on stage. How could she bring such strong emotions to the fore at precisely the right moment? She went on to act in *Piku*, the Bollywood movie, with Amitabh Bachchan.

*Verdict* was a thriller. The play began with boring sequences and established the characters. However, as the story evolved, the audience was gripped and soon we closed in on the climax. As the mystery was about to be unfurled, minutes away from the end, a man in the audience asked loudly, "Is there a doctor in the house? This man has collapsed." We, the actors on stage, froze in shock. The ushers rushed in and helped the person out of the hall. The play resumed, but the spell was broken, the story lost, and the climax collapsed. It was a good play, but this event happened on that one night.

I played one of the brothers in Prakash Bhatia's Hindi production of *The Brothers Karamazov* in 1998. It was quite an experience. Outstanding actors delivered super performances. The play was repeated several times over the years. In 2000, Poile Sengupta wrote *Mangalam*, a story in two parts. The first was located in traditional Tamil Nadu with typical family conflicts. In the second part, the same characters were NRIs set in modern days with similar conflicts. Bhaskar Ghose directed this amazing play, performed with both gusto and enthusiasm. This play also was repeated over the years. In 2003, a sensitive play *Court Martial*, based on the caste system with a background from the Army, was staged. Other groups had staged this play several times earlier. The controversy was that life in the Army was not depicted the way it was presented by the playwright. I played the key character of the Colonel and was criticised severely by friends. The director Prakash Bhatia and co-actors, however, differed.

Yatrik is not merely a theatre group; it is a nursery where actors grow, evolve, and develop. Many actors taking off from the Yatrik launch pad have confidently landed either on a catwalk or on the film screen. The late Jasbir Malik was a great actor. I loved acting with him. The interaction was stimulating and I learnt much from him while watching him evolve a particular character. I followed him to act with other theatre groups. The most memorable roles were four Shakespeare productions. But the one I liked best was a play reading I did with him for Yatrik—*A Walk in the Woods*, in which I read for an American diplomat and Jasbir was a Russian. The setting was in Geneva and the plot showed how diplomats manoeuvred to get results during the Cold War. Jasbir was scintillating. It was a pleasure to watch him develop the character.

My involvement with theatre was and is concurrent with my work with blind people. A few friends and I started an NGO Volunteers for the Blind Foundation several years ago. While this work takes up a huge amount of my time, I have remained committed to theatre and Yatrik over the years. I even roped in Prakash Bhatia once to help train a few blind youths in producing a play enacted by blind children.

With the completion of 40 years of Yatrik, Joy slowly eased herself out of too much responsibility and chose to transfer the leadership of Yatrik to younger hands. The pace set by Joy is hard to emulate, but young people have been given a legacy. They are a capable lot and some are extremely talented. I am confident that Yatrik will continue to be a name to reckon with.

**Prakash Bhatia.** A bird can only fly with two wings, and Yatrik's flight was perfected with the focus on the "Hindi wing". Prakash Bhatia gave it a great boost. He was associated with amateur Hindi theatre in the capital and had a keen desire to join Yatrik. But the eminence of this group was so great, in his mind, that he felt that he could not dare to approach it. His initiation came through a theatre workshop. Soon thereafter, Prakash formally joined Yatrik as its member in 1986. He was nominated to be Yatrik's director for a tenure of two years (2008–10) and has been a member of its executive committee over the years.

Prakash is deeply grateful to Joy Michael for her encouragement, support, and guidance. It is because of her advice that Prakash joined Ebrahim Alkazi's "living theatre" from 1992–94 to do a diploma. Close to Hindi theatre in the capital and respected by Hindi theatre practitioners for his experience and cooperative spirit, he staged significant plays for Yatrik and attracted new theatre audiences.

One of Prakash's memorable productions was Mannu Bhandari's *Mahabhoj* in 1988, which was produced in the course of a workshop. It was a daring attempt on his part to stage such a play with a large canvas and with a large number of characters drawn from various classes. His cast consisted of 40 performers who had already gone through a one-month theatre workshop. Prakash's ingenious approach and his judicious use of limited space were indeed commendable. Joy then encouraged Prakash to do a Hindi translation of Dostoyevsky's *The Brothers Karamazov* in the basement theatre of India Habitat Centre. The passionate philosophical novel is set in 19th-century Russia. It enters deeply into ethical debates of God, free will, and morality. Yet again, with unique originality and innovation, Prakash made a great success of this production.

With Prakash looking after the "Hindi wing", Yatrik has regularly staged Hindi plays. In the 1980s, Shankar Shesh's plays, known for their new and bold ideas, fascinated various directors, and they sought to stage his works. The playwright also tried to examine the contemporary social malaise and class conflicts against the backdrop of mythology, thus illustrating that class conflict has always been prevalent. His play *Ek Aur Dronacharya* is a concrete example of his hypothesis. Prakash directed this play with remarkable finesse, indicating the opportunism prevailing in our existing system. He also staged Shankar Shesh's popular play *Phandi,* which deals with the humanitarian issue of mercy killing.

**Memorabilia**

*Of Mice and Men* (1987); *Ek Aur Dronacharya* (1987); *Mahabhoj* (1988); *Raktabeej* (1989); *Phandi* (1990); *Gourment Babu* (1991 for Sahitya Kala Parishad in their festival); *Rishtey Hi Rishtey* (1994 Hindi adaptation of *The Matchmaker*); *Rashomon* (1997); *The Brothers Karamazov* (1998); *Ek Sapney ki Maut* (1999 Hindi adaptation of *Death of a Salesman*); *Virasat* (2000); *Jaat hi Puchho Sadhu Ki* (2003); *Ballabhpur ki Roop Katha* (2007); *Devdas* (2008); *Meena Bazaar* (2010); *Jis Lahore Nahi Dekhya O Jamiya Hi Nahin* (2016).

**Reminiscences:** In 1986, I read an advertisement in *The Statesman* about a summer theatre workshop to be conducted by Yatrik. I had no professional training in theatre, but had practical experience of acting and directing and was associated with many groups. I went to St. Thomas School and met Meriel Michael, Joy's elder daughter. I was welcomed and I paid 50 rupees as an admission fee. On the first day, as Joy shook my hand, it communicated warmth and affection. I then met Avijit Dutt and Ajay Balram. The participants were introduced to the basic elements of play production—improvisation, movements, stage exercises, and text reading. The production-oriented workshop lasted 21 days, and four short plays were produced and staged in the small auditorium of the school. I directed one play and Joy Michael and Avijit Dutt directed the others. There were 50 participants. When the programme culminated with the stage presentation of improvised productions, we were given a "cast party"—something I had never heard of, let alone participated in.

This was a great experience for me; it was both exciting and inspiring. A whole new world of theatrical art was opening up before me. I was overwhelmed with the treatment Joy gave to the participants. Joy said to me, "Come and do a play for us." I said "yes". It was a momentous event and a great honour. A person of the stature of Joy invited an amateur like me to direct a play for Yatrik! Joy and Avijit gave me several scripts. Finally, a Hindi adaptation of Steinbeck's *Of Mice and Men* was selected, which was staged at AIFACS in 1987.

I did the Hindi adaptation. In fact, at that time, Yatrik had no actors to play in a Hindi production. We selected them from Yatrik's theatre workshop and some seasoned actors from the Hindi stage.

Perhaps, the greatest challenge was *Mahabhoj*. I was asked to stage it in the basement of the Shri Ram Centre (SRC). This proposal seemed to be difficult, especially when *Mahabhoj* had already been staged by the Repertory Company of the National School of Drama under the direction of Amal Allana, with a star cast of Manohar Singh, Uttara Baokar, Rajhuvir Yadav, and Sulekha Sikri, set to the concept of environmental theatre, with the stage set designed by Nissar Allana. When I went to Mannu Bhandari to seek her permission to stage *Mahabhoj*, she was sceptical about the success of the production with a huge cast in the Shri Ram basement theatre (staging of plays at the basement is not permitted now). I assured her that we would not let her down and she agreed.

In fact, ever since Amal's production of *Mahabhoj*, theatre productions all over India were fascinated with this Hindi play that mirrors the stark dichotomy of contemporary Indian socio-economic and political reality. Several directors staged *Mahabhoj* in their own style. Balwant Thakur brought his production from

Jammu and Kashmir, using his usual folk form, and staged it at Kamani Auditorium, Delhi. Devendra Raj Ankur presented it in his "Kahani ka Rangmanch" style at the SRC basement. In Delhi, the play continues to be staged by various amateur groups with varying success, but the content is so strong that, notwithstanding the flaws of the productions, it captures the attention of the audience.

The next challenge was *The Brothers Karamazov*. It was difficult to design a set in the basement for this complex story. Joy insisted that I should work hard and do it. While visualising the set, suddenly it occurred to me that by reversing the layout and taking the acting space to the entrance to the theatre, which had pillars, an appropriate ambiance could be created. The production was a great success.

Finally, I must express my appreciation for Avijit Dutt, who is an excellent actor and director of the English stage, and who is equally adept in acting in and directing Hindi plays. He has always inspired and guided me in my work with Yatrik. It is a great experience to work with him.

*Mahabhoj*, written by Mannu Bhandari, is an immensely powerful play. For Yatrik's production, Avijit Dutt played the pivotal role of Da Sahib, a cruel manipulator and politician in power. With his impressive stage presence and his excellent elocution to deliver dialogue to create a dramatic effect, he gave a performance that captivated the audience, disturbing them deeply. The state apparatus metamorphosed into an instrument of violence to suppress justice and freedom. Prakash Bhatia as Dutta Babu, a publisher with skin-deep conviction and unashamed opportunism, gave a brilliant performance.

Mannu Bhandari was sitting in the audience and she said to Prakash, "Congratulations! I am fully satisfied with the production. It should be staged the way you staged it." Veteran theatre critic Nemichandra Jain critically acclaimed Yatrik's *Mahabhoj*.

*Ballabhpur Ki Roop Katha* was another admirable production by Prakash—the Hindi version of Badal Sircar's original play *Ballabhpurer Roopkatha*. The production presented polished performances and excellent stage management, which "delivered" the ghost in the nick of time. Neeraj Yadav, who played the lead role of Bhupati, the blue-blooded pauper, attempting to sell his ancestral home to pay off his debts and raise funds for setting up a dental clinic in Calcutta, was the pick of the cast with a confident and well-modulated performance, which included enacting his lookalike ghost.

Pankaj Monga, as Sanjeev, plays Bhupati's friend, who is press-ganged to double up as his estate manager. Basab Bhattacharya as Haldar, a soap manufacturer, is obsessed with owning a truly vintage mansion. Ballabhpur is the estate that is up for sale. Bhupati persuades his creditors to open a new line of credit so that he can impress Haldar, his wife Chanda, and daughter Swapna. Haldar falls for the house, which Bhupati quite fancifully traces back to 1560, and books it with an advance of 1 lakh rupees.

Bhupati, fearing the nightly appearance of the ghost of Raghupati, his Sanskrit sloka-reciting ancestor, causes Haldar to cancel the deal, remorseful as he is at having exaggerated the age of the house. The ghost, however, falls in love with Swapna. Chaudhary, Haldar's arch competitor in business and for the house, appears and all hell breaks loose. Everything depends on the appearance of the ghost, who does not disappoint. It goes better with a pinch of salt, which was, after all, Badal Sircar's intention!

A review in *The Statesman* dated 17 August 2001 said:

...There was much that was admirable in the production. First, the sets. Vintage furniture recreated the atmosphere of an old *haveli* and the ghost sported an *achkan* and *pagri* worthy of a Moghul nobleman.

The IHC basement theatre has a very small stage and entries and exits pose problems. Prakash Bhatia and Joy Michael, who produced the play, did well to tackle these issues. They managed to give big stage trappings to the play.

The Yatrik professionalism: Productions bearing the banner of the oldest theatre company in Delhi have a minimum standard of excellence.

*Jis Lahore Nahi Dekhya O Jamiya Hi Nahin* is among the very few Hindi plays, in recent times, which have evoked tremendous interest both in India and abroad. It has been staged in Punjabi, Sindhi, Gujarati, Marathi, Kannada, and English. Besides several venues in Pakistan and India, it has been staged in Washington DC. Some portions of the play have been translated into Hungarian.

Prof. Syed Asghar Wajahat, the eminent playwright, has been honoured with the Sangeet Natak Akademi Award and Shalaka Samman from Delhi.

The tragic tale is set in Lahore in the immediate aftermath of the Partition of India, and the audience is irresistibly drawn into the assertion of humanity in the time of bloodshed. Breaking away from stereotyped themes about the Partition, this play explores the deep recesses of the human heart, steeped as it is in universal brotherhood. Here, the conflict is between the humanistic message of Islam and religious fanaticism. On a broader level, the play highlights the understanding and veneration for different cultures. It is infused with compassion and magnanimity that touch the right chord.

The city is flooded with uprooted, tormented, and devastated refugees. The houses, deserted by their former owners, who had to leave in a desperate hurry, are now being allotted to displaced persons after they have spent a horrible time in refugee camps. One such family that was forced to leave its beloved Lucknow and immigrate to Lahore is allotted a haveli, once owned by a famous Hindu jeweller, Ratan. Mirza, his begum, his son Javed, and his adolescent daughter Tanno excitedly enter the huge haveli and are in for a shock. A haggard old woman appears from inside and accuses the family of trespassing, claiming to be the owner of the haveli. The Mirzas are determined to get rid of the old woman, but she refuses to leave.

The enemies of humanity are on a rampage, spreading the virus of communalism. Pehalwan, a self-styled defender of Islam, represents such a force. As he gets the news of the old Hindu woman inside the haveli, he is furious and demands money from Mirza to eliminate her. Woven into the network of complex characters are poet Nasir Kazmi, who has come from Ambala, and the Maulvi, who represents the human face of Islam. Composing beautiful poems on the theme

The Maulvi discusses matters with the other men

The old woman enjoying a carefree moment with Begum Mirza and others

of human love with a touch of nostalgia and sadness, the poet symbolises the wounded soul of humanity condemned to leave homes, property, and dear friends; all that they are carrying with them are memories of the past. As he wanders all night in the city, a tea stall is his favourite meeting place with common people. Here, he confronts Pehalwan.

With time, the animosity between the old Hindu mother of Ratan and the Mirza family grows into a strong "family" bond. The old woman continues with her routine tasks—she goes to River Ravi early in the morning to take a holy bath and visits neighbours, helping them and recommending home remedies for minor ailments. Begum Mirza, Tanno, and the neighbouring women spend time in the company of the old woman. While Begum Mirza says there is no place like Lucknow, the old woman asserts that anyone who has not seen Lahore is not born yet. The pleasant chatter of women enlivens the scene.

But Pehalwan has not reconciled to the fact that a Hindu is living in Pakistan. He wants to eliminate her. He seeks the help of the Maulvi, who instead persuades him to follow the teachings of Islam that exhort respect for women, especially the elderly and widows. One day, the old woman dies. The Maulvi is called. In the ultimate gesture of humanity, he suggests that her last rites be performed according to the Hindu religion. The good people of Lahore and Mirza, now her surrogate son, light the funeral pyre on the banks of River Ravi. The fanatic Pehalwan kills the Maulvi because of his compassion for the old Hindu woman and his humanitarian vision.

Yatrik's presentation played to full houses. Director Prakash Bhatia created a production remarkable for its intensity, restraint, and sensitivity. Namrata Gupta's debut as the old woman was impressive. All the actors gave commendable performances. However, Shri Chand Makhija as the Maulvi was brilliant. His slow delivery, punctuated with brief pauses, and calm demeanour revealed his inner conviction. Animesh Singhal as Pehalwan was most convincing in his fanatical hatred and violence.

**R.K. Dhingra** received Sangeet Natak Akademi's prestigious award for his contribution to enriching contemporary Indian theatre as "lighting director". He has fond memories of his long association with Yatrik from its inception: during those days, the lighting system in Delhi was primitive. Everything depended on our ingenuity. We didn't even have smoke machines. We would use incense sticks (agarbatti, *dhoop*) and at times we would use a *lohan*—the container emitting smoke from some burning charcoals and herbs, usually carried by a wandering fakir or mendicant.

I recall Meena Williams of NSD working with Yatrik in those days. She was a fine actress. Sanskar Chand was functioning as a production manager. He worked diligently, with an eye for detail. Initially, the shows were staged at the Defence Pavilion, Pragati Maidan. Temporary lights used to be fixed at a considerable height. Major Saheb (Hugh Michael) would hold a ladder to enable me to climb up. There was another problem. Pigeons used to fly frenetically in all different directions. Major Saheb used to bring his gun to scare them away. The cooperation that modest Major Saheb extended was most touching and memorable.

A scene from *Andhera Hone Do* with the light effect through the blinds

Initially, the venue for Yatrik's productions was the Mahadev Road Auditorium, New Delhi. *Azar Ka Khwab*, an adaptation of Bernard Shaw's *Pygmalion*, was staged there. The set was basically built for film screening. There was a small hole through which I had to watch the action in progress on the stage and use the correct light effect. Only by watching through this hole I would fade out the light. I had only

12 slider dimmers, which I was operating single-handedly, using a three-foot wooden rod for fade-out for the lighting of the entire show. Alkazi Saheb (Ebrahim Alkazi) watched me from behind to see how I was functioning. He smiled and left. Similarly, I had to use a dim light in *Andhera Hone Do* in a scene where Salima Raza stabs a character. There is a fade-out, she opens a refrigerator and, in its flickering light, she does the whole act. Even with limited means, Yatrik's productions were remarkable for creating excellent light effects. Later, the British Council donated lighting equipment to Yatrik.

It was a most exciting experience to take Yatrik's productions to Gaiety Theatre on the Mall Road in Shimla. We staged several shows there. Doing plays in Mussoorie had its own charm. During those days, Yatrik, under the direction of Joy Michael, was on the top of Delhi's theatre world. Leading theatre personalities of the country and students of NSD, as they graduated, vied with one another to be associated with Yatrik's production. There was great camaraderie and cooperation in the "family" of artistes, directors, technicians, and stage hands. The Yatrik actresses, Joy Michael, Kusum Haidar, Sushma Seth, and Salima Raza were known for their grace, charm, intelligence, and sensitivity. They portrayed memorable characters in the productions of Yatrik.

Yatrik's productions were known for elaborate sets. The group had built up its own enlightened audience. Tickets and brochures were sold at the box office. As a professional lighting director, I have been in the world of theatre for more than five decades and witnessed great actresses on stage. But I still remember vividly Joy Michael as Hedda Gabler in Henrik Ibsen's play of the same title. Her Gabler was an incarnation of a terribly vindictive and malicious woman. Similarly, I continue to remember Salima Raza's performance as Hajjo in *Azar Ka Khwab.*

**Ramesh Thakur.** Looks like I am lucky to have celebrated 50 years of two theatre groups—Yatrik and Theatre Arts Workshop (TAW), Lucknow. My initiation into Yatrik came from TAW. My mentor Shri Raj Bisaria, founder director of TAW, had mentioned Yatrik to me. I began work with Yatrik sometime in 1976 or 1977 in one of the English translations of German impressionist plays by Tankred Dorst, directed by Sabina Mehta (Jaitly), and staged at Max Mueller Bhavan. In one of them, I played an alcoholic priest.

Yatrik is perhaps the only group where I have been part of almost 25 productions; my contribution has been mostly as an actor. I did some workshops and dramatised readings, besides two televised dramas—*All My Sons* and *The Good Doctor*. I was an executive committee member in the later years. Yatrik has certainly played a major role in my personality development over the years and has motivated my interest in theatre into becoming a passion.

*The Good Doctor*—Sunit Tandon and Ramesh Thakur

*The Man Who Came to Dinner*—Ramesh Thakur with Kristine Michael

I have had the opportunity to play the lead in some memorable productions. To mention a few—*The Devil's Advocate*, *The Road to Mecca*, *Don't Dress for Dinner*, *Musseebat Mara Murari*, and *The Man Who Came to Dinner*. Bhaskar Ghose's *Everything Personal* was a unique and interesting play.

I can also affectionately recall some productions for the unique characters I portrayed in them—a patient and an advertising man in *Cactus Flower*, *The Good Doctor* (in the three short plays that are part of the collection of Neil Simon's plays in *The Good Doctor—The Sneeze, The Drowning Man*, and *Surgery*), *Bedroom Farce*, *Zehrila Nehla Meetha Dehla* (a Hindi translation of *Arsenic and Old Lace*, as a drunk quack opposite Indu Ramchandani and Sinia Dugal playing the crazy sisters), a sozzled English professor in *Keats was a Tuber*, and the psychotic nephew in the repeat show of *Arsenic and Old Lace*.

*The Road to Mecca* and *Arsenic and Old Lace* were challenging, as I was given only 10 days of rehearsal in both. The former was wordy

*Museebat Mara Murari*—Ramesh Thakur

Ramesh Thakur, Sinia Dugal, and Sunit Tandon in *Everything Personal*

with minimal action, the latter a menacing murderer with too much movement. Happily, Yatrik was also the platform where I got the precious opportunity to act with my daughter Nyanu in *Bamboo Flower* and *South Pacific* (the musical). In *South Pacific*, not only did I sing for the very first time on stage ("Bali High"), but also there I was in a coconut-grass skirt and bikini top with red lipstick. Too "saxzy" for words!

Theatre is a platform for friendships and Yatrik has given me many good friends as it has given to the world of theatre and film some wonderful actors and directors. Some amusing incidents come to mind when I recall doing a cameo in *Tamasha* in Hindi directed by Deepak Kejriwal (Qazir). I was playing a servant boy to the leading *Tamasha* lady. After one of the shows, a bunch of NSD students met me to tell me that they were told to come especially and watch me. Some said they were coming again the next day to watch me. After the cast party of *Tamasha*, I met two English guests of Joy. "We didn't understand the language but we understood and liked you as an actor; especially your body language and stage presence, and the mime you brought in-between your scenes." Much later, Deepak Qadir hugged me and said, "What a show! What a performance! You are a fine actor!" A few years later, I was hurriedly walking into Shri Ram Centre for rehearsals when one gentleman stopped me and said, "Sir, I saw you in *Tamasha*. You reminded me of the traditional 'Tamasha' in Maharashtra. Right now, NSD is doing a play *Sainya Bhaye Kotwal*; that play and its central character is meant for you; you should do it. You were good; I had asked many students to come and watch you." When I asked him who he was, his response was, "I am Kelkar. I teach acting in NSD." Again, years later, I was sipping Irish coffee at Prithvi Theatre, Mumbai. Suddenly, a couple of guys called out to me, "Hey! *Tamasha*! Weren't you in *Tamasha*? We are fans of yours." Vijay Kashyap and K.K. Raina (former NSD people) shook my hand and hugged me. And I thought it was just a cameo!

Another strange fact that has baffled me always, and we have joked about often—pairing as a couple with Indu (Ramchandani-Vachani). Indu and I have played a husband–wife team in many plays—*Bamboo Flower*, *Drums in the Night*, *Rumours*, *The Good Doctor* (in *The Sneeze* for both the Hotel Palace, New Delhi, supper theatre show and the SRC basement show).

Half an hour before we went on stage for *The Elephant Man*, we were all backstage, either getting dressed, having make-up done, or reading, and in came our dear friend Dhruv Saikia, completely sozzled. He was totally drunk. While he was obviously in great "spirits", literally and metaphorically, the rest of us were panicking. The majority of the cast wanted to cancel the show. In fact, Joy Michael, the director, was the only one who felt he would pull it off. She spent quite a while with him with mugs and mugs of black coffee, continuously talking with him, massaging his head, splashing his face with cold water intermittently. Then others took turns in this multi-pronged therapy. We were running against time. The show must go on, Joy said with conviction, and so, we mustered up the courage and got on the stage. Keith Shepherd and I were on stage and Dhruv walked in with his opening line, "Hello, Mr Cargom…" and then to our horror, threw up on Keith and me. While we were busy wiping our faces with our handkerchiefs, Dhruv looked at us blankly; then he put his hands on my shoulders. "Hope all is okay around here?" Keith and I were momentarily struck dumb, trying to figure out what to say, when Dhruv walked off and made a sudden dash back to say, "Okay, take care of this place..." Keith then picked up his line and we somehow pulled that scene through. Thereafter, Mr Saikia carried on flawlessly without blinking an eyelid. The show was actually a great success.

Jaipur-based theatre artist and activist **Ranbir Singh**, chief of the apex body of the Indian People's Theatre Association (IPTA), recalls his association with Yatrik:

I was attached to Yatrik at a critical phase of its existence when Joy Michael had gone to the US on an assignment. She gave me the charge of Yatrik. The idea mooted that time was that Yatrik and Shri Ram Centre (SRC) would join hands. It was decided that Yatrik would be the professional repertory. Later, SRC did not understand the aesthetics of a repertory and the working of a theatre group. So the idea was withdrawn. We were left alone. Now the important question was: how to run the group?

Basically, Yatrik was an amateur group. The executive committee consisted of amateurs working in big business houses who were in theatre for their pleasure. On the other hand, Marcus Murch, Barry John, Kulbhushan Kharbanda, and I were professional artists. I served as the manager-director. We sold tickets and the collection was enough to pay our modest salaries. As soon as Joy Michael returned from the US and resumed charge, I left to organise the IPTA.

**Ranjit Mathur** was technically not a founder member, but he joined Yatrik a few years after its formation. He joined it for his sheer love of theatre brought forward from his schooldays and from his previous posting in Calcutta. With Yatrik, he began as a backstage artist and gradually rose to become a fine actor, continuously rejoining the group whenever he was posted to Delhi, with his job in the Indian Railways. He continues to be a regular member of the executive committee of Yatrik, attending it with faith in its objectives and ready to share responsibility entrusted to him.

**Reminiscences:** The motivation that has kept me glued to Yatrik is the diverse activities I have been a part of. As an actor on the English stage in Delhi, I got the opportunity to act in a small part in *Blood Wedding*, directed by Kusum Haidar, whom I knew personally. Then I acted as the lawyer opposite Bhaskar Ghose in Terence Rattigan's *Cause Celebre,* although originally an understudy for the role, and with Ajay Balram in *The Broken Jug*. Other cameo roles came my way—*The Italian Straw Hat, Laughing in Lughnasa, A Tomb with a View, America Here I Come,* and readings and visual enactments from poetry, Shakespeare, and Wilde. Tejeshwar Singh and I were in *Closet Madness,* a short play for a cast of two. A major role I played was Dr Einstein in *Arsenic and Old Lace*, directed by Prabha Tonk, with Indu Ramchandani, Sunit Tandon, Ramesh Thakur, Jacqui Garewal, Sinia Dugal, Jasbir Malik, and others. This hilarious play had many reruns, including in Shimla. I was Advani in Avijit's rerun of *Bombay Bosnia* and the father of the bride when Kusum repeated *Blood Wedding*. I also enjoyed a memorable role in *Mirza Bagh* with several entries, but only four speaking lines. Sabina, who directed this play, also took it to Lucknow and Lahore. At an early stage, I was assigned to record the minutes of the meetings of the executive committee.

Working and meeting together to cooperate and coordinate the working of various departments of a production is most fulfilling. While I was doing backstage work or onstage work in the earlier years, Hugh Michael was always there, sitting quietly, observing that all things were in place. He would give me a little pat on my back, and a smile. This was enough to encourage me. Joy Michael, Kusum Haidar, Prabha Tonk, Sabina Mehta Jaitly—all have been great artists and directors. To work with them has been memorable. Joy has a big heart. Sometimes we might have differences, but her

*Mirza Bagh*—Danish Husain and Ranjit Mathur

love and affection has held us all together—her personal touch is creatively stimulating.

As soon as office hours would get over, I would rush to the venue of a rehearsal or the venue where the play was to be staged. It was exhilarating to be welcomed by the young and old co-artistes, charming Sushma Seth, Sai Paranjpye, Joy Michael, and Kulbhushan Kharbanda, among others. Working with these people, so dedicated and full of enthusiasm, was a great experience. Lola Chatterji has

*Arsenic and Old Lace*—Ranjit Mathur and Rupin Jayal

always been there as a great pillar of strength for all of us playing multiple roles backstage, such as being in charge of make-up, costumes, and props. She is also Yatrik's chronicler and adviser. I enjoyed entering the Ladies Green Room to give a "break-a-leg" kiss to Lola and all the actresses. I have sat enough times at the box office, selling brochures and tickets. The cost for a ticket for the basement theatre in SRC and Habitat Centre was at one time as low as 10 rupees.

There really is nothing like theatre to work together and to know each other. Christmas parties in the Michael home and all cast parties are the memories one cherishes.

I am still an active member of Yatrik, but memories of the past linger. Most of the senior members of Yatrik, who joined at different points of time along this 50-year-plus journey, retain their earlier optimism and enthusiasm to continue. While cherishing memories of the good old days, we all do wish to move forward and be in tune with the changing times giving expression to the original creative impulse. As the drama of human life never ceases to unfold, Yatrik will continue to enact life.

**Rupin Jayal.** So here, I was working in a motorcycle company, Escorts. That raised quite a few eyebrows when I told visiting foreigners where I worked. My work entailed travelling to remote parts of Odisha and Bihar (undivided). Amidst coalfields, various mines, etc., it was an unforgettable experience; but more so in retrospect. I wanted something more enriching to offset the 25 days of dreary monthly touring.

Enter Yatrik, stage left (or right)—my very first play on the Delhi stage. Not my first theatrical experience, though, with lead roles in *Tughlaq* and *Royal Hunt of the Sun* while in school. My entry was with *Arsenic and Old Lace*, directed by Prabha Tonk.

I played the role of Teddy Roosevelt and my enduring memory is of my perpetual battle with a trumpet. On some days, it blew so loudly that nearby countries would go on high alert. On others, all that would emerge was a tired, defeated sigh—probably at my ineptitude. Other than the infernal trumpet and Prabha's reactions, it was a blissful time.

Highlights of this experience were: Prabha, with her delicious husky voice, who would have to put up with me in many plays thereafter. Her unique mix of warmth, toughness, and a laconic sense of humour is deeply missed. "Sinister" Sunit Tandon putting in a virtuoso performance as the deadly Jonathan Brewster, while also teaching himself to smoke. He was to become a lifelong maestro at it. Deepak Mukarji's portrayal of Mortimer's distracted decency. The two delightfully evil Brewster sisters—Indu Vachani Ramchandani and Jackie Garewal—were hilariously nonplussed, but effective. Ranjit Mathur was the plaintively confused Dr Einstein. Jasbir Malik was perfect as the bumbling Police Inspector, whose tendency to forget lines was very much in character, but kept us all alert. These were unforgettable performances. During the journey of this play, I made friends that were a delightful gang to spend time with. And they have been a treasure for me all my life.

Blissful, enriching, joyful, sometimes frustrating, and always rewarding—an invaluable, lifelong gift. Thank you, Yatrik!

**Sabina Mehta Jaitly** is a versatile actress and a sensitive stage director. She was director of Yatrik from 2003 to 2008. She has acted with several theatre groups and has her own group, Dramebaaz. Recently, Sabina has been seen on the small screen in her role as Sanjana Bharadwaj in a Hindi TV serial, *Agar Tum Saath Ho*.

**Reminiscences:** My journey in theatre began in 1971, when I joined Miranda House and Yatrik almost simultaneously. Someone mentioned that Yatrik was holding auditions for a new play and, seeing my excitement, gave me directions on how to get there—a large loft on the second floor in Connaught Place, facing the Embassy restaurant. This was the wonderful home of Yatrik for many years—a space that served as rehearsal space, costume store, stage, and auditorium, and it was here that I arrived to audition for *Servant of Two Masters*, to be directed by the rising star on the theatre horizon—Barry John.

On one side of the large space, M.K. Raina was rehearsing his *Inquilab*, and on the terrace, leaning on the parapet and looking down at the Connaught Place traffic, stood the taciturn Barry, smoking a cigarette. I introduced myself and told him why I was there. He nodded and went back to his cigarette and contemplation of the traffic. Uncertainly, I stood in one corner, anxiously looking at my watch. The hostel gates at the college would shut at 7 pm sharp, and it didn't look as if any auditioning was going to happen any time soon. Finally, I heard loud laughter and banter and in walked Prabha Tonk, Rebecca, and Raghu Sudon, all venerable stars of Delhi's English theatre, followed by Joy Michael. My heart sank. Audition in the presence of these stars? I wanted to run away, but Joy saw me trying to tiptoe away and told me to pull up a chair and sit down. Fortunately, that evening we just read the play and dispersed for the day. The next day, Joy Michael sent a message to college that I was selected to play Beatrice and asked me to show up for rehearsals every day at 4.30 pm.

To cut a long story short—Barry continued to be taciturn and communicated only through unbroken silences, which we learned to interpret. The formidable "stars" turned out to be wonderfully warm people who went out of their way to help me find my stage feet, becoming close friends over the years. We travelled with the play to Lucknow, where it was received with much applause. Soon thereafter, Joy cast me as Mrs Manningham in *Gaslight* with the veteran actor

Marcus Murch playing my sinister husband. Working under Joy was such a different experience. She was decisive, brooked no nonsense, but, at the same time, was open to questions, was sensitive to the needs of the entire cast, guided us, and firmly but with great diplomacy kept Marcus' volatility in check.

By getting me to assist her with costumes and sets, Joy taught me a lot about improvising and creating illusions with odd bits and pieces—lessons that I would continue to learn and put to good use in the several plays I did in college and at St. Stephen's College.

Then came a break of three years, as I graduated from Delhi University and went to the National School of Drama, where we were not permitted to work outside the School. At NSD, I specialised in Direction under the guidance of Ebrahim Alkazi and graduated in 1977 with the award for "Best Director".

This was followed by a spate of plays with Yatrik, which by now had shifted from its "lofty" abode to the auditorium in St. Thomas School. Making up for lost time, I acted in *The Broken Jug, The Devil's Advocate, Antigone* (all directed by Joy), and directed translations of *German Expressionist Plays* for the Max Mueller Bhavan. Then came my first big directorial venture—*The Good Woman of Szechuan*, which stood out for the immensely hummable music composed by Eric Helms, the effervescent performance by Sinia Dugal in the eponymous role, and the delightful vignettes by the talented cast, propelled no doubt by Ajay Balram's delightfully acerbic observations and by the "spirited" contents of Dhruv Saikia's bulging briefcase.

Then I got married and left with my husband for foreign shores, where I continued to do and teach theatre. Back on a home posting, in 1985, I adapted and translated Pinter's *The Lover (Pehlu)* and *The Collection (Intezaar)* and directed them as a double bill and acted, along with Prabha Tonk and Kusum Haidar, in an evocative production on *Sylvia Plath*, directed by Joy Michael, which we took to Ahmedabad and Mumbai.

*Sylvia Plath*—Kusum Haidar and Sabina Jaitly

Another six years away from Delhi—in Geneva and Islamabad, teaching drama. On my return in the early 1990s, Bhaskar Ghose directed me in *Blind Date*, along with the enormously talented Shyama Halder; Joy directed me in *Excerpts from Oscar Wilde* and in the riotous *Six Degrees of Separation*, which had a huge cast of talented young newcomers, some of whom then went on to do several plays with Yatrik. Shortly after this, I directed and acted in *Death and the Maiden*, a script that I had wanted to direct for a long time and had been waiting for Bhaskar to find the time to act in. This was followed by several plays with other theatre groups and a successful dramatised reading of *Skylight*, which Bhaskar and I did for Yatrik.

In 2003, Yatrik celebrated its 40th anniversary and Joy requested me to take over the mantle of directorship from her, which I did, never having been able to refuse Joy. I knew well that it would be a tough endeavour to fit into the large shoes she had worn for 40 fruitful years.

*Thus Spake Shoorpanakha*—
Sunil Gupta and Sabina Jaitly

In the five years that I was director, Bhaskar directed Sunil Gupta and me in *Thus Spake Shoorpanakha*, which was followed by Joy's *Excerpts from Arthur Miller*, and several delightful poetry readings devised by the creative Giti Chandra. In 2004, Yatrik travelled to South Africa under the aegis of ICCR with several plays. We took an old production 9 *Jakhoo Hill*, directed by Sunit Tandon, to The Hindu Theatre Festival in Chennai.

In 2005, I began adapting Brian Friel's *Aristocrats* and *Mirza Bagh* emerged. As I was reading "Aristocrats", in my mind's eye, the play uncannily, almost of its own volition, set itself in an Awadhi kasbah or citadel. The entire transposition happened so naturally—each situation finding a corresponding one, each character its counterpart. The piano sonatas found their resonance in the *chaiti* and the thumri; the funeral dirge in the Marsiyas sung at the Fateha; and the love for popular music translated to our own lifelong and inextricable linkage with "filmy" songs. The Irish love for poetry, the lilting speech, and love of storytelling recognised corresponding passions in the Awadhi heartland.

With a host of new actors and some Yatrik veterans, *Mirza Bagh* opened in March 2006 in Delhi at the Shri Ram Centre with four shows to great audience and critical response. In September, it was invited to perform in Lucknow by the Ministry of Culture, Government of Uttar Pradesh. Performing this play in the milieu in which it is set was an exhilarating experience and the audience response was overwhelmingly appreciative. In November 2006, we were invited to stage two shows at the World Festival of Performing and Visual Arts 2006 in Lahore and we were sponsored by the ICCR. Both shows received standing ovations and wonderful press reviews.

In 2007, *Mirza Bagh* received the Sahitya Kala Parishad award and accolade as one of the "Best Plays of 2006", and we were invited by the Parishad to perform at the Bhartendu Natya Utsav. In September that year, we staged the play at the Taj Palace Hotel in Delhi to raise funds for Palna, a child welfare NGO. For me, it was easily the most fascinating and demanding production of my theatrical journey. I was fortunate to find a talented and committed cast, for whom peeling away the layers of the script to locate its core and proceeding from there to arrive at the truth of their own characters made rehearsals incredibly enriching. Travelling with the play to Lucknow and then to Lahore threw up new challenges. Getting the Sahitya Kala Parishad annual award was the cherry on the icing on a rich cake.

For various reasons, in 2008, five years after I took over from Joy and 37 years since my first play with Yatrik, I resigned. As I said earlier, the shoes didn't fit. Nonetheless, Yatrik continues to hold a special place in my heart and I owe to the group and to Joy a huge debt of gratitude for all they taught me and all the affection they showered me with.

***Mirza Bagh* plays to standing ovation**—By Halima Mansoor, Dawn, Lahore, 13 November 2006.

*Mirza Bagh*, an adaptation of Brian Friel's play *Aristocrats*, reveals one of many things—how large aristocratic families often preserve themselves in homespun glorification of the family and try to retain the titles and the honour of a family long past its prime.

Performed by an Indian troupe, the play grasps the audience as an illusion of theatre by presenting reality on stage.

Set in the mid-1970s, when landowners were losing face along with property, the play opens with a monologue by one of the protagonists, Farhan. Married into this once rich and prestigious family, he unfolds the play's setting: the wedding of the youngest daughter of the crumbling household. One of the five siblings, equally complex and well-threaded characters, the bride-to-be Aliya seems to suffer from clinical depression and loses herself by playing the piano or singing when something disturbs her equilibrium. This theme of music is fluid and constant throughout the play, as various climactic moments are preceded or triggered by classical Brahms or Strauss. For her wedding, four siblings return, while the absence of one underlines the state of their father.

The once-legendary judge, father of five and husband to a woman of an uncertain past, now almost senile, is quartered in a room, while his eldest child, referred to as Apa, takes care of him.

Apa, the mother of a perhaps illegitimate child, who is surreptitiously living in an orphanage, takes care of the once-grand ancestral home that is now crumbling her away with its structure. Zara, the second sister, married to the overconfident and sarcastic Farhan, is an alcoholic who refuses to accept her problem. The third sister ran away to a convent in England and is considered one of the reasons for whom the father completely disintegrates from his awe-inspiring self into a blithering deluded soul, who is only eerily heard through a baby monitor fixed at centre stage. The only brother Qasim, an almost manic personality, tipping towards homosexuality, claims to have a German wife, whose existence the other siblings doubt. A teetotaller, ex-alcoholic uncle threads through this eccentric dysfunctional family as a silent character who has no reason to talk since he need not use his voice to order the bottle any more.

Amidst these characters is a calm logical professor, who is chronicling this once-historic family's saga as part of his research on other such families. The family reveals not even to itself how severe the issues are till the father, who is now ridden by conflicts of the past, takes to his death when he hears the voice of his daughter, the nun, on a tape she sends home. Also with the help of quiet intrusions by the professor, who with a tactful enquiry, brings forth facts that the family refuses to accept.

The entire production, including the live music, the authentic costumes, and the stage management reflect a professionalism and eye for detail. The beauty of the enactment lies in the convincing acting, simple sets, and the feeling that one is looking through a window into the actual lives of a family about to end an epoch of opulent and grandiose living. Full credit goes to the director for presenting to the rapt audience a rare glimpse of true theatre.

Here is a play that must be kept alive for the newness and relevance of its script, superb direction and design, innovative presentation and marvellous performances.

The cast is a mix of Yatrik's old and new. We have Prakash Bhatia playing Baldev Rai, Ramesh Thakur as Qasim Ali Beg, who lives in Germany, Farhan, a former

Naxalite, played rivetingly by Danish Husain, and his wife Zara (Surabhi Goswami), who lives in London. Then there is Inayat Mirza (Tarannum Ahmad), the eldest sister, all as good as ever, and of course, there is Yatrik's veteran Jasbir Malik. In Mahua Sen, we have a versatile singer whose Chaiti, in the very beginning, holds the audience.

Jasbir Malik and Danish Husain in *Mirza Bagh*

**Shyama Haldar.** My Yatrik days began in 1992 with the group's summer theatre workshop. I had nurtured a keenness for the stage since I was in high school, which I'd passed out from a year earlier. At the time, the stage, not the studio, was where one went with acting dreams. To join Yatrik and to be with those who had loved and lived the theatre in Delhi's longest-sustained drama group was, and will remain, a treasure.

Six months later, I was treading the boards I'd longed for: Bhaskar Ghose had cast me in *Blind Date*, a short skit of gentle mischief, the darling first of a warmly recalled series. Avijit Dutt's *Kismet Ya...* with its razor edge and minimalist intensity is outstanding in my memory, as is Kusum Haidar's *Antigone* and its chiselled, tender grace. The cast of *9 Jakhoo Hill*, directed by Sunit Tandon, has still to exhaust our self-deprecating wonder at its decade-long run across several of the Indian metropolises, and in Dubai and South Africa too; this stands

*Blind Date*—Dilip Shankar and Shyama Haldar

Sunit Tandon and Shyama Haldar in 9 *Jakhoo Hill*

unprecedented in Delhi, where one does not see too many plays reviving after their opening weekend.

My most spectacular recall is of playing the title role in Joy Michael's early 2000's production of *Educating Rita.* Growing into the part under the meticulous, unerringly tuned direction of the pioneer and presiding spirit of this city's theatre world was an irretrievably precious experience, as everything about Yatrik will always be for me. There are, of course, regrets, which cannot span the distance of time and space: I wish I could have been in or at least seen *The Curlew's Cry*, one of the earliest attempts at a play in English for, of, and about Indians; I wish I could have known Marcus Murch. I miss being there to get an opportunity to act with Bhaskar Bhattacharji, Prabha Tonk, Jasbir Malik, and Sant Juneja; and being part of the plays that used to be staged at AIFACS in days past, the storied ones of getting by in a tired, timid city, charming it back into evenings of relentless and exuberant life.

**Sinia (Jain) Dugal** has many memories to treasure. She was just 16 and immediately after her Senior Cambridge examination was over, her social-activist mother, Deep Dugal, took her to Joy Michael and requested her to enrol her daughter in Yatrik. She was welcomed to become an active member of the group. Since then, she has never looked back, and under the wings of Yatrik, she has grown from an amateur actress to a professional performer, combining the ingenuity of the amateur with the skill of a professional. Her first role was in *Sinbad the Sailor*, produced by Yatrik. Then she was cast in the role of a maid in Moliere's *The Bourgeois Gentleman.*

**Reminiscences:** I grew up in Yatrik as an actress. Bhaskar Ghose is my guru; he taught me the principles of acting. I also learnt a great deal of my craft from highly dedicated and gifted artists such as Ajay Balram, Deepak Kejriwal, and Madhuri Bhatia. During those days, we used to stage close to five plays a year. The atmosphere in Yatrik

*Cactus Flower*—Lewie Gonsalves and Sinia Dugal

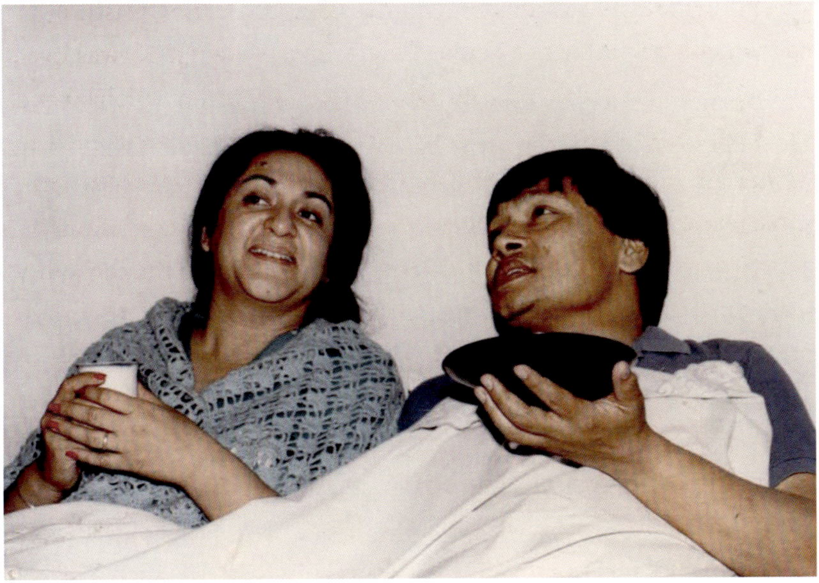

*Bedroom Farce*—Sinia Dugal and Ramesh Thakur

was that of a family, ensuring full freedom to artists. All of us were passionate about theatre and were committed to creating a production that exuded the artists' creativity.

My first major role was in Brecht's *The Good Woman of Szechuan,* which was directed by National School of Drama graduate, Sabina Mehta (Jaitly). In this play, my co-actors included Bhaskar Ghose, Ajay Balram, and Madhuri Bhatia. One of my unforgettable performances was in *Tamasha*, which was directed by Deepak Kejriwal. This was an exciting role, as for three months I underwent rigorous training in the traditional tamasha dance and music form to play a "*tamashe wali*", and the result was amazing. Madhuri Bhatia as a choreographer and actress contributed a lot to make this production one of the masterpieces of Yatrik. My role in *Cactus Flower* was significant. *Bedroom Farce* was a thoroughly enjoyable experience, as was playing the crazy sister Abby to Indu Ramchandani's Martha, during the repeat shows in Prabha Tonk's production of *Arsenic and Old Lace*. Of course, my portrayal of Chitra in *9 Jakhoo Hill* is a landmark for me.

I remember fondly how Sunit guided all the actors to understand the characters, the historical background, and the social context of the script. He also gave us the liberty to rewrite dialogues to some extent in our own way, while he was conducting a workshop. Playwright Gurcharan Das was in full agreement with Sunit's directorial approach. In such a situation, when an actor is given liberty to interpret a character, he or she can create wonders on the stage. My portrayal of Chitra, I believe, was true to the writer's concept of the character.

Bhaskar Ghose also gave his actors the freedom of interpretation of a character, trusting the actors' intelligence and ingenuity—these are the important things that I recall in my long journey with Yatrik. Last but not the least, Joy nurtured me as a mother would, as she has done for all of us who have grown as actors under her wings over all these years.

**Sunit Tandon.** A seasoned actor and director, Sunit Tandon is one of the most creative persons associated with Yatrik. Sunit is an organiser, a sensitive director who has been entrusted with the enormous tasks of the group that were previously performed by Joy Michael. A busy senior officer in the Government of India, he manages to spare time to act as the director of the group. A talented personality, Sunit is an unrivalled actor on the English stage in the capital and hence is much in demand. His recent portrayal of the complex character of Gandhi under the direction of Bhanu Bharati was remarkable for its depth, insight, restraint, and inner intensity, projecting the dilemma that Gandhi faced in the changing political and social scenario, just prior to Partition, marred by opportunism. A thinking actor, he internalises the conflict of his character, making his portrayal intense, probing the complex psychological and emotional world of the character. His performance as Deepak in *9 Jakhoo Hill*, the prestigious production of Yatrik, illustrated his talent as an actor, not to talk of being the director of the production.

**Reminiscences:** I always like to say that I was forcibly propelled into the world of theatre by my late friend and brilliant actor, Bhaskar Bhattacharji. In 1977, I was a shy teenager who had never mustered up the courage to go for auditions for the productions of the Shakespeare Society in my first two years in St. Stephen's College. Bhaskar was two years my senior and was already considered a notable actor. One afternoon, when I refused to accompany him for an audition for the latest annual Shakespeare production, he grabbed hold of my arm and dragged me through the corridors to it. It was an audition for *Macbeth*. I was shocked when I almost beat him to the title role. Eventually, in the toss-up between the two of us, the director Sunil Chand opted for the more experienced Bhaskar, much to my relief. But he cast me in the second longest part in the play—that of Malcolm.

I remember taking to the stage instantly. I discovered that it was auditions I was frightened of, not the stage itself. There was no stage fright even before my very first show, only a pleasurable excitement. Marcus Murch saw that production and immediately cast me in a series of plays for Stagedoor, the company he had started recently after parting ways with Yatrik. In my first role with Stagedoor, I replaced Bhaskar Bhattacharji as the juvenile lead in Agatha Christie's *The Mousetrap* on a tour to Nainital for which Bhaskar was unable to go. The next three years were a rollercoaster ride, with play after play at various venues in Delhi (mostly at Kamani) and tours to Nainital, Mumbai, and Dehra Dun as well, acting with the likes of Bhaskar Bhattacharji, Aamir Raza Hussain, and Salman Khurshid. At that time, we were doing plays at the rate of about four or five productions a year. I learnt a great deal about acting and production from Marcus, but above all, I learnt the thrill of being agile and adaptable on stage. Then Stagedoor ran into troubles and some of us were at a bit of a loose end.

That is when Joy Michael came to the rescue. I had met her some time earlier, when she gave me a lift in her car to Lady Shri Ram College, where I was participating in an elocution competition that she was judging. She had been friendly and warm. Now she called and asked me to act in a major production that she was mounting of Terence Rattigan's *Cause Celebre*. I was a bit hesitant at first, but when I heard that another Stagedoor colleague, Jillian Larkins, was also going to be in the production, I said "yes". Suddenly, I was working with a whole new set of experienced actors. I met, for the first time, Yatrik stalwarts such as Sant Juneja, Ranjit Mathur, and Roshan Seth, all of whom were acting in this production. Then, of course, there was the Michael family—Col. Hugh Michael, Meriel and Kristine, all of whom were solidly involved in almost every production in one capacity or the

*Cause Celebre*—Sunit Tandon with Jillian Larkins

other. Soon, I had met practically all the pillars of Yatrik who came before me, both on and off stage: Bhaskar Ghose, Lola Chatterji, Ajay Balram, Vinay Capila, Rati Bartholomew, Tejeshwar Singh, Madhuri Bhatia, Sinia Dugal, and Ramesh Thakur, to name a few.

And here I was, launched on another rollercoaster ride of productions: Bhaskar Ghose cast me immediately in *Bedroom Farce* by Alan Ayckbourn and, as soon as that was over, Tejeshwar Singh cast me in the demanding title role in *The Night Thoreau Spent in Jail* by Robert Edwin Lee and Jerome Lawrence. This was one of my most satisfying roles on the stage up to that point. Joy also cast me as the Clown in her mammoth production of *The Winter's Tale* for the Shakespeare Society, St. Stephen's College, to celebrate the centenary of the college in 1980, in which several alumni came back to play alongside the present students. These included a host of Yatrik veterans such as Roshan Seth, Shankar Ghose, Nigam Prakash, Kavi Singh, Dilip Sircar, Tejeshwar Singh, and Ajay Balram.

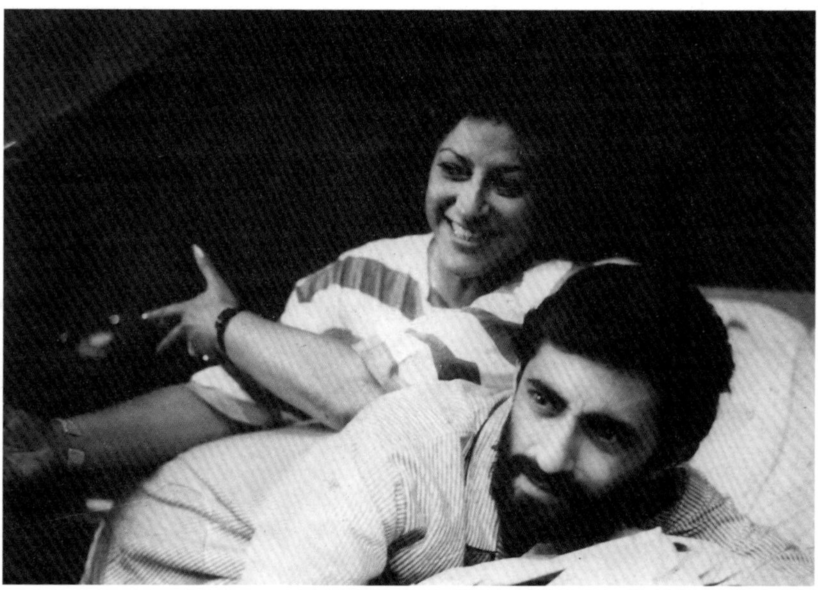

Prabha Tonk and Sunit Tandon in *Bedroom Farce*

Now came the time for me to return Bhaskar Bhattacharji's favour of having propelled me into theatre in the first place. He had also been at a loose end theatre-wise since the hiatus in Stagedoor. I persuaded him to join Yatrik and he agreed. He came and was cast in a small role in *The Night Thoreau Spent in Jail.* This was just the beginning. He went on to act in major roles in several plays, including *Don't Drink the Water, The Curlew's Cry, Uncle Vanya, A Midsummer Night's Dream, Principia Scriptoria, The Daily Truth* and *Antigone.* I was also cast in most of these plays in principal roles, and it was a pleasure to be on stage with him again after college and the recent Stagedoor days. When we lost him at the turn of the millenium, it was a tremendous blow to theatre in Delhi, as well as to many of us personally. He was extremely intelligent, had a marvellous voice and presence on stage, and was the most friendly and generous of co-actors.

Both of us made our directing debuts together. In 1982, Joy Michael persuaded us to select some one-act plays and direct them

Sunit Tandon (right) in *Uncle Vanya*

ourselves for the Shri Ram Centre basement, which was the venue of choice for mounting experimental plays in those days. Bhaskar chose *The Ruffian on the Stair* by Joe Orton, while I chose the first part of *Gallows Humour* by Jack Richardson and *A Separate Peace* by Tom Stoppard.

Naturally, my own memories of this occasion centre on the two plays I directed, since I was busy rehearsing them while Bhaskar rehearsed his play separately. For *Gallows Humour*, I cast the senior Bhaskar, Bhaskar Ghose, whose acting I had admired for long in the principal role with Bindu Tandon (no relation) as the female lead. The chorus I split between two actors, Janaki Bahadur and Sagarika Ghose, Bhaskar's daughter, who was still in school at that time. Bhaskar Ghose was then a senior government officer, a joint secretary, no less, while I was a stripling in my early twenties, starting out on my first job as a probationary officer in a bank. I can never forget his generosity of spirit and professionalism as an actor in not only agreeing to be directed by a young first-timer, but also following my instructions even when he disagreed with me. This was perhaps the basis for the lifelong relationship of trust and friendship, both on and off the stage, that developed between us, acting together in countless productions, directing each other in several plays over the decades.

From the outset, I have never cast myself in any of the plays I have directed, believing firmly that I need to be free from acting responsibilities in order to be able to concentrate on the production. However, on two occasions, I have been forced by circumstances to act in my own productions. The first instance occurred with one of the two plays that marked my directorial debut, *A Separate Peace*. I had cast the young Raghav Behl (who later went on to found the TV 18 empire) as the protagonist of this play. Five days before the opening night, Raghav backed out most apologetically because of some pressing engagement. I couldn't get anyone to substitute for him at such a short notice, and so had to take on the part myself.

The evening of three plays that Bhaskar Bhattacharji and I directed were received well and they gave me the confidence to take up stage direction regularly, all thanks to the warm encouragement of Joy Michael and the tremendous support of the entire Yatrik team.

Having observed at close quarters the kind of rivalries that existed among theatre groups at that time, some of us had resolved to never succumb to them, but to work with as many groups and directors as we could. In this spirit, a few of us got together and formed our own theatre group with the blessings of the other groups we were in touch with. This new group was called Masque. Bhaskar Bhattacharji was the director of the group and I was the president. Many of us had worked formerly with Stagedoor, which had been started by Marcus Murch. Bhaskar and I were already working with Yatrik. Some of us had connections with Theatre Action Group (TAG), which was spearheaded by Barry John, who had also started off in Delhi theatre with Yatrik. We started off with a production of *Twain by the Tale*, based on the hilarious stories of Mark Twain, which I directed. Some of the costumes for the production came from Yatrik and some from TAG.

Over the next five years or so, in the early to mid-1980s, we mounted several Masque productions, while also simultaneously working with Yatrik. Almost all these productions were directed by either Bhaskar Bhattacharji or by myself, with both of us taking turns to act in each other's productions. These included plays such as *The Shadow Box* by Michael Cristofer and *Butley* by Simon Gray, directed by Bhaskar. I directed plays such as *Blithe Spirit* by Noel Coward, *I Ought to be in Pictures* by Neil Simon and *What the Butler Saw* by Joe Orton. Not once did we sense any negative reaction about these "independent" activities from Joy Michael or anyone else in Yatrik. In fact, Joy was extremely supportive and encouraging and many Yatrik stalwarts worked with us in Masque as well. Tejeshwar Singh directed *A Day in the Death of Joe Egg* by Peter Nichols for Masque. Prabha

Tonk played the female lead opposite me in this play. Prabha played Ruth in my production of *Blithe Spirit* and designed the wonderful costumes for it as well, while Sushma Seth's daughter Divya played Madame Arcati brilliantly.

An interesting footnote to the Masque story: wanting to have some relief from the directorial burden of our plays, Bhaskar Bhattacharji and I decided that we should encourage some younger members of the group to direct for an evening of one-act plays at the Shri Ram Centre basement theatre, much as we had been asked to do so by Joy Michael for Yatrik just a couple of years previously. Among these first-time directors was Bhaveen Gosain, who chose a play called *Stops Along the Way* by Jeffrey Sweet. He cast a young actor who was just out of school as one of the two actors in this play. While helping out during rehearsals, I was immediately struck by this actor's seriousness of approach, his intensity, and his concentration. The boy's name was Shah Rukh Khan. He was later to go on to working with Barry John and TAG and then, through the world of TV serials, to films. But his first play for a paying audience was probably this Masque production.

This was also the time when another influential theatre group of Delhi, with which I have had a long association, came into being. In 1981–82, Yatrik produced a dramatised reading of *Deathwatch* by Jean Genet, directed by Dilip Sircar, in which it was a delight for me to act with two of my favourite actors, the two Bhaskars, as we used to call them: Bhaskar Ghose and Bhaskar Bhattacharji. After one show in the SRC basement, three strangers came up to us and congratulated us on our performances. They said that they were staging the same play in the original French in the main theatre upstairs the very next day. Naturally, all of us went to see it and it proved to be a production in a different, more physical and more abstract style. Among the three actors was K. Madavane, who founded the Chingari theatre group shortly thereafter, mostly composed of students of French at the

Alliance Francaise. They included Rajat Kapoor, now a noted film and theatre actor and director and, a bit later, Atul Kumar, also now a noted theatre director. Since Masque was established at about this same time, we took great interest in each other's fledgling groups, sharing workshops, and going to each other's rehearsals. Years later, I had the privilege of being the sole male actor playing about six roles in Madavane's production of his own play *The Mahabharat of Women*, an experience I cherish.

It was about the same time in the mid-1980s that I directed the first of several annual productions for the Shakespeare Society of St. Stephen's College, where theatre had begun for me just about five years previously. I directed George Bernard Shaw's *You Never Can Tell* in 1984 and Shakepeare's *The Merry Wives of Windsor* in 1986. This latter was the diamond jubilee production to celebrate 60 years of the Shakespeare Society and featured Divya Seth, Sagarika Ghose, Smeeta Chakraborty, and Lalit Vachani, among others. All this was happening thanks to Joy Michael and Yatrik pushing me into stage direction in 1982, for which I shall remain ever grateful.

All this while, my activities and involvement with Yatrik had not diminished in any way. Looking back, I marvel at how much theatre we managed to cram into our lives almost continuously, while holding on to full-time jobs as well. Among the memorable productions of this time that I recall with great affection was *The Curlew's Cry* by Kamal Kapur, directed by Bhaskar Ghose in 1982–83 (the same year in which I made my directorial debut). This bilingual play was a fascinating look at contemporary romantic relationships and it marked one of the few times I played an entirely Urdu-speaking character on stage, that of a young *shair* who is in love with a married woman.

As a complete contrast, in the same year I played the aged Professor Serebriakov, married to a young, beautiful, and restless Kusum Haidar in Chekhov's *Uncle Vanya*, directed by Joy Michael. This was, of course, done in English. The next year, in the 1983–84 season, I played the

*The Curlew's Cry*—Sunit Tandon with Chitra Ramachandran

comic role of Father Drobney in Woody Allen's *Don't Drink the Water*, directed by Ajay Balram. I also directed a production of Tom Stoppard's *The Real Inspector Hound* with Arjun Raina and Divya Seth, among others, along with reviving my earlier production of *A Separate Peace*, with Bhaskar Ghose thankfully relieving me of the role of the protagonist. These two plays were put up together at the Shri Ram Centre main theatre as a Stoppard double bill, with Joy Michael herself handling production details with her characteristic enthusiasm and efficiency.

With the next season of 1984–85, I acted in *Blues for Mr. Charlie* by James Baldwin, directed by Joy Michael (in which the future fashion designer Tarun Tahiliani also played a role). I did the sound design and execution for *A Gown for his Mistress* by Georges Feydeau, directed by Tejeshwar Singh, which marked Prabha Tonk's return to the stage after a long gap. I also ended up doing a walk-on in a crowd scene of *The Queen and the Rebels* by Ugo Betti, directed by Bhaskar Ghose, which I had gone to see as part of the audience. Going backstage to wish the cast "break a leg" before the show, I found a frantic Bhaskar bewailing the fact that some of the actors for the important crowd scenes had not turned up. Naturally, he dragooned me into giving up my seat and going onto stage. Equally naturally, I agreed. This production also marked my first meeting with Avijit Dutt, who had recently come to Delhi from Calcutta, and with whom I was to go on to share some memorable moments on stage.

Prabha Tonk also became a good friend and co-actor. Despite the difference in our ages, I enjoyed playing many roles opposite her. When she decided to direct her first play, she ensured that she cast me and Avijit in the main roles, because, as she said, "I don't need to direct you!" The play she chose was *Principia Scriptoriae* by Richard Nelson. It was a stimulating experience acting with Avijit in this rather intense play set in an anonymous South American country. Bhaskar Bhattacharji also played a cameo role in this play.

In the same year (1987–88), Joy cast me in a role I could never have imagined I would play so early in life. I was still in my twenties. She cast me as Prospero for her production of Shakespeare's *The Tempest*. It was a challenge I relished, playing the central role of the aged philosopher in this great classic, with Yatrik stalwarts such as Tejeshwar Singh, Pankaj Mohun (both of them my seniors in the world of TV newscasting), Ajay Balram, and Dilip Sircar also in the cast, all playing characters younger than myself.

It was a year of large-scale productions, for in the same season I played an enjoyable part in Tejeshwar Singh's *The Daily Truth*, which he had adapted from *Pravda* by David Hare and Howard Brenton.

Sunit Tandon as Prospero in *The Tempest*

The next year, Prabha Tonk, who had by now gained more confidence as a director, decided to direct that old war horse among comedies, *Arsenic and Old Lace* by Joseph Kesselring. I must say I thoroughly enjoyed playing the comically evil role of Jonathan, originally created by Boris Karloff. It was a joy to play comedy with actors and friends of the likes of Jacqueline Garewal, Indu Ramchandani, Jasbir Malik, Ranjit Mathur, Deepak Mukarji, and Rupin Jayal and to have Prabha's characteristically acidic directorial interventions to enliven rehearsals.

It was entirely due to Prabha's persuasiveness that I agreed to co-direct a play for the first and only time in my life. After the success of *Arsenic*, she wanted to tackle a similarly macabre comedy, but wanted a more experienced hand to help her tackle it. She settled upon *A Tomb with a View* by Norman Robbins, a play I did not much care for. I have to say that I was not too happy with the result and swore never to be inveigled into co-directing ever again if I could help it.

It was certainly more pleasant to choose a comic play that had a bit of substance and to direct it myself. This is what happened with *The Last of the Red Hot Lovers* by Neil Simon, which I directed next for Yatrik, with a wonderful cast of Deepak Mukarji, Jacqueline Garewal, her daughter Rahat, and Indu Ramchandani. We did several repeat shows of this play, including a sponsored charity show for the benefit of the building restoration fund for my historic old school La Martiniere College, Lucknow. This was also the last time I recall doing a play at the old AIFACS theatre, which was the only auditorium in Delhi built on the lines of the old English theatres, with its raked wooden stage, lighting booth in the wings, spiral staircases leading to green rooms above the stage, steep balcony, and near-perfect acoustics for unamplified stage voices.

We were now in the early 1990s. This was the time when Yatrik experimented with supper theatre. Joy had directed a production of *The Good Doctor* by Neil Simon, based on the stories of Anton Chekhov. Its admixture of the charming, the hilarious, the sad, and the touching was thought to be appropriate for this style of presentation when we were approached by the Taj Palace Hotel to do a play at their coffee shop, Isfahan. It worked rather well as far as the audiences were concerned, but the actors found the setting and the constant chinking of cutlery and glass quite distracting, so much so that we didn't try this format again.

By this time, I had had a surfeit of comedy and lighter plays, not having done a truly serious play since *The Tempest*. I told Joy that I wanted to direct a good classical verse tragedy *Phaedra* by the great French playwright of the 17th century, Jean Racine. I had come across a wonderful English translation in verse by the American poet Robert Lowell and my heart was set upon it. Joy was, as usual, enthusiastic and told me to go ahead, albeit with a restricted budget of just about 20,000 rupees. I was elated and set about casting, designing the sets and costumes, devising the soundtrack, and working out all the details with great enthusiasm. The legendary lighting specialist R.K. Dhingra (or Dingy, as he is fondly known), who was well aware of the budgetary constraints, generously offered to do the lights for free.

This was among my most satisfying productions as a stage director. Dingy's lights were superb. I had designed every detail of the sets and costumes. I devised the entire live soundtrack by using a variety of effects produced solely on a pair of timpani (or kettledrums) to punctuate the play: soft taps, drum rolls going up in crescendi and down in decrescendi, sudden crashes, rhythmic patterns loud and soft. I managed to borrow the two large timpani from Gautam Kaul of the Delhi Symphony Society and found a player from the Naval Band whom I could instruct in the score. I was quite pleased with my score—the closest I have come to composing. And the cast of Prabha Tonk, Jasbir Malik, Indira Joshi, Ashwin Juneja, Indu Ramchandani, Rupin Jayal, Shibani Lulla, and Sonia Faleiro did a wonderful job. While the comedies of Moliere have been popular over the years on the Delhi stage, the classical tragedies of the somewhat younger Jean

Indu Ramchandani, Prabha Tonk, and Jasbir Malik in *Phaedra*

Racine have been ignored. This was the only production of a play by Racine that I can recall in my 40 years of theatre in Delhi.

Memories of my production of *Phaedra* inevitably evoke a tremendous sense of loss. In the untimely passing away of Prabha, I lost a very dear friend and cherished co-actor. She had a marvellous voice, superb diction, and a wicked sense of humour. All of this made her one of my favourite persons to do theatre with. Jasbir Malik, or Bunny, as all of us knew him, was another such person—a thorough gentleman with one of the most powerful voices I have ever encountered on stage, combined with a commanding presence. Looking back, I feel grateful for having had the opportunity to work in so many plays with them and, particularly, to have directed them both together in *Phaedra*.

The next year, 1994, Joy decided to put together an evening of excerpts from Oscar Wilde at the British Council to commemorate the 140th year of his birth. Excerpts from *Salome* and *Lady Windermere's Fan* were performed. Roshan Seth did a moving reading of excerpts from *De Profundis*. But for me, the highlight was playing the part of Algernon in the first act of *The Importance of Being Earnest*, partly because I got to show off that I could play the piano live on stage, but mostly because, for the first time in decades, Joy decided to act herself as well. She played the role of Lady Bracknell. This was the only time I, or anyone else for that matter since the 1970s, had the opportunity to act with Joy on stage. It was truly memorable doing the famous interview scene with her.

Throughout the years, Yatrik did not only produce plays. Spurred on by Joy and Lola Chatterji, the group also organised many poetry and prose-reading sessions. Around Christmas time, Joy would inevitably organise an event featuring seasonal poetry, prose, and carols, prefaced by a dramatised reading of Charles Dickens' *A Christmas Carol*. I was inevitably cast as Scrooge in all these events. All of us recall with particular affection the deftly and intelligently scripted thematic poetry readings orchestrated by the brilliant Giti Chandra, which were greatly enjoyed by readers and audiences alike. We could never have enough of these.

There were also many dramatised readings of plays put on with no budget at all. I recall directing at least two such dramatised readings myself, one of Christopher Fry's *The Lady's not for Burning* and another of Anuvab Pal's *Chaos Theory*. And then there were the summer theatre workshops organised by Yatrik under Joy's direction, assisted ably by Avijit Dutt and Prakash Bhatia, at which many of us took sessions with the young participants. These became a wonderful means for infusion of new blood into the group.

By the mid-1990s, Yatrik had kept up its healthy tradition of doing Indian plays in Hindi and Urdu along with translations and adaptations of Western plays. However, with a few notable exceptions, almost all the English plays were Western. There was a

*The Importance of Being Earnest*—Sunit Tandon and Bhaveen Gosain

growing and confident middle class, for whom English was also an Indian language. The settings and situations of most Western plays (with, perhaps, the exception of the classics) began to seem glaringly alien and of little relevance to our everyday lives in a resurgent India. Having directed a variety of plays from Shakespeare to Shaw to Stoppard and from Racine to Coward and Neil Simon, I came to a resolve that even while continuing to do plays in English, I would henceforth try and direct Indian plays that had a greater audience connect. Many of us felt the same way. Luckily, at about this time, Gurcharan Das offered Bhaskar Ghose a play he had written decades earlier, but which had never been performed. Bhaskar, who was a secretary to the Government of India by that time, was too busy to direct or act and passed it on to me. This was the first draft of the play that eventually became *9 Jakhoo Hill.*

> ***9 Jakhoo Hill*, a landmark in the history of Yatrik.** For an entire decade, from 1996 to 2006, hardly a year went by when this production was not being revived for shows in Delhi or for tours within the country and abroad: it was staged in Mumbai, Calcutta, Chennai, Shimla, Dubai, and South Africa in a five-city tour, including Johannesburg, Durban, Pretoria, Cape Town, and the Grahamstown Arts Festival, where the play was selected as a "Pick of the Festival". It became the longest-running and most popular play ever staged by Yatrik.
>
> However, none of us had any inkling of this when we first held two rounds of readings of the script in Gurcharan's presence. As a result of the discussions that followed the readings, Gurcharan made significant changes to the script, including adding a whole new scene with which to end the play. Eventually, Gurcharan

said that he had done as much as he could with the script and told me that we could change it as we liked for performance. His trust was so great that, years later, when a collection of his plays was to be published, he asked me for the acting version of *9 Jakhoo Hill* that we had prepared from his script and that was the version that was printed.

I'm glad to say that we did not betray the trust Gurcharan reposed in us. I started rehearsals in March 1996 as soon as Bhaskar Ghose retired, because I was adamant that he had to be in the play. I workshopped the entire script with the actors, using the "hot seat" technique. Many changes were made. Whole speeches written by the actors themselves, little details of character, of language and motivation were ironed out. When we finally staged the play for the first time at Kamani Auditorium later that year, I was still extremely apprehensive about its reception. I first realised that the audience was totally with the play during the intermission, when the applause and the buzz took me by surprise. I remember running from the lights booth, where I was operating the sound (Zuleikha Allana was doing the lights) to the green room to tell actors excitedly, "They seem to like it, they're not walking out!"

The original cast of six remained fairly constant for the more than 60 or so shows that we did of this play over the next 10 years. Bhaskar Ghose, Kusum Haidar, Sinia Dugal, Shyama Haldar, and Ajay Balram continued with the play over the years, with a few exceptions. For some shows, when Kusum or Ajay could not make it, Salima Raza and Sunil Gupta stepped into their respective roles. For the last few shows, the late Pooja

Mukherjee replaced Shyama Haldar, who was by then busy raising a family. The major change that took place immediately after the first run was that Rupin Jayal, who had played Deepak, had to drop out at short notice from our first tour to Mumbai. I was left with no option but to step into the role myself, learning the lines on the Rajdhani Express as we made our way westwards. After that, I was stuck with the role for all subsequent shows, much against my wishes and original intention.

Joy Michael was indispensable as producer, especially on our tours. She somehow managed to put the furniture and props together, whichever city we were in. Vinay Capila did outstanding work in ensuring that our precious sets, designed by the eminent artist Anjolie Ela Menon, were always transported carefully and were put up on time. He even painstakingly devised the most marvellous lightweight, collapsible sets for our South Africa tour, which unfortunately got lost in transit. Anjolie herself came along with us on several of our tours to put the finishing touches to our sets. Ashish Paliwal, who had earlier assisted Zuleikha, took over the lighting from the second or third run onwards and stayed on as an essential member of the crew thereafter. Amarjit Singh, or AJ, as he is universally known, operated the sound (since I was now required on stage as an actor) and kept us all in good humour. The actors gradually took complete ownership of their parts and the play became tighter and more effective over the years. The entire team became a well-oiled machine. *9 Jakhoo Hill* was truly a unique and treasured experience for all of us who were involved with it.

Sunit Tandon, Shyama Haldar, Sinia Dugal, and Salima Raza in *9 Jakhoo Hill*

The Yatrik trend of doing new Indian plays in English continued. Avijit Dutt was already writing his own plays. Bhaskar Ghose directed several exceptional plays by the noted playwright Poile Sengupta, including two in which I acted: *Mangalam* and *Keats was a Tuber*. In the former, all of the cast played two roles, one each in the two halves of the play. I particularly enjoyed playing the role of a 60-year-old traditional Tamil brahmin in the first part, for which Bhaskar's wife, the brilliant Bharatanatyam dancer Valli, had to teach me to tie the lungi. Bhaskar Ghose later also directed *Everything Personal* by senior journalist-turned-dramatist Nilanjan Mukhopadhyay.

Earlier, in 2001–02, I directed *Come As You Were*, a new play about the new generation by a new voice Nicholas Bernard Kharkongor, which was received very well indeed. Nicholas went on to write a couple of more plays before moving to the world of cinema, writing and directing his first feature film *Mantra*, which released in 2017.

It was again Bhaskar who directed a play on Pushkin, entitled *Pushkin's Last Poem* by Achala Moulik. He cast me in the challenging role of Pushkin. This play was first staged at Kamani Auditorium in 2007–08. It was later revived in 2009–10 for a tour to Moscow and St. Petersburg, this time directed by Avijit Dutt. Taking an Indian play in English about the great Russian poet to Russia has to be one of the more startlingly implausible, but nevertheless memorable experiences of our lives.

At the same time, Yatrik did not forsake Western plays that could be said to have some universal dimensions. Acting with Avijit in his production of *The Virtuous Burglar* by Nobel Laureate Dario Fo in 1997–98 was a most enjoyable experience. This was another of our more successful productions, gauged in terms of audience response and revivals. It was staged several times over the years and we even took it to Dubai. And indubitably, one of the most ambitious and most lauded productions of Yatrik in the second decade of the 21st century has been *Metamorphoses* by Mary Zimmerman, directed by Kusum Haidar. This play, based on Greek legends, takes place around an actual water pool, which is a huge challenge to construct. It was staged first in 2012–13 and was subsequently invited for NSD's Bharat Rang Mahotsav as well as the Sahitya Kala Parishad Festival of the Best Plays of the Year. It was a most satisfying experience for me, working once again with Kusum, the most active of our founder members in recent times, and to play two roles in the play, apart from designing the complex and crucial soundtrack for this production.

The unique nature of Yatrik as a group has been that it has never cabined, cribbed, or confined its members. Over the years, I have continued to work with other groups and directors as well, including Stagedoor, Masque, Chingari, Ruchika, Scene Stealers, TAG, Primetime, Teamwork, Natwa, Akshara Theatre, Katyayani Productions, and the Shakespeare Society, St. Stephen's College.

*Metamorphoses*—Shena Gamat, Reuben Israel, and Sunit Tandon in the pool of water

*Metamorphoses*—Sunit Tandon as Midas

I have benefitted immensely from working with directors such as Mohan Maharishi, Bhanu Bharati, K. Madavane, Gopal Sharman, Jalabala Vaidya, Anasuya Vaidya, Sohaila Kapur, Lillette Dubey, Arun Kukreja, and Vivek Mansukhani, to name just a few. I have valued this freedom and have remained true to Yatrik at the same time. After all, Yatrik has been my home base for nearly four decades.

**Vinay Capila,** actor, stage manager, and a brilliant designer of sets recalls: my first contact with Yatrik was in 1964 when I was associated with Theatre Group, Mumbai, as the stage manager for their production of *Exit the King* (which they brought to Delhi), directed by Pearl Padamsee, with Alyque Padamsee playing the lead role of the king. Subsequently, in 1965, I participated in a couple of Yatrik's productions, basically as a stagehand or in helping Marcus Murch to paint the sets. This was just after finishing college and I was at a loose end. By mid-1965, I had got my first job and was posted out of Delhi.

It was only 13 years later (in 1978) that I was again firmly established back in Delhi with a job that gave me ample spare time for becoming involved in theatre. For the next 25–30 years or more, I was actively involved with Yatrik, participating in over 60 of their productions in some aspect or the other: mostly for the production of sets and as stage manager, but also in acting, direction, handling of lights and sound, and what have you. For about 20 of these years, I also acted as treasurer for the group.

As an actor, I can remember doing roles in *The Night Thoreau Spent in Jail*, *The Queen and the Rebels*, *Don't Drink the Water*, *Ring Round the Moon*, *The Happiest Days of your Life*, *Mahabhoj*, *Arsenic and Old Lace*, and perhaps a few more. I also did the sets and stage management for all these plays. I directed two plays—*The Elephant Man* and *The*

Vinay Capila in *The Queen and the Rebels*

Stage set for *Arsenic and Old Lace*

Stage set for *Don't Drink the Water*

*Happy Marriage*, and co-directed a few others. However, my forte was making sets for plays and stage management.

Some of the most challenging sets that I had to make were for *The Happiest Days of your Life*, *South Pacific*, *Daily Truth*, *The Herbal Bed,* and *9 Jakhoo Hill.* The first three involved frequent change of sets to represent different locales and therefore required quick removal and assembly techniques within a limited time span. *The Herbal Bed* was a normal "fixed" set, but I also had to create a multilayered garden, for which I grew over a hundred appropriate plants in my garden over two months and put them on stage for the production. For *9 Jakhoo Hill,* I had to construct a sort of "Mechano" set—which could be quickly put together and dismantled and packed into small boxes for transporting to different locations. The play ran for over 30 productions in five cities in India, five in South Africa, and also in Dubai. In 2003, I received the national award for Stage Craft by the Chaman Lal Memorial Society.

# MOVERS AND SHAKERS...
## THE GEN-NEXT

*Good my lord, will you see the players well bestowed?*
*Do you hear, let them be well used, for they are the abstract and brief chronicles of the time.*
*After your death you were better have a bad epitaph than their ill report while you live.*

**Act 2 Scene 2, *Hamlet*,**
**William Shakespeare**

> Yes, this is the next generation, and the future of Yatrik. They have today the best of both worlds. Having come into the fold with the guidance and training from the stalwarts of the group, they have the background and support to combine with the energy and the zeal to forge ahead…

**Arti Nayar** says some things are destined. I realise now, as I sit penning down my thoughts going down memory lane, how grateful and fortunate I am as a member of Yatrik. I remember being persuaded by my good friend Sonali Sharma to join the Yatrik summer workshop at IHC way back in 2002. Her mother happened to read about it in a brochure and the two of us joined the two-week programme, just for the fun of it. Little did I realise how life-changing it would be. Those 14 days exposed me to the wonderful world of theatre. I discovered my passion in this art form. And the rest is history. Since then, I have been part of various productions from modern to old classics, contemporary, and with both Western and Indian origin; I have enjoyed travelling abroad and participating in various prestigious festivals. I owe all this and more to that workshop, as it also introduced me to the "best" in the theatre world.

Yatrik is the longest active theatre group in Delhi and its senior members are all stalwarts. Each member is a "master" in his or her skill, and I have been extremely fortunate to have worked with them. Among the endless names are Joy Michael, Kusum Haidar, Avijit Dutt, Bhaskar Ghose, and Sunit Tandon. I have got great experience in various departments, including backstage management, production, sound, and costume, and training to improve my skills involving voice modulation, movement, and various technical aspects. Some of the Yatrik productions I have been part of are *Virasat*, *Blood Wedding*, *Bombay Bosnia*, *Breaking News*, *Yerma*, *Inner Laws*, *Everything Personal*, *Metamorphoses*, and *When Five Years Pass.*

*Blood Wedding*—The entire cast

*Everything Personal*—Arti Nayar and Sonali Sharma

Arti Nayar (left) in *Party*, a dramatised reading

My favourite production to date is *Metamorphoses*, directed by Kusum Haidar. It was an extremely enriching, challenging, and unforgettable experience. I have several vivid memories linked with our trip to Russia with Avijit Dutt while staging *Pushkin*. Directing my sole production, a dramatised reading of *The Chairs*, in the group's endeavour to promote young talent was challenging. My most beautiful and cherished memory, however, is singing Christmas carols with the Yatrik family at Joy Michael's place. That epitomises tradition, bonding, and celebration. That is *family*—and my best wishes spread out to the Yatrik family.

**Priyanka Nagpal** recalls: 15 years ago, my dearest friend Priyanka Sivanandan (then Gupta) casually suggested that we enrol in the summer workshop that Yatrik did at the time. Little did I know that would be the start of an eternal love affair with the group. The pleasure of working with, and learning from, some of the finest theatre professionals such as Bhaskar Ghose, Sunit Tandon, Swaroopa Ghose, Maya Rao, Kusum Haidar, Prakash Bhatia, and of course, Joy Michael remains a cherished experience of my life.

Yatrik gave me opportunities to portray a range of fulfilling roles. Productions such as *Mangalam*, *Keats was a Tuber*, *Pushkin's Last Poem*, *Ghera*, *Virasat*—all gave me opportunities that actors covet. There are fond memories of backstage experiences with *Educating Rita*, *Alipha*, *So Said Shakuni*, *Thus Spake Shoorpanakha*, among others, that taught me a lot about bringing a production together.

*Mangalam* remains close to the heart. The role of a 30-year-old scheming woman in an orthodox Tamil family was really challenging. The theatre knowledge that the director Bhaskar Ghose gave us remains invaluable. I loved being part of *Pushkin's Last Poem*, another one of Bhaskar's directorial efforts. Understanding the Russian context and working with Sunit Tandon was a great experience.

*Party*, a dramatised reading—Priyanka Nagpal and Isha Joshi

*Inner laws*, under Joy Michael's direction, was incredible. Acting with nine other fabulously talented and fun-loving women made this comic play even more fun for all of us.

Apart from the great work that we were all privileged to witness and be part of, the friendships and connections we made through Yatrik is what makes it a special association. We are lucky to be part of an extraordinary fabric made of lifelong friends and mentors who are strung together through the Yatrik family.

**Shekhar Murugan.** I joined Yatrik through the Yatrik summer workshop held at India Habitat Centre in 2002, and have been actively associated with the group ever since. I had always been enamoured with arc lights and the stage and I got immensely enthused after watching musicals such as *Fiddler on the Roof*. I was more focused on dancing initially, having been with Danceworx in the early years, and after having got the initial heady experience of being on stage with my first musical *The Chorus Line*, directed by Vivek Mansukhani.

My debut into Hindi theatre was with Prakash Bhatia in *Virasat*, where I played the main lead in an ensemble cast. My first English play was the hugely successful *Bombay Bosnia*, directed by Avijit Dutt. Then I went on to do many more plays—including *Ek Sapne ki Maut* and *Devdas* in Hindi, and *The Virtuous Burglar* and *Noor Jehan: An Empress Reveals*. I have also donned the hat of producer for various Yatrik productions—*Abducting Diana*, *Comedy About the End of the World*, which also toured Europe, *Noor Jehan: An Empress Reveals*, which was showcased successfully in Delhi, as well as in Calcutta and Hyderabad. All the plays are special in their own way, but I would rate Dario Fo's *Abducting Diana*, directed by Avijit Dutt, a favourite.

A "dream theatre" initiative by Yatrik Theatre Group and Old World Culture was a special and original concept. Working closely with Avijit, the two of us gave this project all its momentum. Old scripts or original new plays were presented. These were read by actors in a "dramatised reading" and were directed both by first-time directors and established directors in two "sessions" for each play at the Habitat basement or the amphitheatre. For a play, session I was on a particular day in a month, solely directed and designed by the first-time or new director. Session II was a repeat of the same play under the same format on a different day in that particular month, but this time directed and designed by the mentor or by an established director. For more than a year, from 2011 through to 2013, many dramatised readings were staged. *The Chairs* by Arti Nayar, *The Dumb Waiter* by Shekhar Murugan, *The Caretaker* by Prashant Sehgal, *The Man in a Case* by Isha Joshi, *The Lover* by Zoya Hussain, *Afterlife of Birds* by Oroon Das, *The Green Room* by Vani Vyas, *The Toy Cart* by Sonali Sharma, and a play by Sohaila Kapur were showcased under the Yatrik banner at the India Habitat Centre basement.

*The Virtuous Burglar*—Pranay Manchanda, Sunit Tandon, Shekhar Murugan, Shibani Bedi, and Vandana Kilim Datta

*Toy Cart*, a dramatised reading—Shekhar Murugan (second from left) and Arti Nayar (on the floor), along with other actors

Over these years, I have worked with Avijit Dutt, Sunit Tandon, Bhaskar Ghose, Prakash Bhatia, Joy Michael, and Sabina Jaitly. I am an office bearer of the executive committee as secretary. I would not hesitate to say that my association with Yatrik has got me a lot of respect in the fraternity, a lot of memorable and valuable moments, and friends to cherish.

**Sonali Sharma,** one of the young, dynamic members of Yatrik, says: I joined Yatrik in 2002. I needed a creative outlet and it so happened that Yatrik was conducting its Theatre Workshop at IHC. So I dragged my dear friend Arti Nayar, and we joined the workshop. Since then, there has been no turning back for either of us.

Yatrik has been my training ground for theatre in every possible way. Everyone who has worked with Joy Michael talks enthusiastically about his or her association with her. I have had the "bestest of the best" to learn from, heralded by none other than Joy Michael herself. For me, Yatrik and she are synonymous.

My role play in Yatrik was a multitude. It ranged from performance to lighting to helping out in production and finally into directing my first dramatised reading of *Mricchakatika* or *The Toy Cart*. Yatrik gave me the platform to work with different directors and theatre groups. It has been and still is a fascinating journey where I have been fortunate enough to play a variety of complex characters and experience different genres and scripts.

I have had the fortune of working with stalwart directors such as Bhaskar Ghose, Joy Michael, Avijit Dutt, Kusum Haidar, Sabina Mehta Jaitly, Sohaila Kapur, and Abhijit Sengupta, and each of them has helped me to grow and to learn the craft better.

It is hard to pinpoint my favourite production, for there are so many. But some of my most memorable moments are from *Pushkin's Last Poem*, for it was my first play to be directed by Bhaskar Ghose and then by Avijit Dutt, who took it to Russia. What a trip that was! Avijit had assigned me the dual task of both acting and lighting. In Moscow, after enacting my part, I had to run to the tech room to help out with the lights. Since there was no rear exit, I had to run past the entire carpeted corridor outside the auditorium doors, fully dressed for the character on stage, in a flowing gown and bedecked with jewels, much to the astonishment of people outside. And I simply couldn't remember where the tech room was in that beautiful old building.

*Pushkin's Last Poem*—Sonali Sharma with Sunit Tandon in rehearsal

A collage of scenes of a story in *Metamorphoses*

Did I need to turn right and go up the stairs or turn left? Had I taken the wrong turn? With a thousand panic buttons rearing their ugly heads, I just took the nearest turn and ran up the stairs and thankfully landed straight in front of the tech room. There stood Avijit smiling patiently. If only he knew.

I still remember when I started out rehearsing for *Pushkin's Last Poem*, I was fairly new to the craft, and there was still a feeling of shyness of playing the character of Mistress Elizabeth Vorontsova. So I mustered up the courage to approach Bhaskar and ask him, "Are you planning to stick to the script literally or is there scope for adjustment and going with comfort level, because I'm not sure if I can."

Bhaskar smiled at me and said, "Don't worry, my dear, Sunit is harmless and a thorough professional." The role went on to be one that I will forever cherish, and yes, I learnt the art of how to "cheat" onstage. And Bhaskar was right. For me, it was enough that he said post the show, "You did me proud."

A scene from the dramatised reading of *Toy Cart*

Then there was an all-women comic satire scripted by Poile Sengupta, *Inner Laws*, directed first by Joy Michael and then by Abhijit Sengupta. Rehearsing with 10 women was a total laugh riot. There was so much camaraderie that we all wished it would never end.

I must mention two women directors whom I have had the fortune of working with often—Sohaila Kapur and Kusum Haidar. They have pushed me beyond my limits again and again. Kusum will always be the woman who gave me my voice in theatre. For me, a Lorca production is synonymous with Kusum Haidar.

Thank you, Yatrik, for giving me wings!

**Vani Vyas** joined Yatrik in 2007 as part of Avijit Dutt's production on *Pushkin's Last Poem,* which travelled to Russia. The play had originally been directed by Bhaskar Ghose and staged at Kamani Auditorium in Delhi. It was well received. But for taking it to Russia, Avijit Dutt stepped in, recast some of the parts while retaining most of the original principal characters, and edited the play a little more.

Vani recalls: It was a delightful experience as the group performed in Moscow and St. Petersburg. We have many tales to tell from that trip. We almost missed our flight back from St. Petersburg because we girls were too busy shopping at Zara. And yes, Sunit Tandon was right there, shopping for his black overcoat. We all ran a marathon to reach back to the hotel. Sunit reached well on time. But, had Arjun Fauzdar not been there, Zoya Hussain and I would have definitely been lost and would be trying to make our living showing reruns of *Pushkin* to the Russians. There was a lot of madness that prevailed in those seven days both with and without Vodka shots. After this, I have played many memorable roles, including *Breaking News* and *Abducting Diana*, both plays directed by Avijit.

*Metamorphoses*, a visual delight, with some of the finest talent that I have ever worked with, directed by Kusum Haidar, ran to full houses. Somehow, I remember Arti Nayar had a big fall during a technical run. We had a pool in the middle of the stage, as a part of the set and Arti slipped and fell right into it, hitting her face badly. We were all scared that she could have broken her tooth.

But the gods had blessed our Myrrha and she was to look beautiful for the show. I played the conniving Aphrodite in this one. There was a stunning poster of Arti and me, right in the middle of the NSD festival, and that picture remains etched in my heart.

In 2016, I played Noor Jehan for Avijit Dutt's *Noor Jehan: An Empress Reveals*, which was an incredible journey into history. We travelled to Hyderabad and Calcutta with this production. The best show was in Calcutta for 1,500 school kids with raging hormones, who whistled and clapped incessantly during any love scene between Jehangir and Mehrunisa. They really make the best audience.

My first independent "directorial" venture was the dramatised reading of *The Green Room* at the India Habitat Centre's basement

*Metamorphoses*—Arti Nayar and Vani Vyas

*Metamorphoses*—A collage of scenes from *Myrrha*

theatre, under the "dream theatre" initiative by Yatrik Theatre Group and Old World Culture. Interestingly, my daughter Smriti Vyas also made her theatre debut at the age of 9 with Yatrik in 2009, when she acted in a major role in *The Secret World of...*, directed by Zoya Hussain, my close friend, who was herself all of 19 at the time. Smriti and I acted together as mother and daughter.

I have made the most wonderful friends through my association with Yatrik. For me as a young girl, Yatrik held a special place in my heart, one that seemed like a dream. With such coveted and respected people as the core members of Yatrik, I still find it difficult to believe that I am a part of this iconic theatre group.

**A Special Acknowledgement**

Yatrik has always welcomed all who wish to work in theatre in any capacity with open arms. Over the years, many, many persons who may or may not find a mention in this book also contributed to Yatrik's journey in measures large and small, some for a production or two, some for substantial periods of time. It is sadly impossible to name them all. We would like to gratefully acknowledge their contributions to the group—those named below, as well as those countless others who most regrettably may not have been mentioned:

Abhay Manas, Adhiraj Katoch, Ambika Shukla, Anhad Anand, Aniruddh Nair, Anjolie Ela Menon, Arjun Fauzdar, Arjun Raina, Asha Thomas, Ashish Paliwal, Ashish Puri, Ashok Sagar Bhagat, Ashutosh Prakash, Ashwin Juneja, Ayushi Sagar, B.P. Singh, Basab Bhattacharya, Bhaveen Gosain, Bindu Tandon, Chitra Ramachandran, Damandeep Singh, Dayanita Singh, Deepa Grover, Deepak Mukarji, Dhruv Jagasia, Dhruv Saikia, Dilip Shankar, Dilip Sircar, Divya Seth, Geeta Sudan, Gilles Chuyen, Giti Chandra, Himanshu Koirala, Indira Joshi, Isha Joshi, Jacqui Garewal, Jai Chandiram, Jai Pathak, Janaki Bahadur, Jillian Larkins, Joya Chatterjee, Jyoti Nanda, Keshav Moodliar, Koel Purie, Kriti Pant, Lalit Vachani, Latika Nath, Leela Caleb, Lewie Gonsalves, Mandira Kapoor, Neeraj Yadav, Nicholas Bernard Kharkongor, Nilanjan Mukhopadhyay, Nirmala Matthan, Nyanu Thakur, Omkar Goswami, Oroon Das, Piu Dutt, Pooja Mukherjee, Pranay Manchanda, Prashant Sehgal, Preeti Batra Singh, Priyanka Gupta, Priyanka Jhajaria, Radhika Singh, Raghu Sudon, Rahat Raza, Rais Rice, Renuka Narayanan, Reuben Israel, Sagarika Ghose, Sai Paranjpye, Sanjeev Popley, Sharon Lowen, Shena Gamat, Shibani Bedi, Shibani Lulla, Shibani Puri, Shiv Jha Mathur, Sonam Kalra, Sonam Sharma, Sonia Faleiro, Sridhar Rajan, Sudeep Singh, Suhel Seth, Sukesh Arora, Sunil Gupta, Suniya, Luther, Sushma Ramaswami, Swaroopa Ghosh, Tannishtha Chatterjee, Vaishnavi Sharma, Vandana Kilim Datta, Vidushi Mehra, Vishaal Sethia, Vivek Manshukhani, Vivek Tandon, Zohra Sehgal, Zoya Hussain, Zuleikha Allana.

# TRIBUTES

## They Left the Stage of Life ...but are not Forgotten

*Our revels now are ended. These our actors*
*Are melted into air, into thin air... We are such stuff*
*As dreams are made on and our little life*
*Is rounded with a sleep.*

**Act 4, Scene 1, *The Tempest*,**
**William Shakespeare**

*They were with us in this journey, but when it was their time to move on, they did. We pay tribute here to Ashish Puri, Dilip Sircar, Jai Chandiram, Ramesh Venkataraman, and Zohra Sehgal, as well as others, and the few friends we have written about here.*

**Bhaskar Bhattacharji.** Greatly talented, versatile, a brilliant and outstanding actor and media personality. Started his acting career while at St. Stephen's College, where his rendering of *Macbeth* is remembered. He distinguished himself in many important leading roles in theatre to which he brought great sensitivity, understanding, and distinction. Bhaskar was our "Man for all Seasons", greatly loved and respected.

Bhaskar Bhattacharji holds centre stage in *Salome*

*The Curlew's Cry*—Bhaskar Bhattacharji and Chitra Ramachandran

**Jasbir Malik—Bunny.** A charming and perfect gentleman, and a brilliant actor. His wife Anjali (Bitti, as we know here) says: every worthwhile theatre lover of our generation recited, at some stage, the lines of the melancholy Jaques in *As You Like It*: "All the world's a stage; And all the men and women merely players; They have their exits and their entrances, And one man in his time plays many parts, his acts being seven ages."

As Bitti continues, "I knew Jasbir, my husband, Bunny, through most of those seven ages, not least and most vividly when 'Sighing like furnace, with a woeful ballad/Made to his mistress' eyebrow', he proposed to me some 62 years ago!"

But Bunny played many more parts than Jaques could dream of. He was a wonderful, caring and loving son, husband, brother, father, and grandfather; "Dada" to some, "Bhaiya" to others; a Mensa-level mathematician who longed to enthuse others with his knowledge of this subject; a senior executive of what was once called the Imperial Tobacco Company and, later, ITC.

Jasbir Malik and Prabha Tonk in *Lettice and Lovage*

The incarnation in which he truly found and fulfilled himself was as an unpaid teacher for some 20 years in Mirambika, the school in Delhi that is inspired by Sri Aurobindo's teachings. And this was not surprising. Bunny had a great and instinctive empathy for others: succeeding generations of children from that school treasured him as both their guru and dear friend, and the respect was mutual.

His debut on the Delhi stage was with *The Daily Truth*, directed by Tejeshwar Singh. It was a harmony of the baritone voices of the director and actor, so to say…and blending with their voices was the resonance of Bhaskar Bhattacharji's voice. That was the beginning; Bunny was much in demand. We have no track record really of his various stellar performances. He was hysterical as the bumbling Inspector in *Arsenic and Old Lace*. But as the voice in *Mirza Bagh* he created his own unique presence. Everyone loved Bunny. Indeed, his capacity to empathise with others, to enter their minds and souls, was also the secret of his considerable skill as an actor on the stage and in films, in college, in Calcutta and in Delhi. And who but he could make even Jinnah understandable—and possibly likeable—to an audience in Delhi, in a play on the Partition of India?

Such was his natural self, his infinite charm, and his capacity to bring joy to the lives of others—high and low, rich and poor, aged and young. He was equal with all.

**Prabha Tonk.** Her dry, British sense of humour, accompanied by the sparkle in her eyes, often fooled those who did not know her well. As a director, she was as tough on the outside as she was soft on the inside. Caring and scathing all at once, she could be terrifying. An excellent actor with the perfect diction and suave demeanour…she

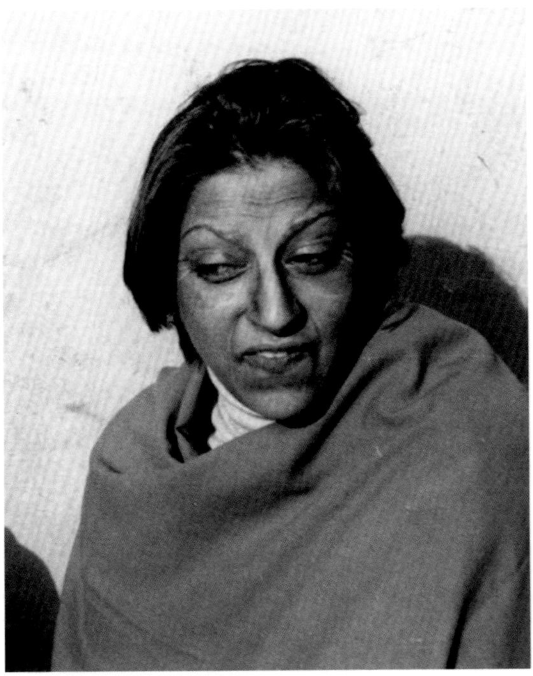

Prabha Tonk in *Gitanjali in Five Times*

held the audience as she dominated the stage. Prabha acted in and directed plays with Yatrik for many years.

Meriel Michael says that Prabha was especially memorable in her role as Dolly the matchmaker in *The Matchmaker* and as the lead doctor's assistant in *Cactus Flower*. In *Gitanjali in Five Times*, playing the old Gitanjali, which involved a lot of movement, she jokingly remarked that the creaks of her knees threatened to drown out the voices of her co-actors.

Indu Ramchandani recalls: Prabha called upon me for backstage help often and then directed me in *Arsenic and Old Lace* and *A Tomb with a View*. I acted with her in *Phaedra*, and during the 40 years' celebrations, we were together in the revival of *Gitanjali in Five Times*. Those were memorable experiences.

Prabha's husband Paul Tonk reminisces: As I recall, Prabha did not show any interest in any of the performing arts while in school in Delhi initially, and later in England. Perhaps, she was more involved

Prabha Tonk (right) in *Cactus Flower*

in readjusting to life in India after the family returned from postings in the US and UK. It was only later when she joined Miranda House that she first got involved in college theatre activities, and then was also invited to participate in St. Stephen's plays, mainly under the Shakespeare Society. I suspect that Bhaskar Ghose and Rajan Chetsingh were the main motivators.

Once Prabha found her interest in plays put up by the university, and then returned to Delhi from a further stint of three years of academic life in London, she found herself more and more involved in Delhi theatre, watching plays performed by the various local groups which were active at the time (Yatrik being the main one then).

The many plays over the years that Prabha initially acted in, and later participated in backstage, speak of her love of theatre and the people involved in it in Delhi. She was always willing to be involved in any production, whether it be acting in any role, or behind the scenes in designing costumes, makeup, front office, ticketing…anything as long as she was a part of the overall effort. With time, she took up direction with successful comedies like *Arsenic and Old Lace*, which travelled to other cities as well. In fact, as less and less suitable parts were available, age-wise, she made more sincere efforts to participate in every aspect of Delhi theatre.

Even when we shifted from the heart of Delhi to Gurgaon, and the inconvenience of having to put up with travel distances between the two, she never lost her enthusiasm for theatre. I think Prabha, like most other theatre people, enjoyed the camaraderie that exists among all theatre lovers, and the "in-depth" discussions that take place to get to the heart of a character or the author's views—whether the play be serious or not. In the years of her association with theatre in Delhi, Prabha formed a number of warm and close associations with people.

**Sant Juneja.** He was very much there, for several years. He acted, helped backstage, and most importantly was supportive and encouraging at every occasion. Everyone who knew him talks of this soft-spoken and gentle person and holds him in high regard. Sant was quiet, but eloquent with his demeanour. He made it a point to attend all executive committee meetings, was apologetic on the rare occasions that he could not make it, and made sure he was heard when an issue was of great importance to him.

As Bhaskar Ghose recalls, Sant protested vigorously when someone suggested that we drop some old members and bring in younger people. His point was that old members could contribute because of their memories of Yatrik and its history. He played, effectively, the part of the old General in Bhaskar's production of *Pushkin's Last Poem* for Yatrik.

**Tejeshwar Singh.** The classic "tall, dark and handsome man" with a statuesque appeal, known best for his deep baritone voice. He was famous as a Doordarshan newsreader in the 1980s and early 1990s, when cable TV was unheard of in India. If anything drew you to listen to the daily news, he did. In 1981, he founded, along with George and Sara McCune, the Indian arm of the international publishing house SAGE Publications. But capitalising on his good looks, he made a brief foray into Bollywood, essaying the role of a villain Deen Dayal or "D.D." in the Naseeruddin Shah starrer *Jalwa* in 1987. Although offers were still coming in, he decided to do what he was best doing, and settled down in the publishing business, and he led from the front to make SAGE a leading publishing house. In 2004, Tejeshwar played a resounding cameo role as Ravi Uncle in Manu Rewal's *Chai Pani etc.*

It was in 1989 that he came forward to direct *Daily Truth* for Yatrik. This was a magnum opus production, and had a huge and impressive cast. Along with Jasbir Malik's debut with Yatrik, the play had Bhaskar Bhattacharji and Sunit Tandon. Many students from Lady Irwin College were part of this large production, based on the story of a leading newspaper.

# Plays Staged by Yatrik... The Theatrical Journey

While every attempt has been made to make this list as accurate as possible, it is not claimed that this is a comprehensive and complete list of past productions.

**1964–65**
All the King's Men
Sabrina Fair
Our Town
The Government Inspector
Hotel Paradiso
Who's Afraid of Virginia Woolf
Five Finger Exercise
Azar Ka Khwab
The Matchmaker

**1965–66**
Khyal Hai Demagh Ka
A Taste of Honey
Dial M for Murder (Hindi)
The Little Hut
After the Fall
The Knack

**1966–67**
Tartuffe
Rahoon-ke-na-Rahoon
The Merchant of Venice
Alice in Wonderland
The Theban Plays
Festival of Short Plays
The Seagull

**1967–68**
Saleeb per Mariam
Tambaku ke Nuksanat
Evam Inderjit
Luv
Moon on a Rainbow Shawl
Victims of Duty
Aai Bala ko Taal Tu
The Land of Cards
Blood Wedding

**1968–69**
Desire Under the Elms
The Four Seasons
Next Time I'll Sing to You
Gandhiji's Sadhana (Hindi)
Awaj-ka-Raaz
Nayak Vinayak
An Evening of Mime
The Sleeping Beauty
Promise in Leningrad
Ek Chaadar Maili Si

A Flea in Her Ear

**1969–70**
Andhera Hone Do
A Delicate Balance
The Bald Soprano
The Chairs
Hedda Gabler
Giddh
The Ungrateful Man

**1970–71**
Goa
Arms and the Man
Aik Tamasha Acha Khasa
The Snow Queen
Shrimant
Cactus Flower
Dancing Donkey
Medea

**1971–72**
Room Service
Ashadh-ka-ek-Din
Tango
A Festival of Hindi Plays
Trudi and the Minstrel
Sleuth

**1972–73**
Inquilab
The Servant of Two Masters
An Enemy of the People
Lok Katha Aaj Ki
The Royal Pardon
Kranti and Parten
The Exception and the Rule
War

**1973–74**
Lower Depths
The Shoemaker's Prodigious Wife
Gaslight
A Doctor In Spite of Himself
Oliver (Musical)

**1974–75**
The Mother
Vyaktigat
The White Liars
Black Comedy

**1975–76**
Six Characters in Search
of an Author
A Shakespeare Evening
Sinbad the Sailor
The Prodigious Snob
Kadi Baabe Dian

**1976–77**
The Fantasticks (Musical)
Suddenly Last Summer

**1977–78**
The Broken Jug
Modern British Theatre
German Expressionist plays

**1978–79**
The Devil's Advocate
The Good Woman of Szechuan
Antigone
Cactus Flower

**1979–80**
Venus Observed
Tamasha
Cause Celebre
Bedroom Farce

**1980–81**
The Night Thoreau Spent in Jail
Two German Plays in Hindustani

(The Great Denunciation at the Town Wall and The Curve)
Jai Baba Gopinath
Don't Drink the Water

**1981–82**
The Crucible
Beejan-Teejan
The Happy Marriage
The Maids and Deathwatch

**1982–83**
The Curlew's Cry
Ruffian on the Stair
A Separate Peace
Gallows Humour
Ek Roshan Awaaz
Too True to be Good
Uncle Vanya

**1983–84**
A Midsummer Night's Dream
The Matchmaker
The Elephant Man
Don't Drink the Water
A Separate Peace
The Real Inspector Hound

**1984–85**
Blues for Mr. Charlie
A Gown for His Mistress
A Christmas Carol
The Queen and the Rebels
Balamji Tum Agey Mein
Peechey

**1985–86**
Three Penny Opera
Samjhauta and Pehlu (Hindi)
Ring Round the Moon
Kuch Door To Kissa Jayega
Spring Awakening (Hindi)
Sylvia Plath

**1986–87**
About Face
Play it Again Sam
The Happiest Days of your Life (musical)
Taking Steps
Of Mice and Men (Hindi)

**1987–88**
Principia Scriptoria
The Tempest
Daily Truth
Approaching Lavender
Closet Madness
Of Mice and Men

**1988–89**
Drums in the Night (Hindi)
Mahabhoj
Gitanjali in Five Times
Arsenic and Old Lace
Ek Aur Dhronacharya

**1989–90**
Phandi
A Tomb with a View
The Man Who Came to Dinner
Bamboo Flower (Hindi)
Museebat Mara Murari
South Pacific (musical)
Christmas Carols & Readings

**1990–91**
Towards Zero
All My Sons
Lettice and Lovage
Mahabhoj
Government Babu
Bedroom Farce

**1991–92**
The Good Doctor
Mahatma Mar Gaya
The Last of the Red Hot Lovers
Ek Kishore ki Dastaan

**1992–93**
Dancing at Lughnasa
Phaedra
A Betrothal
The Road to Mecca
Blind Date
Kismet Ya
The Lady's Not for Burning
A Walk in the Woods

**1993–94**
Bombay Bosnia
Rishtey Hi Rishtey
A Wilde Evening
Salome

**1994–95**
Six Degrees of Separation
Antigone
Rishtey-hi-Rishtey
A Christmas Carol & Poems
The Dumb Dancer

**1995–96**
Verdict
Death and the Maiden
Don't Dress for Dinner
9 Jakhoo Hill
Let Us Go Then (poetry readings at IIC)
The Matchmaker (Hindi)
Christmas Carols & Readings

**1996–97**
The Matchmaker (Hindi)
Bombay Bosnia
A Walk in the Woods
Unbeatable Shakespeare
Love in the Time of Protest
9 Jakhoo Hill
Borderline

**1997–98**
9 Jakhoo Hill (Dubai)
Verdict
The Brothers Karamazov (Hindi)
The Virtuous Burglar
Harvest

**1998–99**
The Herbal Bed
Ek Sapne ki Maut
9 Jakhoo Hill
Virasat
Christmas Carols & Readings

**1999–2000**
Bombay Bosnia
The Virtuous Burglar
9 Jakhoo Hill
Christmas Carols & Readings

**2000–01**
Mangalam
Getting Away with Murder
Ballabhpur Ki Roop Katha
I Am Not Sheikh Chilli

**2001–02**
America Here I Come
Hippolytos
Come As You Were
Educating Rita

**2002–03**
Ek Aur Dronacharya
Educating Rita
Two plays by Poile Sengupta
(Thus Spake Shoorpanakha,

So Said Shakuni & Alipha)

**2003–04**
Keats was a Tuber
Skylight (DR)

**2004–05**
9 Jakhoo Hill & Alipha (South Africa)
Gitanjali (revival)
Mangalam (revival)
Ek Aur Dronacharya (revival)
Scenes from Azar Ka Khwab
Bombay Bosnia (revival)
Come As You Were (revival)

**2005–06**
9 Jakhoo Hill (Chennai)
Mirza Bagh
Inner Laws
Josh Malihabadi Evening

**2006–07**
Chaos Theory
(Dramatised Reading—DR)

**2007–08**
Blood Wedding
Pushkin's Last Poem

**2008–09**
Publish or Perish (DR)
Devdas
Breaking News

**2009–10**
Short Circuit
Pushkin's Last Poem (Russia)
Poetry Reading
Breaking News
Meena Bazaar

**2010–11**
The Secret World of…
Everything Personal
The Toy Cart (DR)

**2011–12**
A Few Characters in Search of
an Author (DR)
The Caretaker (DR)
The Dumb Waiter (DR)
Party (DR)
8 Authors in Search of a City (DR)
The Lover (DR)
Afterlife of Birds (DR)
The Chairs (DR)
The Green Room (DR)
The One Percent Agency (DR)

**2012–13**
Metamorphoses
The Man in a Case (DR)
The Green Room

**2013–14**
Abducting Diana
Of Frogs Expiring and Other Marvels:
An Evening of Dickens Readings

**2014–15**
The Virtuous Burglar
Metamorphoses
Comedy About the End of the World

**2016–17**
Noor Jehan: An Empress Reveals
Jis Lahore Nahin Dekhya

# INDEX OF NAMES